Immortal Memory

IMMORTAL MEMORY

Burns and the Scottish People

CHRISTOPHER A. WHATLEY

First published in Great Britain in 2016 by
John Donald, an imprint of Birlinn Ltd

West Newington House
10 Newington Road
Edinburgh
EH9 1QS

www.birlinn.co.uk

ISBN: 978 1 910900 08 6

British Library Cataloguing-in-Publication Data
A catalogue record for this book is available
on request from the British Library

Typeset by Hewer Text UK Ltd, Edinburgh
Printed and bound in Britain by TJ International, Padstow, Cornwall

Contents

Contents

List of illustrations

Preface and acknowledgements

Living in Scotland, it is virtually impossible to be unaware of Robert Burns. He's there on tea towels, whisky bottles and a myriad of other products, not least banknotes. Statues abound. And late in January there's the Burns Supper season – now for children as well as for adults.

My own awakening happened in the late 1960s, as a student at what was then Clydebank Technical College, taking a crash course in university entrance qualifications. (I'd left school some years earlier, with only a single 'O' grade to my name.) Even though time was tight, a group of us put together an end of year concert that included a Burns performance – in which I appeared as a second rate John Cairney, the Scottish actor who had recently released a double LP on which he had played Burns. My interest in and appreciation of Burns was further aroused during lectures on Scottish literature at the University of Strathclyde. It was then that I adopted as my 'party piece' Burns' 'Holy Willie's Prayer', which for many years I recited, usually dressed in a nightgown and with a candle in my trembling hand, at the Open University's summer schools at Stirling University.

But that's as far as it went. In my final years as an undergraduate I had abandoned literary studies and specialised in economic history. It was this that I taught before a period spent at the University of St Andrews when I metamorphosed into a Scottish historian. My interests widened too, to include political, social and cultural history.

Throughout these years, however, I had maintained a close friendship with Kenneth Simpson, whom I was privileged to have had as one of my literature tutors at Strathclyde – and who had revealed for me the power of Burns' language, his words as weapons. By the early 1990s Kenny and colleagues had begun to organise an annual Burns conference at Strathclyde and, aware of the new directions of my research, invited me to speak at a couple of these, on Burns' social background, and what his views on the Union of 1707 might have been. This was in the 1990s. Conscious that there were those who knew much more than I ever could about Burns, his life, writing and literary achievements, I declined Kenny's subsequent invitations.

But in 2007 he approached me once more, to give a plenary lecture at the University of Glasgow's Centre for Robert Burns Studies' forthcoming conference in January 2009 to mark the 250th anniversary of the poet's birth. Flattered but anxious about what I could offer at such a momentous event that hadn't been said before, I decided to explore something I'd long been intrigued by: the ubiquitous statues of Burns there are in Scotland, and what lay behind this remarkable phenomenon. Kenny approved of the result, but suggested I should not stop there. He was convinced there was a job for a Scottish historian to do in exploring Burns' legacy and the impact of his contested memory on Scottish society.

Sadly, Kenny died in 2013. But, for kick starting the project that has resulted in this book, my debt to him is immeasurable.

Following the 2009 conference, Professor Murray Pittock of the University of Glasgow suggested I join his Arts and Humanities Research Council (AHRC) funded Global Burns Network. From this sprang the AHRC-funded project he led, 'Robert Burns: Inventing Tradition and Securing Memory, 1796–1909'. I was co-investigator, along with Murdo Macdonald, also of the University of Dundee. Murray's enthusiasm, and his initiative in seeking AHRC funding, have been major factors in getting this book written. The Dundee research assistant was Katherine McBay, whose labours on our behalf were immense, as were those of her co-researcher Pauline Mackay. Katherine's endeavours supplemented those of several University of Dundee undergraduates whom I employed in summer vacations between 2008 and 2014: Laura Paterson, Julie Danskin, Nicola Cowmeadow and Barry Sullivan.

Without the generous assistance of archivists, librarians and other custodians of relevant records, books like this cannot be written. My thanks are due therefore to Eddie Bonar, Dundee Burns Club; Steve Connelly and his colleagues at Perth and Kinross Council Archives; Neil Dickson, Stirling Council Archives; Heather Dunlop and Ross McGregor, Burns Monument Centre, and Dick Institute, Kilmarnock respectively; Linda Fairlie and Bruce Morgan, Dick Institute, Kilmarnock; Sandy Fleming, Longforgan; Patricia Grant, Mitchell

Library, Glasgow; David Hopes, Robert Burns Birthplace Museum (National Trust for Scotland); Pamela Logue, Information Officer, Heritage Centre, Paisley Central Library, Renfrewshire Council; Christine Love-Rodgers, New College Library, University of Edinburgh; Hazel McLatchie, Mitchell Library, Glasgow; Sue Payne, Perth Museum; Graham Roberts, Archivist, Ewart Library, Dumfries; Fiona Scharlau and her staff at Angus Archives, Restenneth Priory, Forfar; Joanne Turner, Dumfries Museum; David Weir, Central Library, Paisley; Sandy Wood, Collections Curator, Royal Scottish Academy of Art & Architecture; the staffs of the National Records of Scotland, and the National Library of Scotland. Overseas, special thanks are due to Twila Buttimer of the Provincial Archives, New Brunswick, Canada, Philip Hartling of Nova Scotia Archives, Rose Wilson, of the State Library, Adelaide, South Australia, and Jill Haley, Otago Settlers Museum, Dunedin, New Zealand.

Thanks for other forms of help are due to Mike Bartholomew; David Finkelstein, University of Edinburgh; David Goldie, University of Strathclyde; Christopher Harvie; Murray Frame, Kirsty Gunn, Jim Livesey and Graeme Morton, University of Dundee; Anne Rigney, University of Utrecht; Michael Vance, Saint Mary's University, Nova Scotia; and Mark Wallace of Lyon College, Arkansas. Catriona Macdonald, University of Glasgow, has provided suggestions of sources both primary and secondary, asked searching questions and shared her insights. From the same institution I have been encouraged and assisted by Rhona Brown, Gerry Carruthers, Pauline Mackay and Kirstin McCue (all of the Centre for Robert Burns Studies).

For taking on this book, advising me on style and in other ways bringing it to publication I am grateful to Hugh Andrew and his colleagues at Birlinn Ltd, above all academic managing editor Mairi Sutherland. We had a long and unsuccessful search for a title for the book until my daughter Eilidh came up with what we have now.

I am grateful to the following bodies for permission to use images from their collections: Burns Monument Centre, Kilmarnock; Dick Institute, Kilmarnock; Dumfries Museum and Ewart Library, Dumfries and Galloway Council; Leisure & Culture, Dundee (Dundee Central Library); Glasgow Museums and Libraries (Mitchell Library); Heritage Services, Renfrewshire Council; National Trust for Scotland; Royal Scottish Academy; Douglas Scott, Scottish Federation of Meat Traders; D C Thomson & Co Ltd.

I should thank, too, the organisers of the many Burns suppers I have attended, and from time to time been privileged to address. The effort those concerned put into these heart-warming occasions is unstinting. Their commitment to the preservation of Burns' memory is beyond question, and demands respect.

Last but not least I must acknowledge the support and forbearance of my wife Pat. The final months of a book-writing project are necessarily concentrated. The job done, I'm hoping we can now reconnect, and enjoy life without a deadline. Until the next time.

Christopher A. Whatley

Introduction: dimensions of immortal memory

On a typically overcast, sleet-chilled Thursday in Glasgow in January 1877 a statue of Robert Burns was unveiled in the city's George Square. It had been a long time coming. The date – the 25th – had been chosen deliberately; it had been Burns' birthday.

Witnessing the event – or trying to – were thousands of people in the surrounding streets, almost certainly more than on any previous occasion in the city's history other perhaps than in the months leading up to the great parliamentary Reform Act of 1832.

In the square itself were most of the tradesmen who had formed a several thousand-strong, colourful and cacophonous but disciplined procession that had marched, four deep, from mud-laden Glasgow Green. Tightly packed, they crushed onto the enclosure behind which a large party of elite citizens of the second city of the empire were congregated, and where the flag-draped statue stood. Even rooftops had been commandeered as viewing positions for the plucky. Perhaps as many as half a million people in Glasgow and its surrounding towns stopped work, although as west central Scotland was in its heyday as the workshop of the world, for most the respite was for part of the day only.

Glasgow's enthusiasm for Burns was in many respects astonishing. He had not been born in the city, nor was it somewhere he had lived. He had died in Dumfries.

Yet what happened in Glasgow was not without precedent. A Burns festival near Ayr in August 1844 had attracted anything from 50,000 to 80,000 visitors (crowd size estimates in the nineteenth century are notoriously unreliable), overwhelming the burgh's resident population of just over 5,000. Fifteen years later, in hundreds of Scotland's towns, villages and even some hamlets, but also in many parts of the English-speaking world, most notably North America and Australia, tens of thousands of people turned out to mark the centenary of Burns' birth. This can be classified as a Scottish variant of a Europe-wide phenomenon – the public commemorative festival designed to bring people together in civic spaces 'to act out their loyalties in a pleasurable way'.[1] Yet 25 January 1859 was one of the most extraordinary days in Scotland's history. Ever. Contemporaries – especially from south of the border – were astounded at the extent and exuberance of the occasion. And – in relation to Burns – not for the first time.[2]

The year 1859 was important too in that, although not immediately, it led to the move for a statue in Glasgow. Less than two years after the Glasgow statue's unveiling, in September 1878, in Kilmarnock, the procession that had preceded the laying of the foundation stone for a Burns statue there was so long that the only comparison older inhabitants could make was with the 'extraordinary gatherings' associated with demands for parliamentary reform earlier in the century. Incredibly, eight years later, in 1886, 30,000 people returned to the site – Kay Park – to commemorate the centenary of the publication of a book: the first, Kilmarnock, edition of Burns' poems.

Visual evidence points not just to immense crowds but also to seething surging passionate crowds. Comparing some of the public Burns' celebrations in Victorian Scotland with most of those overseas, the emotional energy they unleashed was striking. It hints at a particularly intense relationship between ordinary Scots and the ploughman poet.

Burns of course was not Scotland's first heroic figure. This honour had fallen to William Wallace as early as the fourteenth century.[3] It was in the nineteenth century though that Wallace's reputation reached a peak.[4] Unveiled in 1869, and standing over 220 feet high, the colossal monument on Abbey Craig near Stirling for the Scottish patriot warrior is grander and more prominent than any of the Burns memorials.

But Burns wins hands down as far as the numbers of large-scale monuments, including statues, are concerned. Three memorials were constructed in relatively quick succession in the early nineteenth century, in Dumfries (1819), Alloway, near Ayr (1823) and Edinburgh (after 1831). These are discussed in chapter 1. The most active period of memorialisation, however, was between 1877 and 1896, with Aberdeen, Ayr, Dumfries, Dundee, Irvine, Kilmarnock, Leith and Paisley (and Glasgow) being swept along in what was an apparently unstoppable wave of Burns statue construction.

Remarkable too was the speed with which some of the statue projects were completed. Five years was how long it took the Glasgow statue's promoters to bring their project to completion. Kilmarnock was faster: not much more than two years from the point at which a Burns statue for the town was first seriously mooted. Dundee too moved rapidly, and well within four years of a firm proposal being made had a statue in place. The campaign for a memorial to Sir Walter Scott was launched within four days of the writer's death on 21 September 1832, but fifteen years were to pass before the monument to and statue of Scott in Edinburgh's Princes Street were completed and inaugurated.

Comparison with Sir Walter Scott is instructive in other respects too. Both Scott and Burns were much esteemed by their countrymen in the decades after their deaths. Aptly, Stuart Kelly used the term 'Scott-Land' for the title of his study of Scott's remarkable impact on the country of his birth, not least the part his writings had played in turning Scotland into a tourist destination by providing visitors as well as his fellow Scots with a usable – romantic – past.[5] Similarly, Burns' cultural 'afterlife' (which began in 1796 as opposed to 1832 for Scott) continued to pulse strongly many decades after his death. However, in some respects Scott's star began to wane even prior to the celebrations to mark the centenary of his birth. There is no sign in Burns' case of the 'commemorative fatigue' that Ann Rigney has suggested may have accounted for the more muted Scott festivities of 1871. Instead, efforts to celebrate, commemorate and perpetuate the memory of Burns intensified rather than diminished as the century wore on. Almost impossible to quantify are the numerous statuettes, busts, plaques, tablets and other smaller memorials that were being placed in town halls, libraries and other appropriate locations, including Poet's Corner in Westminster Abbey in 1885.[6]

Very different too were the constituencies to which the two writers appealed: Scott had countless admirers at home and abroad, but again, as Ann Rigney has remarked, 'his fan base was above all genteel'.[7] Burns' appeal was global too, but different. As far as the everyday lives of vast numbers of Scots in the nineteenth century and even the first decades of the twentieth were concerned, Burns' influence was much greater, and recognised as such by many outside observers of Scottish society.[8] More will be said about this in the chapters that follow, and should serve to justify the praise lavished on Burns in 1896 by William Robertson Turnbull for the galvanising effect he had had on Scotland's 'toiling poor', who 'found in him the best organ for their suppressed feelings or inarticulate longings and desires'.[9]

The Burns statue movement – for this is what it appeared to be even though there was no co-ordinating individual or body until the formation of the Burns Federation in 1885 – spread far beyond Scotland, across the Irish Sea and over the Atlantic to the United States. America was home to one of the earliest statues of Burns erected outside Scotland, unveiled in 1880 in New York's Central Park. Others came later, at the turn of the twentieth century and through to the 1920s, not only in the USA, but also Canada and the more distant lands of Australia and New Zealand – which between them had six by 1913.[10] Ultimately there would be some fifty life-sized or larger statues of Burns worldwide.[11]

We should not get this out of perspective. 'Statuemania' is the term historians have used to describe the period when Britain – from the time of the death of Sir Robert Peel to the end of Queen Victoria's reign – went 'statue mad'.[12] So too did Ireland and mainland Europe, above all France and Germany where such activity peaked between 1870 and 1914.[13] America (of course) had the world's biggest statue – the French-conceived, French-built Statue of Liberty, that stood 32 metres tall. Scotland had nothing on this scale – the Wallace Monument came closest – but here too public statuary flourished as never before (or since). In Glasgow alone a new statue was unveiled on average every three-and-a-half years.[14] Proportionate to its population, Edinburgh had more public memorials than anywhere else in Britain – forty-four just after the First World War, most of them Victorian.[15] Yet the sheer number of Burns statues and memorials – large and small – cannot be gainsaid. Indeed, as we shall see in chapter 4, for the city fathers of Scotland's Lowland towns, to be without a statue of Burns could be a cause of civic angst.

Similarly, we must not exaggerate the significance of the vast turn-outs there were for unveiling and other ceremonies associated with Burns. Most entertainment at this time was public and participative. Throughout much of Europe the nineteenth century was an age of monster meetings, mass demonstrations and thronging crowds. What drew them ranged from celebrations of coronations, through birthdays of monarchs and their relatives and rejoicings at the news of military successes, to funerals of leading statesmen and esteemed local employers.

But again, the numbers for Burns are consistently at the high end of the scale.

* * *

Monuments are the most public and permanent signs of Burns veneration. Very different, and usually held behind closed doors, were the Burns' 'dinners', now usually called suppers. Within five years of Burns' death, the first of these had been convened, when nine friends of the poet dined (on sheep's head and haggis), drank toasts, sang and recited their own verse at the cottage where he had been born, in Alloway. Anniversary dinners or 'feasts' to commemorate departed poets were in themselves unremarkable. Shakespeare, Stephen Duck and Scotland's James Thomson (who wrote the words of 'Rule Britannia'), had all been the focus of such entertainments. What is remarkable in the case of Burns is that the quasi-masonic ritual of the Alloway dinner of 1801 was the model for similar events that have been held ever since, although women are now more likely to be included than they were initially. We now know from Clark McGinn's exhaustive researches that Burns suppers – initiated by Scotsmen – began to be held in England (Oxford was first, in 1806), and the British colonies. Bombay – now Mumbai – was the first in India, possibly in 1810. In North America Burns was acknowledged in toasts at St Andrews Day gatherings from shortly after his death, with the first dedicated Burns supper having been held in Philadelphia in 1816. Canada, Australia and New Zealand were not far behind.

In short, by the middle of the nineteenth century, Burns commemoration was a global practice and by the turn of the twentieth century had even reached Shanghai. Scots abroad used Scottish ethnic associations as a 'harbour of stability and familiarity', with Burns, in the words of Tanja Bueltmann, being 'one of the most effective glues that bound Scots together around the world'.[16] On 25 January 2009, the 250th anniversary of Burns' birth, an estimated nine million people in over 80 different countries participated in Burns suppers worldwide.[17] The words of 'Auld Lang Syne' may not be fully understood, but they are universally sung.

But there were other, less obvious ways in which Scots demonstrated their affection for Burns, and by which his memory was preserved after his death in 1796. Paintings and engravings of Burns himself, his characters and scenes with which he was familiar – a research topic in its own right – proliferated.[18] The endless cascade of editions of his poems and songs are another instance, with some publishers building their reputations around their Burns catalogues.

Relics – items Burns had used or even touched – were viewed or handled as if they had belonged to or were connected with a holy man, suffused with his spirit and capable of renewing his disciples' faith in his good works. Morbid curiosity and a desire somehow to connect with the deceased poet induced an unseemly frenzy to collect – even steal – items associated with him. There was the shameless pilfering of mementoes from his birthplace in Alloway – 'a tabernacle of clay', which overnight became a shrine for literary pilgrims.[19] Used as an alehouse even before the end of the eighteenth century, its proprietors made as much as they could of the Burns connection as a means of attracting the custom of curious visitors, and satiating – at a price – the thirst of weary pilgrims.[20] The cottage is now part of the National Trust for Scotland's Robert Burns Birthplace Museum.

Alloway Kirk, where Burns' father had been buried in 1784 and famously the scene and centrepiece of 'Tam o' Shanter', also attracted early visitors, as did the nearby Brig o' Doon, their close proximity making this a mecca for Burns' devotees.[21] By 1819 nothing of the roof or rafters or 'any other part of the wood work' of the ruined church was left, much to the dismay of those hoping to secure their own fragment of association. One disappointed visitor even made public his complaint that he had had to use his penknife and consequently suffered a blistered hand in his effort to saw off a slice of the gnarled tree that overshadowed the kirk.[22] Such behaviour is to modern eyes one of the less desirable aspects of the relatively new phenomenon of literary tourism, and the unscrupulous search for souvenirs. That the two chairs in which the principal speakers at the first national Burns festival held in Alloway in 1844 were proudly proclaimed as having been carved from what remained of the kirk's rafters, and occasioned no adverse comment, is indicative of different mores than today's.

Burns' grave too was on the itinerary of literary pilgrims. Long before the erection of the mausoleum in 1818 in St Michael's churchyard in Dumfries, the plain stone slab that marked the site of his coffin had drawn a steady stream of visitors, including William and Dorothy Wordsworth in 1803. The grave induced feelings of both reverence and disappointment, as many felt Burns deserved better in what was already a crowded graveyard. Burns' resting place was disturbed on several occasions following his first burial in 1796. The first two (when his grave was re-opened to allow for the coffins of two of his sons to be placed with their father) were little noted. By 1815, however, when Burns' body was moved to accommodate the mausoleum, his remains had taken on a quasi-sacred meaning. On sight of the opened coffin, where were exposed Burns' bones and skull with its 'lordly forehead, arched and high . . . and the teeth perfectly firm and white', the workmen who were present 'stood bare and uncovered', 'their frames thrilling with some indefinable emotion, as they gazed on the ashes of him whose fame is as wide as the world itself'.[23] But the exhumation as well as the re-interment, beneath the mausoleum, were kept deliberately low key and out of public view. And just as well. In 1818 what were thought to have been the bones of Robert the Bruce, Scotland's fourteenth-century king and the hero of Bannockburn, were discovered in front of the former choir at Dunfermline Abbey. To satisfy public interest they were displayed in the Abbey prior to their re-interment. However the volume of material comprising Bruce's body and associated objects that was eventually placed in the new pitched-lined lead coffin in November 1819 was rather less than had been dug up the previous year: teeth, finger bones, nails and fragments of cloth and the original coffin all disappeared in the throng of visitors – although some items turned up for inspection, and sale, later in the century.[24]

This was more like the level of interest that was aroused by a further exhumation of Burns' bones in March 1834. The body of Burns' wife, Jean Armour, was to be laid alongside what remained of her husband. The night beforehand, two phrenologists measured and felt the bumps on Burns' skull. Their conclusions, that the skull was larger than average and that Burns had indeed been a genius, were 'revelations' that attracted attention nationwide.[25] Not even burial was sufficient to deter hero worshippers from digging deep and performing acts of partial resurrection with the man who would later be venerated as Scotland's secular saint.

What relic hunters collected could be serendipitous, but there were those zealots who by bearing witness, so to speak, had a clear purpose in mind: to secure in perpetuity the memory of Burns. A telling example is James Gould, an Edinburgh post office employee who gifted his lifetime's collection of materials relating to the Burns centenary of 1859 (and much more besides) to Glasgow's Mitchell Library. Quite consciously Gould called his contribution 'a pen and ink Monument' of the remarkable proceedings of that year. Like his fellow collectors, Gould was tenacious, his search according to his obituary writer taking him into 'the obscurest corner of every British settlement', as well as to 'the most sequestered portions of the American States, Africa, and India'. The holograph letters, autographs, photographs, newspaper cuttings and ephemera he gathered were Scotland's equivalent of the Dead Sea scriptures, from which future scholars of Burns would find truth and inspiration.[26]

It was not long before the moneymaking opportunities from the manufacture of Burns memorabilia were identified and exploited.[27] Pauline Mackay and others have demonstrated the scale and extent of the commercialised material culture of Burns' memory making, a hobby that in the eyes of a disapproving Elizabeth Ewing (in 1943) had become a business and then degenerated into a racket.[28] Medallions such as those produced by the Paisley modeller John Hemming (1771–1851) were popular but costly (Plate 1).[29] So too were busts – available for one guinea in 1828 – and portraits. But there was a wide range of domestic ware such as plates, vases and drinking vessels, as well as personal items such as wooden snuff boxes decorated with characters and scenes from Burns' poems and songs and much else, which after 1810 became known as Mauchline ware, after the name of the town where such objects were manufactured.[30] It is upon paraphernalia of this kind that the bawdier aspects of Burns' oeuvre were illustrated, subjects deemed unsuitable for public art (Plate 2). Titillating images of youthful buxom witches from 'Tam o' Shanter' for private consumption contrast sharply with the wizened dancers depicted, for example, on the more macabre bas relief panel of the same subject on the pedestal of Albert Hodge's Burns statue in Stirling, unveiled in 1914.

Other than for the most gullible it was widely understood that 'made from the wood of' was what Murray Pittock has called a tokenistic attribution, not a serious guarantee. Exploitation went on long after the nominal source could have been reliably identified, or indeed lasted.[31] Even so, over the course of the two centuries and more after 1796 there have been countless perfervid Burnsians who were prepared to pay small fortunes to possess one of an impossible number of drinking glasses, rings, watches, clocks, pens, walking sticks, pistols, masonic aprons or snuff boxes claimed to have belonged to Burns – so many, Ms Ewing dryly remarked, as 'would . . . have won [him] as distinguished a place among eighteenth-century collectors as among poets'.[32]

This of course was what happened after his death.

* * *

Signs of Burns' charismatic appeal, however, had begun to be apparent during his lifetime. His eventful sojourn to Edinburgh that began at the end of 1786 following the publication of and critical acclaim for the first, Kilmarnock, edition of his *Poems, Chiefly in the Scottish Dialect*, has often been described. Before the year was out the *Poems* were being read – or more often heard – by friends of the Stirling-born physician Dr John Moore in London.[33] Little more than a year later individual poems as well as William Creech's Edinburgh edition of the *Poems* in 1787 were in the hands of Scots émigrés in Boston, Philadelphia and New York (and thereafter in Canada and further afield).[34] At the end of the same decade, verses about Burns were to be found in chapbooks, although poems attacking him were also printed in these.[35] From the outset and notwithstanding the praise that was showered on him, Burns was also a controversial figure.

By the early 1790s, by which time his fame as a dialect poet had grown, along with his reputation as a sympathiser with the revolutionaries in France, Burns had begun to attract a stream of admirers. These were often brother poets from nearby Ulster, who could relatively easily find passage over the North Channel.[36] Demand in Ireland was such that editions of the *Poems* were printed in Belfast and Dublin in 1789, with reprints the following year.[37] Likenesses of his head and face appeared in several publications, the first being John Beugo's engraving – done from life – in the Creech edition.[38] Even before he died, Burns was probably the most recognisable commoner in Scotland.

Through Burns, who had rapidly graduated from being the self-styled bard of Ayrshire to that of Scotland, Dumfries was beginning to be included as a stopping off point for travellers on the Scottish version of the European Grand Tour. In June 1796, only weeks before Burns' death, the Ossian-adoring Reverend James Macdonald, in search of Scotland the sublime and Romantic, was at pains to visit and dine with the 'heaven born Genius' who despite his avowed republicanism waxed lyrical about the so-called Pretender, Charles Edward Stuart. For Macdonald, fervently Scottish and mildly Anglophobic, Burns was one of the wonders of his age, along with a colliery steam engine at Joppa and David Dale's vast mills at New Lanark.[39]

Only weeks later Burns was on his deathbed. Allan Cunningham, the future poet who as a young apprentice stonemason was in Dumfries during Burns' later years, noted the anxiety felt by all ranks.[40] On the day of his funeral the burgh was 'like a besieged place', with those present conscious that Burns had been a man 'whose like we can scarce see again'.[41] His fellow townsman William Grierson forecast that his 'immortal works' would live forever.

Further editions of Burns' poems and songs cascaded from the printing presses. Scarcely a year went by without a Burns publication of one kind or other, some of it – political poems, religious satires including 'Holy Willie's Prayer', and his bawdy productions like the 'Merry Muses of Caledonia' – posthumously.[42] How Burns' work was disseminated and became so widely known is discussed in chapter 2. Here, too, we will begin to explore what Burns meant to growing numbers of ordinary Scots, how he was read and understood, a task that requires us to know something of the *mentalité* of his audiences.[43]

The public's appetite for Burns was insatiable. Before long, he was being read in translation in many parts of mainland Europe – although here it was in the second half of the nineteenth century that interest in Burns blossomed on the back of his radicalism, non-parochial nationalism and as someone who had proclaimed through his work the primacy of folk tradition and native language.[44] By the early twenty-first century there were well over 3,000 editions of Burns' works in foreign languages, many more than his near contemporaries such as the fellow poet Lord Byron or the political economist and moral philosopher Adam Smith.[45] In the Soviet Union where he was portrayed as a peasant revolutionary, one Russian translation sold an incredible 600,000 copies, with other versions being produced for several of the post-USSR republics. In Japan and China, too, he has many admirers, as evidenced by the sale of 100,000 copies of a translation published in Beijing in 2005. However, although Burns had – and has – a vast audience amongst non-Scots in many parts of the world, the constraints of space mean that it is the relationship between his 'afterlife' and the Scottish people mainly at home with which this book is concerned. Burns and the Scots abroad would fill another volume.

Burns, as we have noted already, was not the Scots' only hero in the nineteenth century. But amongst them all he was *primus inter pares* – first amongst equals. The question is why. For it is certainly not immediately apparent why it was that a poet from the rural south-west, whose flexible use of the 'almost untranslatable' Ayrshire vernacular created difficulties in understanding in other parts of Scotland, let alone south of the border or further afield where Lowland Scots was heard even less often, should have become the object of so much veneration.[46]

We will be disappointed in our search for an answer if we turn to Scotland's historians. Few have paid serious attention to what might be called the Burns phenomenon. Burns' cultural and political influence has largely been left to literary scholars. In itself this is not a concern: the work of Burns experts who have explored the multiple contexts in which he lived and wrote and was read, such as Robert Crawford, Thomas Crawford, Leith Davis, Gerard Carruthers, Colin Kidd, Nigel Leask, Carol McGurk, Liam McIlvanney, Murray Pittock, Kenneth Simpson and others, is compelling.

Burns, though, is not solely a literary figure; a central proposition in this book is that he belongs in the mainstream of Scotland's history. Judiciously, James Coleman, the author of an otherwise comprehensive history of Scottish commemoration in the nineteenth century, acknowledged Burns' over-riding cultural importance, but decided to concentrate on the other inspirational heroes who underpinned Scottish nationality in the Victorian era – William Wallace through John Knox to the Covenanters and the Jacobites. His conclusion was that to do Burns justice would require a book in its own right.[47] What you have in front of you is a step in that direction.

But what follows is not just about commemoration. Once again, comparison with Scott is revealing. If Scott 'invented' the Scottish nation, Burns mobilised it. We will explore this theme in greater detail later – primarily in chapters 2, 3 and 4: it is sufficient here to say that Burns spoke to, gave succour to and inspired his countrymen at a time when power was largely in the hands of the landed classes, and the voices of ordinary people were little heard. Democracy was an ideal that only began to gain any currency in the last years of Burns' life, largely through the writings of Thomas Paine. But it is difficult to exaggerate the impact that certain of Burns' poems and songs had on the generations that followed him, above all the notion that 'A Man's a Man for a' That'. Clichéd now, and taken for granted perhaps, in the context of the social order of the nineteenth century the lines of this song were utterly transformational. As Charles Scott, an Edinburgh advocate, remarked at a Burns supper in the capital on the evening of the unveiling of Glasgow's Burns statue, 'there was no man in Scotland who was not entirely different from what he had been had Burns not lived', a net he afterwards widened to include women.[48]

Yet as a moving force, an *agency*, someone who played a part in shaping the course of history, Burns hardly registers. His impact amongst the Scottish diaspora is better understood, as is the effect of his writing and some of his ideals in America.[49] Few, however, have appreciated how intensely Burns mattered to Scots at home.[50]

When Burns does appear in Scottish histories, it is usually fleetingly, the treatment casual. The author of one of the most comprehensive histories of Scotland in recent decades recognised Burns' popularity, but confused the steep rise in the number of Burns clubs affiliated to the Burns Federation between 1885 and 1911 with Burns' appeal for non-members. The measure is useful but misleading if it causes us to ignore the profound impact Burns had on Scotland's artisans and the emergent middling ranks much earlier.[51] One Marxist labour historian clearly had a sense of this, claiming that 'Scottish plebeian radicals [in the early nineteenth century] shared Robert Burns' vision of a new epoch in man's struggle for freedom'.[52] Unfortunately, however, he provided little in the way of supporting evidence, a failing we will go some way to redress in chapter 2. Christopher Harvie on the other hand provides not a scrap of evidence in support of his breathtakingly assured assertion that it was from 1886, the centenary of the publication of the Kilmarnock edition, 'that the modern Burns cult essentially dates'.[53] Clearly – as the evidence already outlined in this Introduction shows – we have work to do to get the story right.

Better evidenced (and fairly well known) is that Burns was often on the reading lists of the first Labour leaders who emerged from the turn of the twentieth century – perhaps the best example being Labour's long-serving Secretary of State for Scotland in the 1960s and 1970s, Willie Ross (1911-1988), whose speeches were often laced with lines from Burns.[54] According to Bill Knox, Burns' idealism was one of the 'most important formative influences' for such men, along with Karl Marx, Keir Hardie, the Bible, Robert Blatchford and William Morris.[55]

Apparently at odds with this association of Burns with the early socialists is what has been argued by Richard Finlay, namely Burns' importance for Scotland's middle classes, many of whom were advocates of *laissez-faire* liberalism and promoted Burns as a 'paradigm of Scottish bourgeois virtue', the 'lad o' pairts' who by dint of his own merits had been successful.[56] There is much truth in this, as we shall see in chapter 4, but more so for the second half of the nineteenth century. Earlier, it was the country's aristocracy who had adopted Burns. However, as has become apparent from investigations of how other great figures, major events and anniversaries were commemorated in the nineteenth century, the efforts of ruling elites to impose by such activities their own values could meet with opposition.[57] Christine MacLeod's study of the celebration by Victorians of the leading inventors of the Industrial Revolution, for example, has revealed that the virtues of particular inventors, extolled by the middle classes and their allies in government, were not necessarily those emphasised by working people.[58] The process of consensus stretching also applied in the case of Burns.

This will be a recurrent theme in what follows. Cultural memory is not neutral, uniform or static. It is worked, as an orator – whether a politician or a comedian – works a crowd. The nation's conservatives in the decades immediately after his death promoted Burns not only as a loyal Briton but also as the 'heaven taught' ploughman poet who had risen to prominence from within the existing social order, and also accepted his place within it. Poems like 'The Cotter's Saturday Night' were appropriated as a source of literary ballast, a means of maintaining the *status quo* at a time of profound change in the nature of society and politics. Burns, however, was not easily moulded. We shall see this in chapter 1, when we discuss the Ayr festival of 1844. What was being presented was a Tory version of Scottish patriotism that owed much to Walter Scott, a Scotland in which a 'sturdy peasantry deferred to a paternalist aristocracy'.[59] Tory attempts to hijack Burns, however, were not unnoticed, or without their critics.

In short, conservative hegemony over Burns' legacy was never complete. By the time of the unveiling of his statue in Glasgow in 1877, Burns in the eyes of many but by no means all Scots had come to represent a very different set of values. But as will be shown in chapter 5, in their turn Scotland's bourgeoisie – the upper segment of the nation's middle class – had to keep the lid on the bottle containing the Burns genie they believed was theirs. Burns' legacy was potent. In life Burns the poet had multiple voices.[60] In death many grasped at, and sought to inherit, his legacy.

It has been said that Burns is 'notoriously elusive'.[61] He is. But the essence of what he represented can be identified. Although Burns was recruited for many causes, there were fewer of these in the nineteenth century than at the end of the twentieth century, when he had become what one commentator has called Scotland's 'elastic symbol'.[62]

* * *

What becomes clear is that in order to understand in all of its complexity what George Rosie has somewhat dismissively labelled 'Burnsmania' – or a baffling 'cultural quirk' – we are going to have to look beyond mainstream Scottish history, and incorporate into our analysis ideas from elsewhere – from other places and different disciplines.[63]

The French historian Pierre Nora has argued that, in the pre-modern world, the past was intertwined with the present and so there was little need to actively cultivate memory. Modern societies, however, were to a greater extent torn loose from their traditional moorings. Accordingly, across Europe there emerged from the later eighteenth century a desire to stabilise the present by celebrating key anniversary dates from the past, whether this was a notable battle or the birth or death of nationally important figures. Allied to this was the cult of commemoration, the celebration of centenaries, bi-centenaries, tercentenaries and even octo-centenaries for more venerable heroes and heroic events, ensuring that neither the past nor the great deeds and doers of the present were forgotten.[64] This created what have been termed *lieux de memoire*, or 'realms of memory', that is, actual locations and material objects – memorials – which became, intentionally, repositories invested with historical meaning.[65]

In Scotland the period with which this book is concerned was one of rapid and sometimes deeply unsettling economic, social and political change – modernisation is a useful single word for describing this. There were revolutions in industry and agriculture. The process of transition to fully fledged capitalism was for those in the driving seat dynamic, forward-looking and in its way triumphant, but for large numbers of people it was conjoined with a pervading sense of loss, both real and imagined.[66] In experiencing disruption of this order of magnitude, Scotland was at the extreme end of a process of transformation that was affecting much of Europe, albeit unevenly. The pace and scale of change were without historical precedent. In such circumstances the past provided a sheet anchor.

Accordingly, in part, Burns' appeal can be accounted for by virtue of the fact that many of his poems vividly captured this rapidly disappearing world of rural and small town Scotland. It is in this context that historian Tom Devine has knitted Burns into his narrative on post-Union Scotland. However, influenced perhaps by what Burns became in the twentieth century rather than what he was in the century beforehand, his emphasis is on Burns' role in slaking what he calls a thirst for nostalgia amongst nineteenth-century Scots, severed from their past by the sword swipes of modernity.[67] This takes us so far, but there was more to it than that, as the short section on agency, above, indicated. Longing for what had been left behind was commoner amongst Scots abroad than those who were still in Scotland.

John Wolfe has argued that great deaths, where the deceased was a national figure whose passing was deeply felt, could challenge a people. The loss, however, could be overcome by 'the assertion of a transcending reality', the death a prompt 'to the intensified expression of the shared values and convictions of the group as a whole'.[68] This, it will be argued, is what happened in the case of Burns. He was a poet, but Scotland was not alone in establishing as the national bard a 'peasant' (which is how Burns was commonly portrayed), whose 'life describes an arc from birth in poverty and obscurity to the summit of fame and social success, then tragedy and disgrace in his final years'. The words quoted here, however, are not about Burns but refer to Jacint Verdaguer, Catalonia's leading nineteenth-century poet. Like Burns, Verdaguer produced poetry of 'rare intensity' and had 'an unusual awareness of his country's history and his own poetic destiny'.[69] It may be significant that both Scotland and Catalonia were once independent nations that had been absorbed by more powerful neighbours, the former by England in two relatively peaceful stages in 1603 and 1707, the latter, Catalonia, conquered by Spain in 1714 at the end of the same global war that had been instrumental in ending Scottish independence seven years earlier. In such circumstances poets such as Burns and Verdaguer assume greater political and cultural significance, although in heralding a poet as a national figurehead and symbol of their respective cultures, the Scots and the Catalans were by no means alone. Virtually everywhere writers were in the vanguard of a phenomenon that has been termed cultural nationalism (although in Scotland's case the honours hitherto have been awarded to Scott rather than Burns).[70]

In this respect England may have been the exception, according to a *Times* correspondent contrasting the heady excitement of the inauguration of Glasgow's Burns statue with the muted tercentenary celebrations of Shakespeare's birth in 1864, an event that had roused little national interest: it 'is not of authors we are more proud', he had concluded.[71] Elsewhere, though, it was often around poets and other writers that nations' identities were forged and consolidated. Take the case of the Russian Romantic poet and playwright Alexander Pushkin. The chronology and character of his commemoration shadowed those for Burns. Born in 1799, Pushkin had, like Burns, died relatively young, in 1837. The idea for a permanent monument became a firm proposal in 1857, around the time the Glasgow Burns statue was first mooted. It was unveiled in Moscow in June 1880 in front of a crowd that was similar in size to Glasgow's – although the celebrations went on for three days.[72] For Russians, who were denied political recognition by the Tsarist state (which has a parallel in the complaint of many Scots that England was largely indifferent to Scotland's distinctiveness and needs), Pushkin became the 'validator of their [the Russian people's] self-worth'.[73] Indeed in the Soviet era he was described as 'a living, active force, a mighty factor in . . . literature and art', and the 'founder of our aesthetic code'.[74] There are grounds for believing that Burns performed a similar function for the Scots, stateless despite their strong sense of nationhood. As one of the world's 'fragile' nations, its relationship with England a source of internal tensions and, periodically, of national angst, perhaps in Scotland commemorative acts were more than ordinarily required to mask divisions and create a coherent national memory. And, arguably, more than anyone else, Burns kept alive and added further luminosity to the patriotic flame that despite surges during the Jacobite risings had in the post-1707 era flickered only faintly until the publication in 1760 of the poems of 'Ossian' by James Macpherson. By 1805, however, these had been shown to be fraudulent. The 'bardic mantle' passed to Burns, whose poetry and songs that were steeped in Scotland's heroic past provided much of the cultural capital to sustain the sense of nation that by the later 1880s had become a powerful movement for Home Rule.[75]

For many Scots in the nineteenth century, language was the essence of Scottishness; Burns' use of it in much of his best work gave legitimacy to the way most ordinary Scots thought and spoke, and added another bulwark against the tide of Anglicising North British-ness that had flowed north since the union of 1707. Unionist-nationalism is the term coined by Graeme Morton to capture the notion of growing Scottish assertiveness within the framework of an uncontested union, although more recently Colin Kidd has referred to 'banal' unionism. The union, according to Kidd, was akin to familiar wallpaper, with Scotland's relations with England being largely a settled question, an accepted fact of political life from Culloden (in 1746) until the rise of the Scottish National Party in the 1970s.[76] But we should not assume that the wallpaper was to everyone's taste, nor mistake the couthy Kailyard literature of the later nineteenth century with the language of the people as spoken and the radical sentiments it was capable of expressing. Certainly in Burns' hands this was so.[77] The erection of enduring memorials to a figure such as this was an extension of the struggle over speech: in effect, nation building.

* * *

It is worth digressing briefly to outline how important large-scale monuments were in the era of 'Statuemania'. Nowadays we have become inured to the presence of the statues that line our streets or even sit centre stage in town and city squares and gardens. Photographs and other types of illustrations that began to appear in the press and magazines from the later nineteenth century meant that one function of portrait statues – representation as close to 'real' life as possible – was redundant. Now often overshadowed by taller buildings than were common in the nineteenth century, these statues are hardly noticed. But it was not always thus. In some parts of the world there have been memorials and statues that so offended deep-rooted sensitivities that they were either desecrated or in some cases toppled. Nearer to home, in Ireland, street monuments including statues became the focus of bitter conflict. Several, unsurprisingly those representing British monarchs and imperial governors, have been pulled down or blown up.[78] In Scotland, where nationalism was of a different character and violence had rarely been adopted as a means of political expression, most public statuary survived unscathed. Even so, sentiments that would not have been out of place in Ireland were being articulated in the early nineteenth century.

One side of the argument was exemplified in Archibald Alison's plea for a National Monument on Edinburgh's Calton Hill, a campaign for which had begun in 1819, with building getting under way – for a short time – in 1826.[79] It was right, Alison declared, that 'the Scotch should glory with their aged sovereign in the name of Britain' and the 'united whole' that had extended and upheld the British Empire. But, he went on, it was equally important that Scotland's 'ancient metropolis', Edinburgh, 'should not degenerate into a provincial town'. An independent nation, once rivalling England, should remember with pride 'the peculiar glories by which her people have been distinguished'. Otherwise the 'good effects' of the rivalry between the two nations would be lost, and the 'genius of her different people ... will be drawn into one centre, where all that is original and characteristic will be lost in the overwhelming influence of prejudice and fashion'.[80] For Alison, Burns was one of Scotland's geniuses, in the promotion of which he was in the forefront. At the same time, unionists like Alison were conscious of the dangers of playing too enthusiastically the patriotic card, and aware that fanning the embers of Anglophobia could result in the eruption of full-blown nationalism.

From a somewhat different perspective but coming to a similar conclusion was a correspondent to *The Scotsman* in September 1833. The Scottish capital could boast three 'colossal' monuments, he observed, of Henry Dundas (Lord Melville), King George IV and, just unveiled, William Pitt. Imposing as they were, the writer protested that not only were the statues of the monarch and Pitt poorly executed (by Sir Francis Chantrey) but they did Scotland no honour. On the contrary, they were useful only as emblems 'to remind us of past degradation'. It was the 'illustrious' dead of Scotland, currently ignored as far as public memorials in Edinburgh were concerned, who, the writer urged, should in future be commemorated, so ensuring that 'our public monuments will not . . . be a reproach to our patriotism'.[81]

Yet such monuments in Scotland have had a bad press. In her seminal *Strange Death of Scottish History* the late Marinell Ash concluded that many of those raised were 'meaningless or highly selective images of Scotland's past', the consequence of an historical failure of nerve and loss of confidence amongst Scots intellectuals in the nineteenth century.[82] Cairns Craig has challenged this last proposition, not least by demonstrating the vitality and modernity of Scottish thought in science, psychology and anthropology.[83] The evidence presented in this book will cast further doubt on the validity of Ash's assertions.[84] A central contention is that Burns memorials were redolent with meaning. Or meanings. Certainly they were selective but it was the fact of their selection that indicates their meaningfulness.

In Victorian and early Edwardian Scotland there was a cadre of thoughtful, intelligent and well-read Scots who not only held their nerve, but who through Burns nurtured the self-conscious sense of Scottishness that emerged strongly during the nineteenth century. Several of Scotland's more influential public intellectuals – such as John Stuart Blackie, Andrew Lang and Charles Rogers – had no hesitation in singing Burns' praises and acknowledging his influence. The 'amnesia' Colin Kidd has identified as a cause of the neglect of Scottishness by some Scots in the nineteenth century was far from a universal condition.[85] The rapturous reception given to speakers at commemorative occasions who proclaimed Burns' association with and significance for Scotland is indicative of a vigorous sense of nation at the popular level.

Which takes us to Home Rule. It has been suggested that the pressure for this was parliamentary rather than popular.[86] The evidence suggests otherwise. By the 1850s Burns had become unquestionably the 'poet of the [Scottish] people'. In this capacity – as a patriotic icon – Burns played a similar role to the one for which William Wallace was appropriated, sometimes by exactly the same small coterie of individuals who were Burns' leading exponents.[87] One of these was Archibald Primrose, 5th Earl of Rosebery, Scotland's 'uncrowned King' who in numerous speeches acknowledged the importance of Burns' role as a carrier of Scottish nationality. Burns was so wrapped up with Scotland's sense of itself that by the end of the nineteenth century and the first years of the twentieth century the issue of *how* he should be represented in statues became a matter of intense public debate, as is discussed in full in chapter 6.

* * *

Carved from stone or cast in metal, memorials are works of art in their own right as well as having a role in confirming the myths with which people – and peoples – make sense of their lives.[88] That monuments are now being 'read' by historians of art and architecture such as Johnny Rodger, their mnemonics interrogated for the designer's or sculptor's meaning, is enormously helpful for our present endeavour. But essential – and revealing – as such analysis is, it tells us only part of the story; missing is how the statue got there, why and in what ideological or political interest and, too often overlooked, what it meant for contemporaries.[89]

Without visitors or viewers, a memorial is an arid piece of carved stone or moulded bronze bereft of social significance.[90] A key question is whether it achieved the aims its promoters – and the artist – sought. We will 'listen' too (by reading), and judge where we can what the participants' responses were to what was said by platform speakers at unveiling ceremonies. By such means we will better appreciate the multiplicity of meanings such occasions could evoke on the part of onlookers.[91] Investigations in the field of what is known elsewhere as memory studies have demonstrated not only the fluidity of 'national' memory but also the extent to which it was contested: pluralist – kaleidoscopic and fractured by factors such as class, religion, gender and ethnicity – and even contradictory.[92] All of this applies to Burns.

Prior to Victoria's reign, few statues had been erected in Scotland's public places (most of the medieval statues that had mainly served religious purposes had been destroyed after the Reformation). The remark is not pejorative. Until the Napoleonic Wars ended, there were not many public memorials in England either.[93]

The move to public statuary (as opposed to non-figurative memorials) was at first cautious. That Glasgow's Napoleonic War hero Sir John Moore – the first in George Square, in 1819 – would be commemorated in the form of a statue was by no means a foregone conclusion when the project was first mooted: an early suggestion for an obelisk was rejected not on aesthetic grounds but because the city already had one, in Glasgow Green, commemorating Lord Nelson, of Trafalgar fame. Similar issues came to the fore during the heated debates in Edinburgh after Sir Walter Scott's death in 1832 about the most appropriate form of memorial with which to immortalise him. There had been strong support for William Playfair's proposal for a 60-metre high Egyptian obelisk – aimed to be the world's tallest – on a 13-metre-high pedestal to be sited at the west end of George Street, on Charlotte Square. Height, harmony with its surroundings in Edinburgh's classical New Town, durability, dignity and timelessness were amongst the reasons advanced for its adoption. Backers of Thomas Rickman's 'Gothic' structure on the other hand (which was supplanted at the planning stage by a design by the architect George Meikle Kemp) pointed to the similarity of an obelisk with the growing number of factory chimneys that were to be seen dominating the skylines of industrial towns like Manchester and Glasgow, something to be avoided in the Athens of the North. The Gothic style, too, was fitting for an author who had historicised Scotland.[94] But above all what the promoters wanted was a *representation* of Scott, preferably life-sized at least and thereby recognisable, which an obelisk was not. The answer was the portrait statue.

But it was not only to record the likeness of the deceased that sculptors were engaged. They also performed on behalf of their patrons (or so it was hoped) a pedagogic role by fixing in the public consciousness the primacy of certain ideological beliefs and values.[95]

Accordingly, what we need to know more about in the case of Burns statues is who commissioned them, and what they had in mind when doing so. And as they were so integral to the public commemoration of Burns, we should – and will – pay some attention to the artists who designed the statues of the bard.

The promoters of Burns monuments were certainly zealous. Few people had the stomach or degree of dedication required to become involved in enterprises that were fraught with difficulty – whether this was statue construction or the compilation of a paper memorial. Much was left to key individuals – avowed Burns enthusiasts, like Gould in Edinburgh. Yet we know surprisingly little about the more avid collectors of Burns manuscripts, small artefacts, editions of his works and masses of print and other material relating to Burns. Or of the ubiquitous Burns clubs with their more modest collections of what became known as Burnsiana. Other poets – including Browning, Shakespeare and Wordsworth – had inspired the formation of clubs and societies, but none had as yet 'approached anything like the universality of the Burns Club', as Wilhelm Meister observed in 1891.[96] Burns club members, we shall see, played a hitherto little regarded part in the physical manifestation of Scottish national consciousness in the nineteenth and early twentieth centuries, inasmuch as Burns was a contributor to this. It is also significant that the most important Burns clubs were town-based.

In Scotland, without a parliament since 1707 – a 'stateless nation' – and central government headquartered in London, there was no state agency north of the border to influence collective memory in a bid to secure loyalty and obedience.[97] Towns therefore often spoke for the nation.

The effectiveness with which they did this in part depended on the number and grandeur of their statuary. Walter Scott's death in 1832 had inspired calls in some places for commemorative statues. Edinburgh, Glasgow, Selkirk and Perth all sought to become the guardians – and beneficiaries – of his memory.[98] Wallace too induced rivalry between some of Scotland's towns. But it was the race for Burns' statues that instigated the fiercest competition.

* * *

Graeme Morton's observation that 'There is something for everybody in Burns', is probably true.[99] Today. But it was not always thus.

When Glasgow's statue of Burns was unveiled, much was made of its seminal importance as a very public and permanent symbol of what was a particularly strong relationship between the Scottish people and *their* poet – the people's poet. However, there were reservations about the apparent narrowness of this appellation, with one writer preferring to call Burns the poet of mankind, given that the middle and upper classes, too, had contributed substantially to commemoration projects.[100]

But there was also a very real limit to Burns' inclusiveness, and it concerns gender.[101] We know that women read Burns. They recited his poems and sang his songs. One of the loudest cheers in Glasgow's George Square in January 1877 was for an anonymous woman who, from the roof of a warehouse, gave a lusty rendition of 'Scots Wha Hae'. There are hints, however, that Burns' licentiousness and robust language – and the image of 'rantin, rovin Robin' – may not have been so welcome in some female circles as they were amongst men. If a lack of hard evidence makes this difficult to prove, what is certain is that Burns' commemoration in all of its main guises was male led, and usually designed to appeal to male conceit. Women had their place, as we shall see, but by and large this was a subordinate one. Was this, one wonders, why Burns Cottage in Alloway became a target for suffragettes, one of whom, Fanny Parker, was arrested in an attempt to blow it up in 1914.[102]

Women – or many of them – wanted to participate in Burns legacy making. There were, however, Scots who wanted no part of him, or his memory. 'Burnomania' (oddly, without the 's'), was the derogatory term applied to Burns hero worship by one clerical critic of the Burns cult as early as 1811. This was the Reverend William Peebles, minister at Newton-on-Ayr, who had felt at first-hand the sting of Burns' words when the poet was still alive.[103] Across the country, according to Scotland's leading social historian of religion, 'over a thousand parish theocracies ... [had in the eighteenth century] imposed a compulsory culture of conformism.'[104] Offenders – and Burns was one – were not only publicly humiliated but also liable to pay fines, and ostracised within their communities. Burns had no qualms about writing anti-clerical satire. But at the same time he was at pains to ensure that copies of his more extreme verbal darts were circulated privately rather than appearing in print under his name.[105]

Ultimately Burns would be fêted for the part his daring verse played in lifting the repression imposed by the kirk, but this happened despite the ferocious counter-attacks by Peebles and other like-minded clerics. Albeit in dwindling numbers, old school Presbyterian clergymen would continue to condemn Burns, his lifestyle and the irreligious habits he was alleged to have encouraged in the Scottish people. In the eyes of his most severe clerical critics he was the devil incarnate – the Antichrist even.

There is a paradox here. Scotland was a nation renowned for its puritanism in the eighteenth and nineteenth centuries, a land where 'people and church were in unique alliance'.[106] Yet anointed as the embodiment of the nation's values was a man who many churchmen deplored. It was a contradiction contemporaries were acutely aware of. In the wake of the Ayr Burns festival of 1844 Hugh Miller, founder and editor of what after 1843 became the mouthpiece of the Free Church, *The Witness*, pointed to the incongruity of Scotland's renown as 'pre-eminently a moral and religious land', and the 'universally known fact' that Burns was 'an immoral and irreligious man'.[107]

Yet as important were those, clergymen included, who defended Burns against such attacks – especially in the first half of the nine-teenth century when to do so often required considerable courage. Later there were voices that proclaimed him not as a sinner but rather as the leader of a spiritual revival in Scotland, a new Knox, 'God's gift to the Scottish people'.[108]

What requires to be underlined here though – other than the fact that there were numerous tensions over what aspects of Burns life and works should be commemorated (if at all) – is the vehemence of such very public and well-publicised debates. It is unambiguous testimony to how large Burns loomed in the consciousness of Scots in the nine-teenth century.

Unwittingly, the siren voices serve to underline the significance of Burns' legacy, and the principal proposition of this book, that, more than any other Scot, Burns mattered.

ONE

'From scenes like these old Scotia's grandeur springs'

Burns, 'The Cotter's Saturday Night', and Scotland's Tories in the age of revolutions

The shock felt at Burns' premature death was short-lived. Very soon, short biographical sketches and reminiscences began to appear. Maria Riddell wrote the earliest – within a month. She had been a close confidante of Burns and was a woman he much admired. Robert Heron's *Memoir of the Life of the Late Robert Burns* was next, in 1797. Not long afterwards came the first of numerous full-length biographies and commentaries on Burns' work. These included – in 1800 – James Currie's influential and much-reprinted *The Works of Robert Burns; with an Account of his Life and a Criticism on his Writings.*

Editions of his poems and songs poured from printing presses. In addition there were countless pirated copies of individual poems and songs that appeared in the shape of small cheap chapbooks – pamphlet-like publications – that were sold in thousands by itinerant pedlars, or chapmen.[1] These were passed from person to person, and avidly read, even by the labouring poor. Little wonder was it, reflected an editor of the *Glasgow Herald* speaking in Kilmarnock in 1886 at an event marking the centenary of the publication of the first Burns' edition, that 'in a few years the poems of Robert Burns were as well known in the peasant cottages and the bothies of Scotland as the Shorter Catechism'.[2] As we have seen already, the urge to read Burns was not confined to Scotland. 'Wherever there is a Scotsman, there are the volumes of Burns', declared John Commelin in the King's Arms Inn in Dumfries at a Burns 'dinner' in January 1817. It is a claim that at first reading seems hollow but which is supported by harder evidence from places such as Otago, in New Zealand, where Scots settlers – led by the Free Churchmen Thomas Burns (one of Robert Burns' brother Gilbert's sons) and William Cargill – arrived from 1848, with Burns suppers being held soon afterwards.[3] Indeed evidence from Canada suggests that owing to the existence of trading networks and proactive merchants and booksellers in towns such as Halifax, Montreal and Quebec readers there might have found it easier to acquire copies of Burns works from the 1780s than in some parts of Britain.[4]

Dumfries had followed Alloway, Greenock and Paisley in establishing the Burns supper tradition in Scotland. Within a few years – that is by the 1820s and 1830s – Scots were holding these highly formalised celebrations of the bard's life in a host of locations in Scotland, and abroad. It was not long before the suggestion was made that some kind of memorial should be raised in Burns' honour. In fact the Irish *Hibernian Journal* had called for a memorial of a different kind within days of Burns dying, in the form of assistance for his 'distressed and helpless family', that would be a 'monument' of the beneficence of his admirers.[5] A subscription for this purpose was soon established, and by 1804 some £500 had been raised by a group of Burns' friends in Dumfries. By exploiting the patronage networks that bound Scotland to London, posts, one in the Stamp Office and two in the East India Company, were secured for Burns' three sons.[6] However, it was David Erskine, 11th Earl of Buchan, the patriotic Scottish antiquarian, an acquaintance of and enthusiast for Burns, who went as far as having a model of the poet seated prepared by John Smith, a local builder and sculptor, with the idea of situating a stone statue of Burns in the Temple of Muses then (1811–12) under construction on his Dryburgh estate in the Borders.[7] Although Burns never appeared and the cliff above the Temple site was to be dominated by a statue of William Wallace, within months a proposal had come from John Forbes Mitchell – at one of the first Burns suppers to be held overseas, in Bombay, probably in 1812 – that a memorial to Burns be erected in Scotland.

But it was in Dumfries that the first practical steps were taken to erect a more substantial monument, namely a mausoleum 'resembling a temple' that was to be built over his remains in St Michael's churchyard. Initially mooted shortly after Burns' death, it became a serious proposition towards the end of 1813, under the direction of William Grierson and John Syme and other 'friends and admirers of the late Scottish bard'.[8] Following a competition, Thomas F. Hunt from London was appointed as architect, helpfully offering to work without payment. Soon after that the celebrated Belfast-born, London-based artist Peter Turnerelli was invited to design a marble mural sculpture to be placed inside the mausoleum. Burns was depicted at the plough with the 'Genius of Coila' casting her mantle over the poet, a reference to his own pronouncement that Coila had found him 'as the prophetic bard Elijah did Elisha'. In May 1815 agreement was reached that the mausoleum would not be sited over Burns' grave as planned originally (as it was 'so much encumbered with monuments and tombstones ... and a risk that it may still be more obscured by other erections') but over a new burial place for the Burns family.[9] Although the foundation stone was laid in June in accordance with masonic ceremonial, thereafter progress slowed. It was not until 1819, after overcoming problems associated with the standard of work of local tradesmen, Turnerelli's truculence and reluctance to ship the statue from London without being paid his full fee, and a shortage of funds due in part to their tardy transmission from London to Dumfries, that the mausoleum was completed.

News of the inauguration of the campaign for the mausoleum in Dumfries sparked an almost immediate response in Ayr, thereby signalling a competitive edge to the memorialisation of Burns that would intensify later in the century. There is some dispute about whether only one man – Hamilton Paul of Ayr, the gregarious minister who had organised the first ever Burns supper, in Alloway in 1801 – responded to Alexander Boswell of Auchinleck's call for a meeting to discuss a memorial for Ayr. Boswell later told John Galt, the novelist, that he had had to hold the first meeting on his own.[10] The minutes of the Ayr Monument committee record the involvement of five landed proprietors however, including the initiator of the scheme, Boswell, the poetry-writing son of James Boswell, Dr Johnson's biographer. Their purpose was clear. Having regard to the mausoleum project in Dumfries:

> it must be no less an interesting object to us, to raise a Monument to the memory of the Ayrshire Bard, where he first drew breath, and in the County where his genius was fostered and matured; and therefore that a Monument shall be erected at or near the Place of his Birth.[11]

Over the following six years what was always a small committee of prominent mainly south Ayrshire landowners along with the provost

of Ayr and William Cowan, banker, sought subscriptions, organised
the competition for 'an Architect of talent' to design the monument
(for a reduced fee of twenty guineas on the assumption that association with the name of Burns would be reward in itself), and identified
a suitable site. At the end of January 1818 the architect was selected
– Thomas Hamilton, from Edinburgh. Whether altruistic or a shrewd
business move, Hamilton chose to offer his services free of charge for
what was his first major public commission.[12] The builder, John
Connell, was less obliging. The desired location, on David Cathcart,
Lord Alloway's estate, between the old and new bridges of Doon and
almost opposite Alloway Kirk – locus of one of Burns' best-known
poems, 'Tam o' Shanter' – and within a furlong of the poet's birthplace, was settled upon late in 1819. On 25 January 1820, with full
masonic honours and in view of an 'immense' crowd, the foundation
stone was laid by Boswell, who, apart from having become an MP (for
the Devonshire seat of Plympton), was also Worshipful Depute Grand
Master of the Most Ancient Lodge, Kilwinning (Plate 3).[13]

By now Edinburgh had entered the race, even if the starting gun for
the capital's memorial had been fired in Bombay. In April 1819 the
inaugural meeting for the campaign for an Edinburgh monument to
Burns was held in the Freemason's Tavern in London's Great Queen
Street. Prior to this the Bombay backers of the scheme – prominent
amongst whom was Francis Rawdon Hastings, Lord Moira, governor
general of India between 1812 and 1823 (who had assisted in securing
two of Burns' sons posts in the army of the East India Company) – had
not only collected some subscriptions. They had also agreed with the
town council that the monument would be located on Calton Hill.[14]
(Not settled, however, was the exact site, a cause of much anguish
later when it was realised that the Burns memorial would be placed
'lower on the hill than those of less illustrious men'.[15]) The main business in London therefore was to make plans for further fund-raising
and to decide on what form the memorial would take, and its
purpose.[16] What was envisaged for the Athens of North Britain was an
Acropolis of Edinburgh, which would include a monument celebrating Burns but also other Scottish writers and artists.

A few weeks later a second fund-raising event was held in London
– a 'festival' – this time chaired by HRH the Duke of Sussex, at which
£236 was contributed.[17] In accordance with Forbes Mitchell's original
proposal however, John Flaxman, a leading British sculptor who had
worked in Scotland (on Glasgow's statue of Sir John Moore), was

commissioned to produce a life-sized statue of Burns. Initial hopes that this would be in bronze were scaled down; marble – which weathered less well – was to be the medium. Even so progress was slow. The ageing Flaxman, who was in his later sixties when he took on the commission, died in 1826 with the statue unfinished. Where to locate it after it was completed by Flaxman's brother-in-law, who was also his pupil, was an issue too. It was not until 1831 that the foundation stone was laid for a Grecian temple on Calton Hill in which the statue was to be displayed. Hamilton, whose reputation had been greatly enhanced by his Alloway memorial, was employed as the architect, although it was not until 1839, after a fraught and prolonged struggle to raise the requisite funds, that the project was completed.[18]

Two features of the campaigns for these early memorials stand out. The first is their provenance. Most of the initial impetus to commemorate and celebrate Burns came from Scottish aristocrats and others of relatively high social standing – bankers, merchants, lawyers and other professionals, whether in Scotland, England or parts of Britain's overseas empire. It is true that it was Burns' friends and acquaintances from in and around Dumfries who instigated the mausoleum project, but one of the first things they did was enlarge their committee by inviting the region's leading landed proprietors to join it. This was a prudent move. Scotland's landowners and the tenants of the larger farms had been amongst the major beneficiaries of the wars against France owing to rising land prices and rental income, and had money to spare.[19] At the head of the committee for promoting the subscription were the marquis of Queensberry and the Earl of Selkirk, with the largest sums being collected at assemblies such as that held in London in May 1816. This was chaired by the Earl of Aberdeen, with other prominent London-Scots in attendance – including Henry Dundas, Lord Melville, Kirkman Finlay, Scotland's most successful textile manufacturer who had major interests in the Indian trade and was also Glasgow's MP, and the artist David Wilkie.[20] The predominance of landed stock on the Ayr committee we have noted already.[21] London's inaugural meeting for the Edinburgh monument was chaired by the Duke of Atholl, whilst amongst the 'noblemen and gentlemen' present were Lord Keith, and Charles Forbes, MP, sometime head of Forbes & Co., of Bombay, an immensely successful banking and mercantile and shipping business established by John Forbes of Strathdon.[22]

Burns clearly had admirers in high places. The Prince Regent (afterwards George IV) topped the list of individual subscribers in both Dumfries and Ayr by donating just over £50 to each, with Lord Sidmouth the Home Secretary not far behind, contributing £20. Much of the fund-raising effort was directed towards the respective counties. For the Alloway monument, landowners, factors and land surveyors, merchants, and members of the legal and medical professions were the main contributors, along with a sprinkling of small business proprietors including David Auld, an Ayr hairdresser, a few shoemakers and a plumber. If the committee had 'little doubt of the anxiety of all ranks to offer tribute to the Memory of Burns' and asked schoolmasters to collect small sums from ordinary people, contributions from this source are hard to identify – although the ten shillings and sixpence subscribed by 'Mr Muir', a school teacher in Muirkirk, may have been a collective payment. Similarly in Dumfries, while the projectors of the mausoleum claimed that it had been paid for by monies that 'flowed in liberally . . . from lowly peasants and mechanics up to Majesty itself', and enthused at the appearance of 'the name of a lady' amongst subscribers from Huddersfield, there is little sign of donations from the former. This is hardly surprising given that the maximum subscription of two guineas recommended by the committee was more than twice the weekly wage of even the best-paid artisan.[23] Much more significant in both places were periodic remittances from London – which was relatively thickly populated with Scottish professionals, skilled tradesmen and others, not least those seeking employment with the East India Company employment or who as stockholders were its beneficiaries.[24] Liverpool, too, was home to well-heeled, Burns-admiring Scots.[25] Between them they contributed a hefty £135 for Dumfries. In Lancashire over £30 was collected. Explicitly targeted too were Scots serving in the British empire. It was from India that the largest remittance came – £450, although sizeable sums were also sent from Trinidad, Tobago, South Carolina (from 'natives of Scotland and resident there'), Virginia and, closer to home, Greenock.

What was also notable though – and a considerable challenge for the organising committees – were the funding shortfalls. Costs were invariably underestimated and committees struggled to complete their projects on time, none more so than Edinburgh's even though six years prior to the opening of the Calton Hill monument there was reported to have been a shortfall of only £200 or £300.[26] In terms of both subscribers and the speed with which memorial schemes were concluded, the contrast with what would happen later, after Glasgow's

Burns statue was inaugurated in 1877, was stark – although even then, fund-raising was rarely straightforward.

Yet the monuments were built, those in Ayr and Dumfries through the tireless efforts of committed individuals. They had reason to be contented with their endeavours: some £3,300 (c.£140,000 in today's money) was eventually raised for the Alloway monument, for example. And those who did subscribe were generally enthusiastic – more so after the Napoleonic Wars had ended in 1815. Prior to that there had been some reluctance owing to reservations about Burns' loyalty to the British cause, born of his enthusiasm for the revolutionaries in France in the early 1790s.[27] Thus, although the Duke of Buccleuch was eventually persuaded to subscribe to the Dumfries memorial, he declined to join the committee. Not only did Buccleuch dislike Burns' politics, but also, with the war against France still being fought, he felt it was the 'exertions and glorious death of some of our Countrymen who have fallen' that should be commemorated.[28]

The motives of those who did subscribe differed, even if they often overlapped. Aristocratic enthusiasm for Burns was genuine enough, and it was from such sources that most of the largest subscriptions came. But these were also very public acts of generosity that helped assuage the guilt men of this class either felt – or were made to feel – about the circumstances of Burns' death, that is the penury and relative ignominy that marked his last years. These, conceded the Earl of Aberdeen in his speech appealing for funds for the Dumfries memorial, were a reproach to the pride 'Scotland' felt about Burns. The only way to 'discharge this debt is by uniting to honour his tomb'. (Aberdeen's hope was in vain; that the landed elite had turned their back on Burns after lionising him in Edinburgh was a beating stick frequently used in the long struggle against landowner domination of Scottish politics and society in the nineteenth century.[29])

Time and distance from Scotland induced feelings of loss, longing and nostalgia, with an intensity that some contemporaries were convinced was greater than that felt by Englishmen overseas.[30] Nowhere was this truer than in the case of Scots in India, the perilous sea journey from which to Scotland could take up to six months. By the end of the eighteenth century and during the first decades of the nineteenth, there were disproportionate numbers of Scots military officers, doctors, writers and men of business amongst the East India Company's numerous employees.[31] The 'delight experienced from his [Burns'] writings by his countrymen in India' was given as the explanation for Forbes Mitchell's proposal for a Burns memorial, a point reinforced by a former colonial soldier, George A. Veitch who later recalled that the 'name of Burns opened like a charm amid the regrets of banishment . . . in his poetry and songs, we used to triumph over the sorrows of exile'.[32] Allied to this was the way that reading Burns could arouse Scottish patriotic sentiment – as in Veitch's 'Lines Written for the Anniversary of Burns's Birth-Day in Bengal', one stanza of which runs:

> What shields can e'er withstand the blow
> From swords of men who feel the glow
> Of Bannockburn's immortal few
>   Within their veins?
> O! while it swells, let never foe
>   Tell us of chains.

Less martial but similarly deep-seated emotions can be discerned in the letters and poems of Scots emigrants to North America, of which there were several thousand each year. We have seen already that many took with them copies of Burns' works, or bought or heard them once there.[33] Amongst Scots abroad – but even in centres in England where there were sizeable communities of Scots, the 'near diaspora' – there was a strong sense of ethnic solidarity, induced in part by networks created through patronage based on family, kin (even if this was often fictive), town and region.[34] Wherever Scots were congregated, Burns' birthday was often the occasion when such links were renewed, and celebrated, as well as being prompts for fund-raising activity.[35]

Although the sense of being Scottish reported here was a major force behind the adulation of Burns at home too, for those intent on securing Burns' memory in Scotland there were other considerations. Thus while Burns' acquaintances behind the mausoleum venture in Dumfries were genuinely keen to commemorate him in this grander fashion than by the unadorned stone that had disappointed earlier visitors to the graveyard, there was another motive. Scotland's town elites were at this time attempting to enhance the appearance of their burghs by what has been called 'visual aggrandisement', an aspect of the process of urban improvement that had been in vogue from the 1740s. And although nothing like the blueprints for local economic growth that would flow from local authority planning departments in the second half of the twentieth century, they had a keen awareness of opportunities there were to stimulate town economies. Dumfries, one of a number of the country's burghs that were heavily in debt by 1816, was much in need of additional revenue.[36] Thus in an early appeal for support for the mausoleum the Reverend Henry Duncan – who was acutely aware of the undesirable social and political consequences of economic malaise – acknowledged that whilst Burns' political principles might make it difficult for some people to contribute, trumping this was that a 'Mausoleum over the ashes of Burns' would be 'an ornament' to Dumfries, and might well 'conduce to the prosperity of the inhabitants by bringing strangers amongst us in their travels thro' Scotland'.[37]

Indeed so important was this that the Dumfries committee, anxious throughout 1818 about how to pay the temperamental Turnerelli, rejected the sculptor's proposal to raise money by organising a travelling exhibition of his statue to Edinburgh and Glasgow.[38] Not only would this be demeaning to Scotland and Burns, it would also have defeated the purpose of commissioning a memorial to draw visitors to Dumfries. (Instead the committee chose to rely on an additional £150 remitted from the recently acquired sugar-producing slave colony of Demerara, in what is now Guyana. That Guyana should have been the source of funds was also highly ironic however, if, as seems likely, despite his having nearly become a 'Negro [slave] driver', Burns had been sympathetic to the abolitionists' cause.[39]) Literary tourism, mentioned briefly in the Introduction, was becoming big business. It grew with 'astonishing' speed in Burns' case, with guidebooks to Burns country and scenes and locations associated with the poet having been published at least as early as 1805, the trickle becoming a flood as the potential Burns had to become 'Scotia's Shakespeare' was realised.[40] Very much in the minds of the supporters of the Alloway monument was their conviction that Burns was Ayrshire's poet, and should be commemorated – and exploited – as such, in a competition with Dumfries for visitors which carries on today. In Edinburgh, too, at least some of those behind the Calton Hill project were keen that what was built should be 'a permanent ornament to their metropolis' – an embellishment that would enhance Edinburgh's standing and attractiveness. Inter-town rivalry on the basis of Burns-centred business prospects became even more intense as the century wore on.

But behind pragmatism of this sort lay more profound considerations. Put simply, these were language and nation. Thus at an early meeting of the Dumfries mausoleum committee, there was agreement that it was to be regretted that in Dumfries-shire there was no public mark of respect for the memory of the man 'who employed his remarkable powers in giving grace and dignity to the Lowland language of Scotland'.[41] The same resolution also commended Burns for having illustrated the 'manners and character of the Scottish peasantry'. What was meant was not just that Burns had depicted the everyday life of the rural poor, credit-worthy as this undoubtedly was. There was a growing belief in the later eighteenth century, although not confined to Scotland, that amongst the peasant class was to be found the essence of the nation – the folk. It was the aural recollection of the songs of the ancient bards who had sung of Scotland's heroic figures, those who had 'laid down their lives to protect their native land from slavery and dependence', that had preserved 'the nationality of the Scots'.[42] Burns therefore, having in the words of the Earl of Aberdeen in 1816, 'sprung from . . . [Scotland's] very soil', was the authentic voice of the Scottish peasantry – and of the Scottish nation, a nation the integrity of which was at risk. Burns was also a product of Scotland's national educational system and, by extension, of the benefits of a Presbyterian polity.[43]

In this sense Burns functioned as a counterweight to the 'drift towards Anglo-British-ness' identified by Colin Kidd and others.[44] In the early nineteenth century Scotland's 'institutional inheritance' that had survived through the eighteenth century following the parliamentary union of 1707 was widely feared to be at risk.[45] The schools, universities, legal system, poor laws, and banks – all were subject to attempts on the part of London governments to 'destroy peculiarities, and to blend the two countries together'.[46] Many Scots had been far from passive, from the period of the Union itself asserting their country's freedom from conquest, boasting its people's martial spirit and fighting abilities, and in other ways, including the pursuit of antiquarianism (in several guises), defending and arguing Scotland's case.[47] Burns himself had contributed to the growing interest in distinctively Scottish historic sites, not least through his collaboration with the English antiquarian Francis Grose. The inclusion by Grose in his *Antiquities of Scotland* (1797) of Alloway Kirk, was partly due to Burns' prompting, while his 'Tam o' Shanter', composed to accompany and enliven the engraving of the kirk, ensured that, ever since, it has been at the heart of one of Scotland's most iconic heritage precincts.[48] But the concern was for nation, not the narrower cause of political nationalism.[49] Thus the Calton Hill monument became not simply a memorial to Burns, but a record of the heroic role played by Scots in the British defeat of Napoleon. In this context Burns was commemorated as the 'poet of Scotland-in-Empire' – neatly sidestepping the vexed question of Scotland's diminished status within the United Kingdom.[50]

As we have just noted, a particular cause of anxiety was the disappearance of the Scots tongue. This had been intensified in Enlightenment Edinburgh as Scots rushed to cleanse their speech and writings of anything offensive to English taste (and indeed that of Anglophile, socially subservient Scotsmen), so that by the middle of the nineteenth century the Scots vernacular had been all but dropped by the middle and upper classes. Even Burns had been advised to use 'provincial dialect' more sparingly, for the benefit of his English readers.[51] However, for men like the prominent Whig politician Henry Cockburn, Solicitor General from 1830, the Scots' dialect and language were the genetic markers of Scottishness. With their demise, Cockburn remarked, 'we lose ourselves'.[52] Thus from the outset, there was a widespread recognition that Burns had been a major force in rescuing and indeed ennobling Scottish language and song – a process begun earlier by eighteenth-century collectors such as David Herd and John Pinkerton, and the compiler of the *Dictionary of the Scottish Language* (1808), John Jamieson.[53] Language, it has been argued, was not as central to Scottish identity as in other European nations.[54] True, especially for many of the country's elite, but for the ordinary Scots, dialect, patterns of speech and Scottish words and expressions were of its essence.[55] Burns, 'by a bold grasp of genius . . . rescued from oblivion our provincial dialect, and given to the Scotch language . . . energy and a tone unknown and unfelt before', declared James Thomson at the first meeting of Kilmarnock's Burns Club in 1808.[56] Much of this linguistic heritage had been captured in the 373 or so songs Burns collected or composed for James Johnson's *Scots Musical Museum*, and George Thomson's *A Select Collection of Original Scottish Airs*, a labour of love that had absorbed much of his time and energy from 1787.[57] In seeking contributions for the *Musical Museum* Burns made clear that what he was collecting were distinctively Scottish, as opposed to English airs, a venture that was entirely in keeping with his resentment at the intrusion and negative impact of the British state on Scotland, through taxation on products such as whisky, for example.[58] Burns' songs therefore were of seminal importance in the emergence of the self-conscious and, as important, the self-confident, Scottish patriotism that emerged in the early part of the nineteenth century. It is exemplified by the fact that the appellation 'high chief of Scottish song', used initially by the Glasgow-born poet Thomas Campbell (1777–1844) in his 'Ode to the Memory of Burns', read out at the Freemasons Hall dinner in 1816, was also printed on one of the main banners carried through Dumfries in 1896 for the centennial commemoration of Burns' death.[59]

* * *

But in spite of what was a more or less consensual appeal to Scottish pride, Burns in the first decades of the nineteenth century was presented and promoted with a distinct Tory overlay. By no means was this at odds with the celebration of Burns' association with Scotland's language and song: embedded within Scottish Toryism in this period was a commitment to the idea of Scottish nationhood, albeit of a romanticised, Celtic, feudal strain, manifested in the Highland-tinged pageant for King George IV's visit to Edinburgh in 1822, masterminded by Walter Scott, and to a lesser degree in Archibald Montgomerie the 13th Earl of Eglinton's mock medieval tournament held – and then abandoned due to incessant rain – on his estate near Kilwinning in Ayrshire at the end of August 1839.[60] Hijacked by Scottish Tories, Burns was incorporated into this invented tradition of Scottishness – to bolster their attempts to inculcate what they feared might become the lost values of paternalism and deference.[61]

As far as possible, stripped out of the publications and speeches of Scots of this persuasion was any sense of Burns as social critic, an occasional celebrant of bacchanalian excess, or that politically he had been on the side of radical reform.[62] 'I suppose it will be thought prudent to avoid all political allusions in the life', wrote James Currie, before taking on the task of being Burns' first major, and posthumous, biographer.[63] Currie felt the same about Burns and religion and left out of his *Works of Robert Burns* poems critical of the kirk.[64] Nor, as a teetotaller, did he have many qualms about expressing his disapproval of Burns' relationship with drink. Similarly, in the preface to his *Reliques* of Robert Burns, published in 1808, Robert H. Cromek clearly had reservations about Burns' Jacobitism and the use to which he had put this, and some of his satires, and declared it proper therefore to omit any compositions which displayed 'a spirit of resentment' that would be 'unjust' to his memory – and that of his targets.[65] Other critics in the same mould – the University of Edinburgh's formidable, fiercely Scottish but radical-detesting Tory, Professor John Wilson for instance – expressed disbelief that the man who had written 'The Cotter's Saturday Night' could also have been a Jacobin. He explained Burns' attachment to democracy as fleeting, born of a Byronic desire to shock, whilst also dismissing the charge as one exaggerated by Dumfries' Tories, at the time fearful of French influences.[66] At core, Wilson declared, Burns was a patriot, his song 'Does Haughty Gaul' embodying more political wisdom, and appealing more effectively to the 'noblest principles of patriotism in the British heart' than any orator either inside or outside Parliament. For good reason this stirring refrain had been used to galvanise the powerful pro-British patriotic sentiment that had broadened and deepened to reach down into the lower ranks of Scottish society in the wake of the threat of French invasion, while other songs of Burns were bowdlerised and embellished in the ubiquitous song chapbooks of the early nineteenth century.[67]

Indeed any doubts there might have been about Burns' loyalism were set aside, with appeals for subscriptions for the three Burns memorials playing on Burns' real or assumed fondness for Great Britain. Much earlier his friends in Ayr at dinners such as that held in his memory in January 1804 had no hesitation about evoking Burns' support for the valiant 'Sons of the Britons' and the defence of Britain in the face of 'Gaul's martial Demon'.[68] The same message was conveyed symbolically for a number of years after around 1818 when the Ayr and Edinburgh Burns Club held what were called annual anniversary meetings in Nelson's monument on Edinburgh's Calton Hill.[69] As with similar events elsewhere, long lists of loyal and patriotic toasts were worked through, as in Paisley where the Burns club also met in June in honour of their local poet James Tannahill, and sang not only Tannahill's songs but also the 'national' songs, 'Scots Wha Hae', 'Rule Britannia' and 'Hearts of Oak'.[70] Towards the end of the Napoleonic Wars and in the immediate aftermath Burns' poems and songs either in whole or part were quoted, but more often adapted to more forcefully register the role of Scots soldiers and their loyalty and service to the British state.[71] Typical of the genre was William Jerdan's 'The After Battle Sang', written for the dinner held in London in 1816, in aid of the Dumfries mausoleum. Sung to the tune of 'Scots Wha Hae', stanzas two and three are unambiguous in their meaning:

Whan to the winds the tartan threw
Its meteor faulds o' changeful hue,
And on thy plain, red Waterloo,
The claymore reap'd the Victory!

Scots o' WELLINGTON's brave band,
O' Egypt and o' Maida's strand,
Let's drain the bowl, and grasp the hand,
And sing the Sang o' Victory.[72]

By shaping Burns' legacy in this way Scotland's political establishment was able to demonstrate its unionist credentials. But we have hinted at another, more pressing concern that caused the nation's Tories to hold Burns tight to their chests. Given his popularity amongst ordinary people, unmediated, he could be dangerous – another threat to the prevailing social order at a time of deep unease about whether it would survive in its current form. That Burns could be an acerbic critic of aspects of the society in which he lived and at times expressed radical sentiments was precisely what had endeared him to many of Ulster's weaver poets, as mentioned in the Introduction.

For reasons of self-preservation then, during the first four or five decades of the nineteenth century his elite sponsors crafted Burns as a social conservative. He was energetically exploited as a counter-revolutionary by leading Scottish Tories and their allies (including Whigs such as Lord Francis Jeffrey), intent on stemming the tsunami of societal unrest they feared would accompany the linked processes of rampant industrialisation, rapid urbanisation – and political upheaval.[73]

In both town and country older ways of working and living were disappearing under the onslaught of aggressive capitalist reforms. The market system and the era of the factory, mechanisation and regimented work had arrived – with a vengeance. The same forces impinged on the countryside, where the long drawn-out process of amalgamating smaller farms intensified after the 1760s in the search for greater efficiency due to the 'craving' of landlords for additional income.[74] The main features of this were the enclosure of land and the re-organisation of labour, which was utilised more efficiently in a regime the prevailing ethos of which was 'order and economy'. One consequence was an exodus of former rural dwellers into the mushrooming towns of Lowland Scotland, above all Glasgow and its 'suburbs', many of which were industrial communities in their own right. But everywhere, time discipline – the use of the clock to monitor long working hours – was becoming the norm, replacing customary working patterns. In the countryside where the bulk of the population had been clustered in ferm-touns of various sizes, cottar households – that might formerly have had access to a portion of land upon which they could keep a cow and grow some of their own food – became more dependent on the wages they could earn.[75] Across rural Scotland the norm was for the larger farms to be dominated by a single tenant farmer – the master – who employed full-time agricultural workers on various terms and conditions. Historians disagree about the extent to which the dispossessed, the former subtenants and cottars who were the new rural proletariat, protested against the process of reform, a topic to which we will return later and again in chapter 2. There is no disagreement though about the pain, anxiety and insecurity the trans-formation created.[76]

With destabilising social changes of the sort outlined here taking place at the same time as political revolutions in France in 1789 but also there and elsewhere in Europe in 1830, Scotland's governing classes suffered from periodic intimations of the dangers posed by the lower orders. One of the most prominent and vociferous members of Scotland's conservative phalanx was Sir Archibald Alison. Alison was the Enlightenment-educated, lawyer son of an Episcopalian minister who in 1834 was appointed sheriff and chief law officer for Scotland's manu-facturing heartland of Lanarkshire.[77] Like many men of his generation, Alison had been shocked and horrified by the French Revolution – which he studied in depth and spent many years writing about, not least so that its lessons would be learned and a similar catastrophe avoided in Britain. Alison also earned a reputation and was attacked in the Radical press as a scourge of the working class. He was also in the front rank of Burns celebrants – as we saw in the Introduction.

As this indicates, Radicals (as several of them found to their cost at the time of the repressive sedition trials of 1793–4), were considered by the notoriously reactionary Scottish judiciary to be especially dangerous. Even so, in the main the Radicalism of the early 1790s was relatively orderly and even respectable, with much support for burgh and parliamentary reform coming from the propertied classes, includ-ing several manufacturers, merchants, lawyers, clergymen and shop-keepers, as well as artisans.[78] After around 1815, however, a different kind of Radicalism emerged, fuelled by the growth of collective consciousness amongst proletarians – the working classes. In 1819 Sir Walter Scott defined the term 'Radical' as 'a set of blackguards a hundred times more mischievous and absurd than our old friends in 1794 and 1795'. He feared that their intention was to seize by a general rising the 'property of the rich'.[79] He was right to be concerned. Crimes against property including the theft of money, food and clothing were increasing rapidly.[80]

The inclination of Scott and his allies was to look backwards to rural paternalism for a model of social relations appropriate for the industrial age. The foundations of social stability they believed lay in the countryside and small-town Scotland. It was a model of society headed by the aristocracy, and held together by bonds of inter-dependence, paternalism and deference – and kept in check by the Presbyterian kirk. This contrasted with the new manufacturing districts, where in years of bad trade the large numbers of unemployed – 'a separate class, a new state' – provided 'excellent materials for the demagogue'.[81] As part of their efforts to counter this threat from the lower orders, and secure their vision of a settled Scottish society, Scotland's Tories and others concerned to maintain their place within it, looked to Burns.

Just how important Burns could be as a word-built bulwark in maintaining the existing social order – and as a comfort to those who feared its demise – is illustrated in an article published in the robustly Tory *Blackwood's Edinburgh Magazine*, in December 1819. This was after several months of savage wage cuts during which Glasgow, Paisley, Dundee and the other manufacturing and mining towns in Ayrshire, Stirlingshire and Fife and elsewhere had been racked as never before by social tensions and violent disturbances.[82] Unrest had begun with the commercial depression of 1816, but by 1819 the turmoil was close to its peak, with dissatisfaction harnessed by working class radicals, many of them weavers. Some advocated tax strikes and political education while others, more ominously, prepared for the armed rebellion that had Scott trembling – what would later be known as the Radical War.

This was the nerve-jangling environment in which 'Emerus' penned 'The Radical's Saturday Night', one of a number of articles published in response to the threatened rising. 'Emerus' was a pseudonym for the aforementioned John Wilson (who also used the pen-name Christopher North), one of *Blackwood's* principal writers. For many years Wilson set the tone of the magazine, galvanising its growing number of subscribers in their detestation of radicalism, republicanism and, above all, revolution.[83]

The lynchpin in Wilson's essay was Burns' 'The Cotter's Saturday Night'. With its portrayal of a humble rural household at the head of which was a pious patriarch, 'The Cotter's Saturday Night' was a Scottish manifestation of industrialising Europe's 'discovery' of the stoical peasant, frugal in habit and industrious to a fault, with commentators like Currie praising the poem for its representation of 'a form of naturalized civil society operating harmoniously with minimum state intervention'.[84]

It was amongst the Scottish peasantry, Wilson and his allies believed, that a sense of loyalty to their social superiors was still to be found. In Scotland alone there existed a 'union of knowledge, morality, and religion, so universal, and so intense ... and solemn, as to constitute National Character', a scenario endorsed it seemed by Burns in the first line of the poem's nineteenth stanza: 'From scenes like these old Scotia's grandeur springs'. 'The Cotter's Saturday Night' then, a secular hymn in praise of the virtue of simple Presbyterianism as practised by 'hard-working country folk', and suffused with the 'spirit of religion', offered a powerful recipe for social contentment and became, in effect, a manifesto for the country's conservative elite.[85] It was a masterful choice. It was almost certainly the most quoted and individually reprinted of Burns' poems while he was still alive.[86] After Burns' death it was for a long time the most lauded, and only lost favour amongst literary critics in the twentieth century.

The visual images the poem conjured appeared in countless engravings, in magazines, books and prints (Plate 4), a nostalgic version of pre-industrialised Scotland that was still recognisable – and comforting – several decades later. It was the familiarity of the scenes vividly portrayed and evoked by Burns, and the wistfulness this induced amongst those for whom this was a world that was disappearing or had only recently disappeared, that partly explains Burns' immense popularity. It was not only in Ayrshire that there could still be detected in the homes of village tradesmen and agricultural workers a serious tone of conversation, where readings from the family Bible were commonplace, the Sabbath was observed, and children were reared with an appreciation of the importance of honesty and obedience, good service and thrift.[87] James Tait, one-time editor of the *Kelso Chronicle*, was in 1889 able to write with conviction about the religiosity of farm households in Roxburghshire earlier in the century, and observed of the smaller tenants and 'peasantry' that they had been the 'chief adherents' of the secession from the Church of Scotland. They continued, he went on, 'to be of frugal habits, simple manners, and evangelical sentiments'.[88]

Wilson's purpose in his *Blackwood's* wake-up call was to demonstrate what would happen should there be any erosion of the virtues found in the 'The Cotter's Saturday Night'. He narrated a dream of arriving, lost, on a stormy night at the door of a cottage near Bothwell Castle in Lanarkshire. Every aspect of the humble abode was the stark opposite of Burns' fondly drawn image. Instead of the 'wee bit-ingle, blinkin bonnily', that had greeted Burns' 'toil-worn' cottar, Wilson's visitor felt cold and clammy. In the gloom, he heard a 'long deep broken groan' evidently uttered by the head of the household, an old man sitting by a 'scanty fire', white haired and with cheeks 'as sunken and wan as if he had risen from the grave'. He then witnessed – again in contrast to Burns' portrayal of the cottar's love-struck daughter Jenny and her suitor – the 'fury and hatred' that existed between the drunken husband and his wife, the daughter of the house. Almost naked, her 'famished breast' was unable to provide sustenance for her unloved child. The head of the household despaired as his son-in-law recounted his evening's work. This had been to level the nearby kirk to the ground, while the pews, lofts, rafters, pulpit and sounding board, 'where the old hypocrite [the minister] used to preach salvation to our souls', were set alight. By 'the bones of Thomas Paine, they made a glorious bonfire!' ranted Emerus' nemesis in an oath-strewn account of radical assaults on more than a thousand church buildings throughout the land, 'a glorious day for Scotland'.

Awaking from his nightmare, the narrator sought succour by attending a sermon delivered by a minister he had been taught to venerate as a boy, in an 'ancient' church sheltered by trees that had stood for centuries – images designed to convey the sense that this was the natural, even fixed, order of things, a recurring theme in *Blackwood's*. His feeling of the 'joyful conviction of the stability of religion' was reinforced by the sight of the parishioners wending their way home, their minds filled with what was a weekly 'treasure of supporting and elevated thoughts' that (in contrast to the Radical) would counter the trials and troubles of life. So long as similar happy scenes were replicated elsewhere, the minister convinced him, 'the RADICAL'S SATURDAY NIGHT would never be in Scotland anything other than – a dream'.[89]

Notwithstanding Presbyterian assaults on Burns such as that mentioned in the Introduction (and to be seen in chapter 3), men like Wilson were convinced that carefully directed readings of Burns in alliance with Church of Scotland sermonising could be a powerful antidote to revolution in the nineteenth century – as to a degree pulpit exhortations had been in the previous century as the Hanoverian state sought to repel Jacobite insurgency in 1715–16 and 1745–6.[90]

The mediation of Burns by his editors was vital to the Tories' mission. At first sight it may seem perverse to conflate 'The Cotter's Saturday Night' with anything other than social tranquillity. With the patriotic flourish of its final two stanzas wherein a 'virtuous Populace' might rise and 'stand a wall of fire around their much-/lov'd ISLE', and God was implored 'never, never' to 'SCOTIA'S realm desert', the poem could appeal equally to Scot and Briton, as a stirring defence of the homeland. However, buried within the poem were some deeply unsettling sentiments. The last seven lines of the third last stanza were especially corrosive. Immediately following his beatification of the religiosity of the humble cottar household, Burns wrote:

> Princes and lords are but the breath of kings,
>   'An honest man's the noble work of GOD:'
>   And certes, in fair Virtue's heavenly road,
> The Cottage leaves the Palace far behind:
>   What is a lordling's pomp? A cumbrous load,
> Disguising oft the wretch of human kind,
> Studied in the arts of hell, in wickedness refin'd!

Wilson of course was well aware of how dangerous such revolutionary lines in praise of the labouring poor could be.[91]

* * *

By the early to mid 1840s there was concern not just about everyday criminality, but over more serious signs of unrest in Ayrshire and elsewhere in the west of Scotland. Opening with revolutions in Europe, the 1830s had been a decade of uncertainty and deep anxiety for the country's ruling elite. The country's Tories' sense of foreboding and loss of control had been heightened by the Reform Act of 1832 – the herald of Scottish democracy that had already transformed Scotland's representation at Westminster from a majority of Tory MPs into a Whig one. Just how explosive Burns' memory could be in the wrong hands can be sensed in the decision of Edinburgh's provost and magistrates in September 1831, when excitement over parliamentary reform was at fever pitch, to ban the proposed procession for the laying of the foundation stone of the Burns monument on Calton Hill.[92] Just over ten years later the establishment Church of Scotland was reeling from the loss of the 454 ministers who had left in the Disruption of 1843, while beyond the ranks of the committed, the Free Church – dominated by the middle classes – saw little to be comforted with. The Sabbath was being increasingly violated, while through much of Scotland there were too many instances of a 'perverse pride' being taken in 'casting off restraint' and blatant disregard for the 'decencies of religion'.[93]

Adding further to upper class unease was the fact that the years from 1837 and through into 1843 marked the deepest and most unrelieved economic depression of the nineteenth century. Consequently, there were serious threats to social stability.[94] These included not only the emergence of physical force Chartism but also major strikes, some of which, including those of the Glasgow cotton spinners in 1837, and the coal miners in Glasgow and the west of Scotland six years later, were widespread, well-organised and had induced the authorities to call on the military – directed by the aforementioned Archibald Alison – to contain them.[95]

Early in 1844, however, Alison was heavily involved in what to all intents and purposes was a very different kind of project, a Burns festival, to be held in Alloway that summer, on 6 August. Although by no means dormant, public interest in Burns had been re-awakened by the placing of a monument in Greenock's Old West Kirkyard to Mary Campbell, 'Highland Mary', with whom Burns had had a short-lived but intense love affair in 1786, months prior to Mary's tragic death, probably from typhus.[96] It was a highly charged incident in Burns' life the sentiments of which tugged long and hard at the heartstrings of Victorian Scots.

Ostensibly the festival was held in recognition of the fact that Burns' three surviving sons were now in Scotland, two of them having returned home after many years overseas in the service of the East India Company. Homage was to be paid by 'an admiring and repentant people', not only to Burns' sons, Robert Burns, Major James Glencairn Burns and Colonel Nicol Burns, but other relatives including his daughter Isabella Begg and two nieces – assuaging the continuing sense of guilt there was that the nation's bard had been permitted to end his days in penury, and as a pariah cast out by those who had once befriended him. In terms of format the model was a grand festival in Stratford that had been held for Shakespeare in 1769: Scotland's literary hero deserved nothing less. The location chosen was fitting: near the place of Burns' birth, and in full view of the Alloway monument – the 'shrine of genius' – and nearby the Auld Kirk in which Burns' father was buried and the setting for his well-known poem 'Tam o' Shanter'.[97] And the proposal struck a chord that resounded through much of Scotland and even further afield. On tour in Europe, Bayard Taylor, the American poet and journalist from the *New York Tribune*, found himself drawn to Ayr.[98] Indeed although it was the 'hallowed ground' of Alloway that had largely determined where the festival would be held, the organisers had also been aware that Ayr was now easily reached by the newfangled form of mass transportation – the steam railway.[99] Ayr had been connected thereby to Glasgow (and Paisley and Kilmarnock) since 1840. For their part, recognising the business opportunity that Burns worship represented, the rail companies put on special trains – although even without the festival the line was an enormous success, with seventy-three locomotives running on it by 1850, compared to eight initially, facilitating passenger travel deep into Burns country.[100] Steamship companies, too, offered sailings from Stranraer and Glasgow on the day of the festival, the earliest, the 'Cardiff Castle' leaving Glasgow's Broomielaw at 4 am. As we saw in the Introduction, there is some uncertainty about how many people attended, but even if the lower number of 50,000 is the accurate one, this was more than eight times the county town's normal population and made for the grandest day in the town's history.

However, that Professor Wilson, with Alison in support, masterminded the festival, hints at deeper motives. At the head of the organising committee was the 13th Earl of Eglinton, who had been responsible for the ill-fated tournament of 1839 that bore his name and was one of Scotland's most influential Tories. The involvement of such individuals in the planning of the festival supports the contention that they believed a well-orchestrated Burns celebration could serve to reinforce aristocratic paternalism in Scotland, and thereby counter the baneful effects of modernity.[101] There was little point in denying Burns' role as a spokesman for the poor, defiantly challenging the notion that 'poverty was a crime or a dishonourable thing to be despised'. But what was to be stressed was that only Scotland could have produced Burns (and celebrated him, despite his humble background), to the extent that an 'intensely national feeling' was expected to pervade – and unite – the hearts of those present, with the prominent display of Union Jack flags in Ayr and on top of the great pavilion by the River Doon presumably designed as a subliminal reminder that Scotland was also British. Both Alison and Eglinton were patriotic Scots, but firm unionists too, and conscious – as we noted earlier – of the danger of arousing the lurking genie of nationalism.[102] However, that reviving cross-class enthusiasm for the Scottish nation was one of the organisers' aims was very publicly demonstrated by the sight in the procession that preceded the festivities on the banks of the Doon of an eight- or nine-foot high thistle, which induced 'loud and unrestrained applause' from onlookers and which was grasped at theatrically by Wilson and his platform party as it was carried past them.[103]

Reinforcing this elision of class interest was the choice of Eglinton – a peer – to preside at what was the commemoration of a 'peasant', 'the most graceful of all possible arrangements', so that all ranks, 'from side to side of social life' would be 'bound and fused together on this illustrious occasion'.[104] There was no need for recourse to radical politics and violence. Persons of 'humble station' – like the 'peasant' Burns – who applied themselves and worked hard, could succeed, and achieve recognition for their God-given talents. In conveying this message the festival's sponsors were at one with the *laissez-faire* inclined economic liberalism of Scotland's emerging manufacturing and commercial elite, who individually and through Burns clubs such as those of Greenock and Irvine, had supported the festival.[105]

In addition to its associations with Burns there was another reason why Ayrshire was a particularly apposite location. Recent happenings in the county had revealed that, behind the apparent quiescence of an agricultural district which was characterised by small family farms and had been relatively late in the creation of a rural proletariat, there lurked the potential for serious unrest.[106] Following the Radical rising of April 1820 in Glasgow and the west of Scotland, including Kilmarnock, James MacQueen warned that Ayrshire was one of those counties where the 'largest portion' of the inhabitants were 'deeply poisoned by the spirit of radicalism', the lubricating essence of rebellion and revolution.[107] In the agitation for parliamentary reform, radicalism, the Chartist movement, bitter hostility towards Tories, and strikes (in the mining industry), Ayrshire was well represented.[108]

Little wonder then that pride of place in the procession – after the town council and trades – was given to the ploughmen and shepherds. With their skill in managing horses, ploughmen had emerged as the new elite amongst the rural workforce on the larger, commercially oriented farms that studded the countryside. And it was as a plough-man that Burns was celebrated. In the Borders and other sheep farm-ing districts the shepherd too was becoming an increasingly important figure.[109] The enhanced status and influence within their communities of the two groups was recognised by the organisers who at least went through the motions of consulting with their representatives on the arrangements for the procession, including inviting them, 'if conveni-ent', to distinguish themselves by donning blue bonnets in the case of the ploughmen, and by the shepherds wearing plaids, and carrying staffs. But highly visible too were tartan bedecked pipers and 'bonnie lasses', and others dressed as Highland chieftains, visual signifiers of the Tories' vision for Scotland that leaned heavily on a part-imagined past (outlined above), in which there was a place too for the 'Glasgow District of the Grand Order of Modern Druids' who arrived in Ayr by steamboat.

All this this goes a long way towards explaining why several of the speeches that were delivered to the well-heeled audience of 2,000 crowded into the great-tented pavilion acknowledged the desirable qualities of the Scottish peasantry. These were first and foremost their 'industry, frugality and contentment', but also their piety and patriot-ism. Sir David Hunter-Blair of Blairquhan, proprietor of an estate to the east of Ayr, went further. These virtues, Hunter-Blair declared, contrasted with the situation in rural England where the 'demon of discontent' was rife. This was a reference to the wave of arson that had been sweeping East Anglia and other south-eastern counties of England prior to and even in the weeks immediately preceding the festival.[110] The *Morning Chronicle* had described as 'cutting satires' the 'old pictures of the kindly . . . almost paternal relations subsisting between the owners and the tillers of the soil'; such was the resent-ment of the last-named that what were currently 'flashes of incendiar-ism' may 'startle us by a general and more destructive explosion'.[111] Such a horrific prospect, Hunter-Blair was certain, would never be seen in Scotland, 'so long . . . as the genius and memory of the peasant Burns continue to be cherished amongst his fellow-peasants, as they are at this day'.[112] The source of what he called the 'beautiful attribute of contentment' was to be found in the Scottish rural worker's household – as depicted in 'The Cotter's Saturday Night'. Hunter-Blair's was a widely held view, the Free Church, for example, commending it as exemplary in its sentiments, but regretting that amongst Burns' productions it was the exception.[113]

In consolidating a renewed sense of Scottishness amongst those present, the festival was an undoubted success.[114] That it was Burns who had inspired the evident pride there was in the nation was not in doubt. Eyewitness accounts tell of unprecedented outpourings of emotion. 'I never experienced the like feelings before', wrote one visitor who, 'although a stranger, felt I was one spirit with the vast assemblage'.[115] *Blackwood's Magazine*, as fearful as in 1819 of signs of political radicalism, delighted in reporting that on striking up the 'beautiful air – "Ye banks and braes o' bonny Doon" . . . the People, as if actuated by one common impulse, took up the strain, and a loftier swell of music never rose beneath the cope of heaven.'[116] And although the organisers had been disappointed that Charles Dickens, William Wordsworth and Alfred Lord Tennyson – to name but three invitees from England – had not come, those who did brave the journey to Ayr had been indelibly struck by the fervour they had seen for Burns, and Scotland.[117]

* * *

Yet as an exercise in paternalist-led class conciliation the festival had its limitations. For one thing, most visitors were excluded from the pavilion where the main speeches were delivered. For the humbler 'pilgrims', entertainment (but nothing 'approaching to frivolity') at a 'cheap rate', was provided by music bands and in enclosures for dancing on the green, the objective being to maintain 'the mental as well as the moral dignity of the occasion'.[118] Even so, one perceptive London journalist was convinced that it was here that the real business of the festival was to be witnessed, remarking that even if there had been no pavilion with its 'tasteful draperies . . . and elevated galleries', 'the manifestation of respect on the part of the people towards their poet, would have been accomplished' and the 'heart-beatings of Scotland, as thoroughly accomplished'. The same writer noted that the arrangements for the procession had been 'the PEOPLE's arrangements'.[119] Presumably these had also included the decision that the three-deep, mile-long procession, led by the band of the 87th Fusiliers would move to the tune of 'A Man's a Man' – by 1844 established as a part of the radical song canon, and that as the marchers passed Burns' birthplace in Alloway they would slow down and remove their caps as a mark of respect to a man of their own class. Not many years beforehand such deferential gestures were reserved for the gentry, which they continued to be in rural society (Plate 5).[120] Processions of civic elites, guilds and trade societies had long been part of the pageantry of urban Scotland: what was relatively recent, however, was the use of the orderly parade as a vehicle by which ordinary people could make known their collective views.[121] This is not to suggest that the crowds of people who thronged Ayr and Alloway during the festival were drawn from the ranks of Scotland's proletarians. Some were but the bulk of those attending had to be sufficiently well off to give up a day's pay and afford even the reduced fares for the day – which suggests artisans, proprietors of small businesses, and professionals, who were 'well-dressed' and able to purchase the medallions of Burns that had been struck for the occasion. Even so, Charles Mackay, the editor of the *Glasgow Argus*, and his companion Patrick Park, a Glasgow-born sculptor, were at pains to understand the adulation there was amongst those present for Burns – in comparison to what they were persuaded was more muted enthusiasm for Walter Scott. The manner of Burns' early death was one reason, they thought. Another was that Burns had human failings. However, more than this, the two men concluded, it was because Burns had been a lover and preacher of independence; but above all, as he was 'a democrat to the bone'.[122]

We will look more closely at Radical responses to the Ayr festival in the next chapter. But it was not only Radicals who had reservations about how Burns was promoted by the festival's main speakers. Eglinton was well received. For Wilson, however, croupier for the day, the proceedings ended in humiliation. Despite his renown as an energetic orator Wilson was forced to abandon his address mid-way through as the audience became not only restless, but also hostile.

We 'did not go there [to Ayr] to listen to a lecture on moral philosophy, beautiful as it is from the college chair', reflected George Veitch, the army officer recently returned from India. Nor, he continued, did we need to be reminded 'for the thousandth time, that Burns had failings as well as virtues', or to learn about the unrivalled power of song.[123] Rather, he and others had come to do honour to Burns as a man, and 'all his sublimity as a poet'. He was less than happy, too, with what he felt was Sir John McNeil of Barra's 'dissertation on English poets', a cringing 'apology for nationality' on an occasion 'when we had a right to be full of nationality at a festival in memory of Burns'. In short, what was wanted was less talk about Burns and more unmediated renditions of his poems and songs.

Wilson, however, was caught on a cleft stick. *The Witness*, the Free Church's newspaper, condemned him for what had actually been a defence of Burns, the paper's editor Hugh Miller evidently being unable to overlook his conviction that Burns had 'sinned grievously, and caused many, very many, to sin'. But it was the festival in its entirety of which Miller and his fellow churchmen disapproved. The writings of Burns which contained so much 'false principle . . . profane scoffing at religious truth, [and] so much of downright undisguised licentiousness' had in the past 'done much mischief to the morals of Ayrshire, as well as throughout Scotland'. Hard to understand was how the author of 'The Cotter's Saturday Night' could have written 'The Holy Fair', with its far from flattering description of what for the kirk was a profoundly significant sacrament – holy communion. The 'somewhat senseless exhibition' at Alloway, it was to be feared, would restore Burns' 'malignant influence' to its 'former vigour'.[124] Miller was pleased therefore that only one clergyman was reported to have attended the Alloway banquet. The names of other churchmen who had sanctioned the festival, or participated, should be named, and shamed.

On the other hand there were those who hoped that the festival would lead to a further weakening of the churches' grip on public morals, intensifying the clash between Burns' admirers and the country's more zealous Presbyterians in the decades immediately after 1844. Indeed, akin to waving a red rag at a bull, published anew in 1852 in Edinburgh, Glasgow and London was a cheap, small, chapbook-like collection of six of Burns' clerical satires under the title, *The Kirk's Alarm: or, A Present For The Priest-Ridden*.[125] Aimed at a wide readership, its purpose was starkly stated: by exposing Scotland's system 'of bigotry, intolerance and hypocrisy, the most narrow-minded . . . the world has yet witnessed', Burns had inspired his countrymen with 'the enthusiasm of mental freedom, and a just and manly self-esteem'. The opening lines of Burns' 'Address to the Unco Guid' set the tone:

> O ye wha are sae guid yourself,
>   Sae pious and sae holy,
> Ye've nought to do but mark and tell
>   Your neibour's fauts and folly!

The availability of the satires in the new format, the publishers boldly anticipated, would 'exercise a wholesome influence over the popular mind in all time coming'. They certainly gave voice both humorous and lacerating that at a popular level challenged Old Calvinist views about predestination and the Elect. Accompanying this from the 1830s were shifts in theological thinking that pointed towards a milder, more loving understanding of faith, although widespread adoption of this awaited developments in science and history that rocked the foundations upon which Biblical certainty had been built.[126]

The year 1844 marked the high water mark for Scotland's Tories' association with Burns. Indeed for Burns, too, it was a pinnacle of a sort, the first national festival to be held in his honour. But it was not the last. Forcing their way into the driving seat of Burns commemoration was a set of men whose backgrounds and interest in Burns and ideas of how his legacy was to be assured were substantially different.

TWO

'The man who first taught the Scottish people to stand erect'

Burns, Chartism and the working classes

Scotland's Tories' efforts to corral Burns were impressive but never comprehensive. There was much in Burns about which there was consensus. Above all was a shared affection for and attachment to a recognisable, largely rural past and, not far behind, the feelings he aroused for the nation, about which there was immense pride and patriotic fervour, especially in regard to Scotland, but for Britain too.

However, they were confronted with the fact that it was not solely through editions of Burns' works such as those produced by James Currie that ordinary people discovered Burns. And even when they did, how they read and interpreted him was not necessarily as his early nineteenth-century promoters would have wished. According to Jonathan Rose, an historian of the reading habits of the working classes, canonical literature that either had an inbuilt ideological purpose or was appropriated for this reason by proselytising critics, could 'ignite insurrections in the minds of workers'.[1] The labouring classes, Rose contends, were not simply receptacles into which the ideas of others could be poured and accepted unthinkingly. Rather, they evinced a determination to come to their own, independent conclusions about what they were reading.

We saw intimations of this in the previous chapter, and we will dig deeper in what follows. First though, we should establish how widely Burns' work was known beyond the landed classes, Edinburgh's intellectual circle and the growing numbers of manufacturers, merchants and professionals who formed the increasingly literature-conscious social elites of Scotland's burgeoning towns and cities.

There was a growing hunger for print, and a consequent 'explosion in reading' as newspapers, periodicals, town directories, histories

– and volumes of verse – became more readily available.[2] By the end of the eighteenth century, subscription libraries were becoming commonplace, along with newspaper reading rooms and coffee houses where the commercial classes and professional men such as doctors, surgeons, lawyers and ministers of the church mingled, shared information and discussed the affairs of the day. Burns himself was involved with the short-lived Monklands Society (set up in 1789), the brainchild of his neighbour and friend while he was at Ellisland farm, Robert Riddell of Glenriddell. Most members were Riddell's tenants and some neighbouring farmers.[3] He was an enthusiastic supporter, too, of a subscription library established in Dumfries in 1792, gifting it with Jean Louis De Lolme's influential *Constitution of England*, first published in 1771.[4]

Although shopkeepers and tradesmen and certainly the labouring poor were less likely to own books (other than a Bible and perhaps Blind Harry's ubiquitous *Wallace*), it seems reasonably clear that from an early date Burns was known about, and read or heard, by more ordinary people than might be expected. Perhaps he was exaggerating, but one of Burns' first biographers, Robert Heron, who was living in Galloway when editions of Burns' poems first became available, 'well remember[ed], how even plough-boys and maid-servants would have gladly bestowed the wages which they earned the most hardly', despite having more pressing needs, 'if they might procure the works of BURNS'.[5] Other sources confirm the impression that there may have been a growing audience for Burns amongst the relatively humble, including coal miners, smiths, masons, tailors and even shepherds.[6]

The dissemination process this points to was facilitated in Lowland Scotland by having, even in the eighteenth century, 'one of the highest literacy rates in the world'.[7] Small tenant farmers and cottagers, but craftsmen too, could read, and did so, avidly, even if most of the reading material was religious in nature. Many were members of the new circulating libraries and reading societies both formal and informal that began to appear in the later eighteenth century. Handloom weavers, though, were in the vanguard. Their shorter working hours up until the 1790s and in some cases even until after the Napoleonic Wars, and the nature of their work – indoors and at a pace set by the operative – gave them time to read, debate, and in some cases write poetry.[8] Paisley was the source of a particularly active group of part-time weaver poets – like Alexander Wilson (1766–1813). Wilson, who would later earn fame as an ornithologist in America, was working unhappily at the loom in 1786 but somehow became aware of and inspired by Burns' *Poems*.[9]

As in Ulster, many of these autodidact poets lived and worked at the same time as Burns, whose stress on the virtues of independence of mind chimed with the values their own reading and insights had inculcated. They shared too the same literary traditions – being familiar with the work of the makars William Dunbar and Robert Henryson, and later Allan Ramsay and Robert Fergusson, as well as verse forms such as the Standard Habbie, 'the six-line elegiac stanza of Scots poetry' masterfully employed by Burns.[10]

*   *   *

There were various means by which Burns' poems and songs became known. Prior to the publication of the Kilmarnock and Edinburgh editions of his *Poems, Chiefly in the Scottish Dialect*, in 1786 and 1787 respectively, Burns' practice was to circulate manuscript copies of individual poems – mainly epistles – to his Ayrshire friends and acquaintants. Several of these – like John Lapraik, Davie Sillar and John Rankine – were brother bards, who like Burns were struggling to survive in Ayrshire's harsh economic climate of the early 1780s.[11]

The 600 or so subscribers to the Kilmarnock edition were largely Ayrshire based. However, very rapidly after the publication of the Edinburgh edition of his *Poems* in 1787, with its 1,300 subscribers (and 2,800 copies), Burns' readership widened from Ayrshire to the national and international. Within days of William Creech's advertisement in the *Edinburgh Advertiser* of the availability, by pre-payment, of the *Poems*, the same paper printed samples of Burns' work, thereby broadening his audience.[12] He continued to write and send off poems to those close to him, but also to the editors of newspapers in Scotland as well as London and Belfast.

The thirst to read more and learn about his life was unquenchable, so much so that by 1805, less than ten years after Burns' death, James Currie's *Works of Robert Burns* had reached its fifth edition, and sold more than 10,000 copies. By 1820 there were eight editions.[13] Pristine copies of the Kilmarnock edition, which had cost three shillings, or Currie's *Works*, were beyond the reach of most of those from the lower classes. From the mid to later 1790s, however, there was a proliferation of reading rooms, trades libraries and artisan book clubs, evidence of the greater emphasis on independent thinking there may have been amongst the labouring classes north of the border. With lower charges, even less well paid tradesmen and labourers were able to participate, albeit in modest numbers in what could be short-lived associations.[14] When they survived, however, they were heavily used. Not unrepresentative was Robert Tannahill (1774–1810), another weaver poet who was involved in a number of literary societies in and around Paisley, and a member of the town's trades library that opened in 1806.[15] It was the small library in Langloan, Old Monkland, where the female poet Janet Hamilton (née Thomson, 1795–1873), a shoe-maker's daughter, found much of the reading matter, including the poems of Fergusson and Burns that would inform her later writing.[16] The pattern this indicates, of greater participation by artisans and the proprietors of small businesses in reading, is to be seen at Haddington's free library (where user records survive), as too is the interest there was in Burns, whose *Poems* was amongst the most popular items borrowed after a copy was acquired in 1804, although in this case more so amongst female than male readers.[17]

Even then, this was no guarantee that Burns would be available. Although probably atypical, in Kilmarnock there was an instance of ministerial censorship at the end of the eighteenth century when the Reverend James MacKinlay of the Laigh Kirk led the opposition to the purchase of Burns' *Poems* for the new library on the grounds that it was an immoral and 'corrupting' book – a stance he may have adopted owing to his having been suspected by his unforgiving parishioners of ante-nuptial fornication.[18] Mostly, though, Burns slipped under the censor's net, which was more likely to catch the more obviously inflammable writings of Thomas Paine or William Godwin.[19] Burns' poems that appeared in radical newspapers like James Anderson's *Bee*, his friendship with reformers and gestures of support for the French revolutionaries did draw the wrath of the authorities at the end of 1792 and into 1793. But as he was driven underground and forced to publish both anonymously and pseudonymously during the years of repression – manifested by the harsh sentences handed out in Edinburgh's High Court by Lord Braxfield – even recent scholars have had difficulty in agreeing which works were those of Burns.[20]

We alluded to the importance of chapbooks in the previous chapter. Mass circulation of Burns was the preserve of the proprietors of chapbook publishing ventures, mainly concentrated in Glasgow, Edinburgh, Falkirk, Stirling and Paisley. Eclectic in their content, and 'disgracefully ignored' by historians until recently, chapbooks were pamphlet-like productions normally eight pages long, printed on coarse paper, sometimes crudely illustrated and costing a penny or less. Affordable therefore, they were the staple reading material of ordinary Scots well into the nineteenth century.[21] Distributed by itinerant pedlars – chapmen – chapbooks flooded town and city streets. At their peak in the century after 1750, some 200,000 chapbooks were sold each year, the equivalent today of a circulation of 600,000.[22]

This is not to suggest that chapbooks and broadsheets were necessarily the vehicles by which Burns' politically unsettling or even his more bawdy work was conveyed. Some was, with editions of 'The Jolly Beggars' and 'The Fornicator's Court' published in 1801 and 1817 respectively, while 'Tam o' Shanter', the Burns poem most often printed in the first chapbooks, could titillate as well as act as a warning against drink-fuelled abandon. Chapbook publishers could also be moralisers and upholders of the political status quo; their publications were rarely radical in content.[23]

Much that was published was pirated. Poems and songs were particularly popular, with chapbooks devoted to these outnumbering those devoted to prose by a factor of two to one.[24] By mid century the chapbooks were being supplemented by cheap editions of Burns' works. In 1859 one publisher claimed to have sold 15,000 poems at 1d each, a format that would enable purchasers to have a complete set of the poems for one shilling. Publishers were not slow in recognising the sales potential of key commemorative dates. People 'are always buying Burns in Scotland', James M'Kie of Kilmarnock was assured as his *People's Statue Edition* of Burns' poems was being printed for sale in Glasgow in January 1877. A 'beautiful' edition on good paper, this would 'sell by thousands' to artisan buyers who could afford one shilling but not a facsimile of the same publisher's Kilmarnock edition that cost ten shillings and sixpence.[25]

But there were also informal ways in which awareness of Burns occurred. Born in 1811, Alexander Somerville was the son of a family of poor agricultural workers in Berwickshire. His parents were intensely religious – adherents of the anti-burgher secession church – to the extent that his father led his family at worship each morning and night, much along the lines described by Burns in his 'Cotter's Saturday Night'. Somerville first heard – rather than read – Burns when he was eleven. This was when James Wilson, a corn stacker with whom he was working at the harvest, recited a number of Burns' poems and songs but also recounted what he knew of Burns' life.[26] Intrigued, Somerville immediately borrowed Wilson's volume of the

Poems, which had been much used, almost certainly by several read-ers. Although his father was wary of the impression Burns could have on his young son, and bought him a copy of *Gospel Sonnets* as an alternative, Somerville had 'felt new sensations so exquisitely delight-ful' on reading Burns, and refused to give him up. The elation felt by Somerville on first becoming acquainted with Burns was an experience shared with many more men and women of his class.[27]

Song was an integral element of Scottish popular culture.[28] Song in the eyes of Professor James Beattie in Aberdeen, and for the enthusiastic song collector Joseph Ritson, was in a country like Scotland the product of the people below – the folk whose significance we alluded to in the previous chapter. Thus collecting songs was, in the context of the revo-lutionary era in which Ritson (and Burns) operated, a radical – and patriotic – activity, and it was certainly a project into which Burns threw himself full-bloodedly.[29] It was not long before, in Ulster as well as Scotland, women workers – often hand spinners operating in small groups in or near the home – were to be heard singing Burns' songs, leaving an audible impression on those who heard them.[30] We know, too, that weavers, notably those by the 1800s who were crowded into noisy, loom-rattling weaving sheds, found solace in song. William Thom, the Inverurie-born weaver and poet, was employed in an Aberdeen weaving factory in the early years of the nineteenth century, and acknowledged the debt he and his fellow workers owed to the 'Song Spirits' as they 'walked in melody from loom to loom, ministering to the low-hearted'. Poets were the weavers' priests, and songs their alterna-tive to sermons. Favourites were the lyrical effusions of Robert Tannahill that conjured up bitter-sweet scenes of loves lost in settings of pastoral tranquillity as in 'The Braes of Gleniffer', or the importance of love in 'Gloomy Winter's Now Awa'. But when hearts were filled with 'every-thing but hope and happiness, and all but seared', it was a rousing rendition of Burns' 'A Man's a Man' that lifted the spirits of the 'fagged weaver'.[31] This song, which Burns had probably written in 1794, inspired by Thomas Paine's *Rights of Man*, had been published posthu-mously, in 1805, and rapidly became a favourite amongst Britain's Radicals.[32] The third stanza is representative of the song's levelling – and stirring – message:

> Ye see yon birkie, ca'd a lord,
> Wha struts, and stares, and a' that;
> Tho' hundreds worship at his word,

He's but a coof for a' that:
For a' that and a' that,
His riband, star and a' that,
The man of independent mind,
He looks and laughs at a' that.

And as we saw in the previous chapter, this was one of the tunes to which the ploughmen and shepherds who formed the procession that preceded the Burns festival in Ayr marched. Much sung too, from 1817 if not earlier, was 'Scots Wha Hae'.[33] The song, Burns' title for which was 'Robert Bruce's March to Bannockburn', is proudly patriotic, but also a defiant rejection of slavery and tyranny, and a hymn to liberty.[34] These were themes articulated by Radicals throughout Britain, including in the Chartist strongholds, a topic we will explore further below.[35]

* * *

The Radical community – and Burns' audience too – comprised mainly skilled, literate, independent, usually protestant, and largely sober members of the respectable working classes, in both town and country. Tens of thousands of men of this description were also freemasons, as Burns had been. Indeed later in the nineteenth century there was irritation amongst the freemason fraternity that his biographers had skirted round Burns' masonic associations, and overlooked 'the 'great propelling power' of freemasonry in his work, above all his 'stern love of independence and brotherhood'.[36] Modern scholars, however, are inclined to see Burns' freemasonry as one of a number of influences. Some of these overlapped with the ideals of the calling. They included the egalitarianism of the son of the 4th Earl of Selkirk, Lord Daer, a friend of Thomas Paine, whom Burns had met and been impressed by in April 1786, and the Revolution Whigs' commitment to civil liberties that Daer also espoused and with which Burns became increasingly familiar owing to the company he kept after 1788.[37]

The emphasis of operative masonic lodges in Scotland, numbers of which had risen six-fold between 1736 when the Grand Lodge of Scotland was founded, and 1800, tended to be on mutual aid, similar to the friendly societies.[38] But they were hardly nests of political disaffection during the period of the Revolution in France.[39] Although a handful had joined forces with branches of Friends of the People, if there was any link between freemasonry and Scottish Radicalism after

1815 it was indirect. Masonic lodges and Radical politics drew separately from the same pool of respectable artisans whose interests in sociability, egalitarianism, democracy and meritocracy overlapped. But most were also constitutional loyalists, which explains why the 'judiciously chosen' date for the laying of the foundation stone for the Burns mausoleum in Dumfries, at which ceremony freemasons were to preside, was 4 June 1815, the king's birthday.[40] Radicals and freemasons, too, saw strength in unity, valued their independence and publicly demonstrated their beliefs through parades and processions. Both adopted 'A Man's a Man' as their anthem, although, as is suggested by the lines below, specially written on the occasion of the laying of the foundation stone for the Burns monument in Kilmarnock in September 1878, for freemasons universal brotherhood was to be restricted to brother masons (although this was no small constituency):

> Ye 'brothers o' the *mystic tie*',
> The *mystic grip*, and a' that,
> Now gather forth, frae south and north,
> Frae east, and west, and a' that;
> And a' that, and a' that,
> Frae near, and far, and a' that,
> Each *Brother* dear his *badge* maun wear
> This day for Burns and a' that.[41]

Even so, and in large part what explains the freemasons' anxiety to promote Burns as a freemason first and foremost, the Kilmarnock edition of his poems had depended almost entirely on subscriptions from his brother masons, while Burns' entry to Edinburgh's elite circle of literati late in 1786 owed much to his masonic connections.[42] His association with freemasonry was therefore something of which his brethren were enormously proud, and is underlined by their presence in vast numbers at most of the ceremonies for laying foundation stones for Burns memorials throughout much of the nineteenth century. Freemasons were involved too in the main anniversary events held in Burns' name which punctuated the period, although increasingly independently, as they sought exclusive ownership of the poet. But it was freemasons who in 1885 were the founding fathers of the influential Burns Federation.[43]

* * *

Somewhat different were the communities of self-taught handloom weavers referred to earlier. These were frequently hotbeds of political discussion, which, not unusually, was combined with earnest Presbyterianism. However, it also contained a deeply rooted radical edge. This was embodied in the principle enunciated with newfound enthusiasm after the Glorious Revolution of 1688–9, that monarchs and governments were not directly ordained by God, but rather that the people were sovereign.[44] The weaver community in Fenwick in Ayrshire is one such example – where, significantly, Burns was venerated over other poets including Milton and Byron.[45] Another was Patiemuir, near Dunfermline, where the grandparents and parents of Andrew Carnegie – later to become a US-based steel and rail magnate and philanthropist – were politically active. What is striking is the importance that was attached to Burns by Carnegie's father, a damask weaver renowned locally as a singer of Burns' songs, so much so that 'even before he could read and write' Andrew was able to recite several Burns poems.[46] Although not in this case, it was in such ways that Burns' poems in Scots – the language of ordinary people and which for this reason had a 'radical irreverent quality' – became part of the everyday life and political discourse of Scotland's working classes.[47]

During his lifetime Burns had associated himself with a number of anti-establishment causes, including the American Revolution, and, for a time, the Revolution in France.[48] Hardly surprisingly, certain of the values and principles articulated in Burns' work, as well as selective interpretations of Burns' life, were appropriated by radically inclined Scots in the first half of the nineteenth century. Manifested first – mainly, but not exclusively – in Chartism, many of the same values were held equally dear by the Chartists' immediate successors, the Radical Liberals.[49]

Prior to this however, and over time, a number of overtly radical poems and songs either written by or attributed to Burns had appeared posthumously. 'A Man's a Man' we have noted. Others included 'Why Should We Idly Waste Our Prime, Or a Revolutionary Lyric' (1834) and 'The Tree of Liberty' (1838).[50] Yet there is little to suggest that the more overtly political productions of this kind resonated particularly strongly with the majority of his readers.

There was sufficient material amongst the standard canon of Burns' work to arouse dormant passions and fire radical ardour. The much-reprinted Kilmarnock edition opened with 'The Twa Dogs', which could be read as a light-hearted questioning of social hierarchy and of the virtues of metropolitan culture or, more persuasively, as a poem that borrowed heavily from Robert Fergusson's 'most politically-barbed' poem, 'The Ghaists'.[51] In 'The Twa Dogs' Burns spoke to and for those on the receiving end of hard-hearted agents or factors, as well as to the dispossessed tenant. The same was true of the 'Address to Beelzebub' and 'Man was Made to Mourn'.[52] Similarly, 'To a Mouse', in which the ploughman (poet) has unhoused a mouse – so breaking 'Nature's social union' – implicit is the shared experience of mouse and man, both relatively powerless in the struggle against the consequences of enclosure, clearance and rack-renting.[53] These poems not only offered empathy, succour and support, but may also have articulated the rumbling resentments that lay beneath the sullen and eerie silence that accompanied the processes of rural commercialisation, proletarianisation, and clearance referred to in the previous chapter.[54] Dignity, self-respect and a sense of self-worth were of fundamental importance for working people in the nineteenth century.[55] In providing a language that captured these feelings, the evidence suggests that Burns' works were a well-thumbed resource. The significance of this is difficult to exaggerate.

One of Burns' poems not to be found in either the Kilmarnock or Edinburgh editions, however, was also much in demand. This was 'Holy Willie's Prayer', an uncompromising attack on the hypocritical, drink-imbibing, fornicating elder from Mauchline, William Fisher, a representative of the Auld Licht wing of the Church of Scotland, which held to the Calvinist doctrines of original sin and predestination. This unforgiving and illiberal wing of the Kirk had long been on Burns' radar, although, as indicated in the Introduction, his apprehension about the censure that would result if he were discovered to have written 'Holy Willie's Prayer' (without question his best-known religious satire), caused him to circulate it in manuscript form amongst his friends and trusted acquaintances only. Indeed, although Burns did publish poetry that ridiculed preachers both canting and smugly refined (as in 'The Holy Fair'), he continued to resist the publication of poems critical of the men he termed 'Bigoted priests'. As a consequence his *Prayer of Holy Willie, a Canting, Hypocritical, Kirk Elder*, was published as a chapbook in 1789, anonymously and probably without his knowledge or permission.[56]

Even though Currie and other early editors of Burns omitted the poem, it was circulating in Glasgow in 1799, with other chapbook versions following in 1801.[57] New Licht Presbyterianism, with its principles of 'private judgement, practical benevolence, universal tolerance, [and] defiance of tyranny' that combined Enlightenment ideas alongside traditional Presbyterian teaching, was on the march. It found growing favour not only amongst members of the Moderate party in the Church of Scotland that had been formed in 1752 but on the ground too. This was above all in the west of Scotland where there was a long-standing tradition of lay resistance to clerical domination.[58] This was the doctrine Burns had espoused and articulated.

However, it was dissatisfaction with Burns' early editors' 'disposition to draw a veil' over this feature of Burns' 'genius' that had led to the appearance, in 1852, of *The Kirk's Alarm*, referred to at the end of the previous chapter. Anti-clericalism was a common theme of working class poets in Victorian Britain. Yet Burns' assaults on 'Priestcraft', and, conversely, his belief in a merciful God and the right of individuals to make their own judgements about the nature of God and creation, and the subsequent 'mental elevation of the people', were acknowledged by numerous commentators in the nineteenth century as one of his most significant and lasting contributions. Testimony to this is provided by the example of Robert Williams Buchanan, the writer, poet and dramatist, who in 1850 had arrived with his parents in Glasgow, and spent much of the rest of his life in Scotland. Struck, as so many incomers were, by how familiar the Scots were with Burns' works, Buchanan was persuaded that Burns' kirk satires had been 'one of the great factors in the disintegration of Scottish superstition'. Without Burns, he found it difficult to imagine what Scotland, 'with its gravitation towards the Sabbatarian and the sunless', would have become.[59]

* * *

Albeit often by inference, we can say more about Burns' appeal for ordinary Scots. His depictions of late eighteenth-century rural life and the society of hamlets and villages with their innkeepers, shoemakers, weavers and beggars, are not simply to be dismissed as sentimental or idealised representations of a fast disappearing world. For one thing, it had not yet gone, certainly not in the first decades of the nineteenth century. (Worth noting too is that, notwithstanding the rapid pace of rural change, concerns of this kind, and regret at the vanishing countryside of the past, were not confined to Burns or even Scottish poets.[60])

As we have seen, rural society in Scotland was changing fast. Yet elements of the old order endured. The more efficient farming units – single tenant farms as opposed to the ferm-touns – were still communities, even if the farmer now ate separately from his servants (many of whom continued to live in), and was better dressed. Farm workers (and their families in the case of married men) continued to move on at the end of their six-monthly or annual term, and to seek employment at hiring fairs. The annual agricultural cycle that began with ploughing and sowing and culminated at harvest time with the various local customs that celebrated the climax to the growing season was timeless. So too, to an extent anyway, were the fairs, holy and otherwise, and the festivities held to mark occasions such as Halloween and Hogmanay – all subjects that featured in Burns' poetry. Images of a mouse disturbed, or a daisy crushed or shows of affection for an age-worn mare conjured up by Burns continued to resonate.

For those who remained on the land, there is ample testimony, admittedly more often second hand, that Burns' poems which captured in verse so much that was recognisable in their everyday lives, gave enormous pleasure.[61] But there are some first-hand accounts too. Robert Davidson, for example, was a day labourer in the Borders who around 1798 first encountered Burns, recounting later (not unlike Alexander Somerville) the 'astonishment and admiration' he felt about the 'poetry and powers of that extraordinary man'.[62] Below, we will see just how powerful Burns' influence was. And there were many rural readers like Davidson. Indeed it was only in the 1880s that a majority of Scots lived in the larger towns, that is those with over 5,000 inhabitants; before that most people were to be found in the countryside and smaller towns.[63]

In other words there were many for whom rural Scotland was real enough. Indeed large numbers of working people who had been forced to find employment and accommodation in the industrial towns returned to the countryside for the harvest and seized what opportunities they could to visit relatives in the surrounding countryside well into the century.[64] Burns' poems and songs – as with the chapbooks and popular publications like *Whistle-Binkie: A Collection of Songs for the Social Circle* (first published in 1832) – provided an emotional anchor as migrants struggled to adjust to an environment that was certainly different from that they had known. The mass of humanity, the steam, smoke, overcrowding, apparent chaos and noise, was for many distressingly alien.[65] A dominant theme of urban culture in

Victorian Scotland was that of a lost world, a rural idyll that contrasted with the cramped environment of the manufacturing towns with their enclosed mills and factories and the regimentation of hard-driving work. Accordingly, rhapsodising about city parks became a distinct and prominent trope in the writing of many working-class poets.

Burns, however, had not simply observed, portrayed and preserved in verse and song a world that was not quite yesteryear. With its stress on unaffected simplicity, and the nobility of the poor, a poem such as 'The Cotter's Saturday Night' bolstered the confidence of the plough-men – in the early nineteenth century valued for their skills and their capacity to look after and manage their horses, which were now crucial to the success of the revolutionised farming system.[66] It spoke, too, to the respectable town-dwelling working classes of the early and mid nineteenth century, the first- and second-generation heirs of Arcadia. Piety, sobriety, thrift and independence – central themes in this and other Burns poems – were codes many of the new inhabitants of Scotland's towns tried to live by. This is manifested in their reading habits and regular attendance at church (primarily as members of the dissenting congregations), and their membership of self-help organisations like friendly societies and savings banks, the numbers of which in Scotland mushroomed during and after the Napoleonic Wars.[67] We will say more about this class of people – Scotland's respectable artisans and the emergent *petit bourgeoisie* – in a moment and in chapter 4.

But if Burns was a salve, he could also inflame in the manner described by Jonathan Rose. For this to happen, reading context was important. Perused in periodicals intent on fostering a popular radical culture, for instance, pastoral sentimentality could take on a sharp subversive edge.[68] One channel through which this somewhat more socially challenging Burns flowed was some of the societies that were founded in Burns' name in the early nineteenth century. Examination (where it is possible) of the membership of these shows that the tradition of keeping alive in a formal sense the memory of, and paying tribute to, Robert Burns was not solely the preserve of Scotland's aristocrats, Tories and others of the social elite who organised and attended many of the early dinners to mark Burns' birthday.

It was proprietors of workshops, shopkeepers and other small-scale employers who were amongst the fifteen members of the committee of Paisley's Burns Anniversary Society, established under the direction of Robert Tannahill in 1805, along with others who had been journeymen handloom weavers or employees in other trades – at which a few continued to work. Indeed Tannahill later expressed his revulsion at the appropriation of Burns' birthday by the 'better sort' into whose pockets 'Fortune has thrown ... five shillings while she has left others with scarcely one brotherless penny.'[69] Some of the Society's members – James Scadlock, James Tannahill and William M'Laren to name but three – had in the early 1790s been identified with French Revolutionary ideals, even if later they changed their minds.

By 1818, however, the club's membership had moved up the social scale to include several successful businessmen, lawyers, ministers, a teacher, an artist, a medical doctor and William Motherwell, newspaper editor, poet and collector of ballads – and a staunch Tory. In fact while the local reformer George Gardner was also a member, in politics the group was largely Conservative, and firmly on the side of order, with at least one of them, Lieutenant James Stewart, serving as a volunteer raised to combat the Radical rising in 1820.[70] Partly as a reaction to this and the alleged 'aristocratic' nature of the Paisley club's Burns suppers, in the nearby weaving village of Kilbarchan, a New Burns Club was formed, also in 1820. Only bread and cheese and water were consumed at the new club's suppers – a menu designed to deny the government tax revenue and force it to 'submit to the views of the inhabitants', although by no means was this weapon confined to Renfrewshire. It was men from similar social backgrounds who were probably instrumental in setting up Burns societies in other smaller manufacturing centres, such as Dunfermline (1812) and Fenwick in north Ayrshire. Although little is known about the Burns Club of Ayr, that in 1836 its president was Dr John Taylor, Ayrshire's Chartist revolutionary, suggests that at least some of its members had radical leanings.[71]

Burns' influence was felt far beyond the confines of clubs of this nature devoted to his memory, however. There were few of them and participation rates were generally low. Some rulebooks banned political discussion, the emphasis being on congeniality – the worm that, as we will see later in this book, metamorphosed into the cult charged with parodying Burns' legacy.

* * *

Quite independently, there were plebeian Scots who took up the verbal missiles that Burns' song and verse could become, and with them engaged in the campaigns that Burns had sided with, or appeared to have done. Carol McGuirk has put this succinctly. Unlike Scott's Scotland, Burns' was 'not over yet'.[72]

One reason for this was to be found in the country's social structure. Henry Skrine was a seasoned traveller who after visits to Scotland in the 1780s and 1790s was astonished by the 'absolute' power of the nobility and 'untitled lairds', and how immense the gulf was between 'the mighty lord and the humble peasant', the last-named mired in poverty and lacking in spirit. This, he asserted, contrasted with England where 'the rights of the peasant are as fully ascertained as those of the prince'. The effect of 'elevating a certain number to so high a pitch', he argued, without ministers and professionals to intervene, insulated them 'too much from the other orders of society, to permit their benefiting the general mass in adequate degree'.[73]

Skrine's assessment finds support from historians who have commented on the unusual degree of quiescence exhibited by Scotland's labouring people during the eighteenth century. The tradition of anti-noble sentiment, strong in France, for example, had not developed in Scotland.[74] Although we know now that there was more protest and disorder than was once recognised, what remains true is that the landed classes in Scotland had inherited enormous power over many centuries. And this was concentrated in the hands of a smaller proportion of landlords than anywhere in Europe. All pervasive, thus was entrenched a massively uneven social structure. Signs of dissent were quickly identified and anything that smacked of a threat was ruthlessly put down, including by force with the use of the army, and a legal system that nationally and in the counties was heavily weighted in the landowner's interest.[75]

Bolstered by the British state with the power of patronage from 1712, leading landowners – the heritors – appointed parish ministers of the established church and the schoolmaster that every parish was obliged to provide. The dependent status of both ensured that they – as 'the mouthpiece of the lairds' – played their part as bastions of social order.[76] Ordinary parishioners had a stark reminder of their lowly status each time they attended church, seated as they were in plain pews (if indeed they could afford to pay) on the ground floor while sitting above, in fine 'lairds' lofts', were the heritors whose principal tenants would also have specially reserved pews.[77] On their way they would have been expected to doff their bonnets and hats when passing a member of the gentry, in what one contemporary called 'an unmeaning expression of respect'.[78] Sermons proclaimed the virtues of the present constitution. Ministers and their kirk sessions in what have been likened to parish theocracies were responsible for the parishioners' conduct, in terms of both civil and ecclesiastical offences, and for deciding whether they were deserving of poor relief, essential during periods of crisis in order for households to survive. Throughout but increasingly in the later eighteenth century and beyond, their main focus became fornication and, less so, adultery.[79] Investigations into suspected cases were invariably intrusive, occasionally barbaric and for those found guilty, deeply humiliating.

The infamous Highland clearances are well known. But Lowlanders too endured a similar process, even if it was piecemeal and longer drawn out in comparison to the systematic eviction of entire communities in the north and north-west.[80] Conditions (money wages are the most obvious measure) in the countryside do seem to have improved over the course of Burns' lifetime; that is for most of those who managed to find a place in the new farming regime. But agrarian reform led eventually to the forced expulsion of what by 1815 had become a surplus army of landless labourers, and a remorseless drift to the towns and cities where even before the recession of 1816 there were too many hands for too little work.[81] Although since around 1760 there had been a general improvement in diet and dress in Scotland, in the towns poverty continued to be an endemic feature.[82] For particular occupations, above all handloom weaving, in the later eighteenth century the single largest employer of more or less full-time – and well-paid – workers, conditions worsened, with savage reductions in incomes that at times threatened starvation, longer hours and, with the emergence of the loom shed and steam-power, loss of the independence once-proud weavers had enjoyed when many had been their own masters.[83]

In circumstances such as these, it is little wonder that many of those who experienced at first hand the destabilising and often distressing effects of unprecedented economic and social change turned to the Bible and Burns, which were frequently reported to have been found in combination in working-class households.[84] During the early years of the French Revolution, Bob Harris has suggested, apocalyptic religious traditions, somehow 'buried' amongst seceding congregations, may have re-surfaced.[85] This makes sense, as from the middle of the eighteenth century there had been an identifiable increase in the incidence of Arminian preaching with its rejection of Calvinist predestination, and a shift to 'salvationist exhortation' from secession and relief church pulpits.[86]

There was a millenarian quality, too, to some of Burns' work, above all in 'A Man's a Man', a song we have referred to already and will again, in which the prayer is offered that 'come it may / As come it will for a' that', 'That man to man, the world o'er / Shall brothers be for a' that.' We can sense something of the sort from a description of a centenary celebration organised by Ayr's Working Men's Reform Association in January 1859. The reason for the gathering, declared the main speaker, a Colonel Shaw of the Queen's India Army, was not to praise Burns' poetic genius or to assess his life and character, but rather to commemorate 'the great Reformer who more than seventy years ago went for "manhood suffrage" – singing "A man's a man for a' that" ', a song that 'like the bird in the morning' had 'soared towards heaven'. Shaw's speech was then applauded and, at his bidding, those present – women as well as men – the 'glorious' song was sung.[87]

Apocalyptic visions were part and parcel of the poetic apparatus of a number of the radical poets who followed Burns, and acknowledged their debt to him. A telling example is the final couplet of the poverty-pressed weaver poet William Thom's 'Whisperings For the Unwashed', which looks forward to a time:

> When the breast glows to Love and the brow
>   beams in Light –
> Oh! Hasten it Heaven! MAN LONGS FOR HIS RIGHT.

Thom's account of his experience of the weaving shed and Burns' enervating impact therein we noted earlier, as well as his own creative work, points to the role Burns played in rallying the spirits of ordinary Scots at a time of dislocation and sometimes despair. Thom is often quoted, but there were many working-class poets of both sexes who were inspired and influenced by, or who imitated, Burns. In their writings is to be found some of the most vivid evidence of Burns' legacy, in terms of the similarities in subject matter, poetic form, language and sentiments. Such work is rarely read today, but much of it survives.

The existence of the Paisley weaver poets demonstrates that Burns was not the only man of his social standing in the second half of the eighteenth century who wrote poetry. There were women too, such as Isobel Pagan (*c.*1740–1821), from New Cumnock in Ayrshire, Janet Little (1759–1813), Janet Hamilton, mentioned above, and perhaps the best example of all, Elizabeth Horne Smith, a Glasgow-born ploughman's daughter.[88] None of these, however, had risen to the heady heights of critical acclaim enjoyed by Burns. Partly encouraged by Romantic notions about the nature of poetic talent, there was a widespread belief (instigated by Henry Mackenzie in his well-known review of the Kilmarnock edition in the *Lounger* in which he announced Burns as the 'Heaven-taught ploughman') that Burns really was of relatively humble origin and uneducated. James Hogg (1770–1835), the 'Ettrick Shepherd', and Robert Tannahill were cut of similar cloth, and had their emulators too.[89] But it was Burns' life according to Alexander Somerville that had 'excited an interest in me far stronger than the recital of . . . two poems'.[90] Not dissimilarly, in the north-east, William Lillie rose to become a clerk and miller, but acknowledged the importance of Burns as an exemplar by calling himself 'Buchan's Ploughman Poet'.[91]

But awakenings of this kind were widespread, with Burns' example (and, to be fair, James Hogg's) inducing a stream of imitators, many writing in the vernacular, sometimes in an anti-establishment vein, but often also in an overly sentimental manner.[92] Prime examples include James Taylor in Fenwick, and Andrew Fisher, formerly a weaver and Chartist who became a colliery worker in Lanarkshire. Fisher's verse not only imitated Burns; he consciously adopted the role of bard of the local mining community.[93] Few, though, went as far as Alexander Anderson (1845–1909), a peasant poet much influenced by Burns and Hogg, who, rather eerily, had his own eyes painted into a portrait of Burns that he owned.[94] The emergence of self-styled 'people's poets' on the public stage was aided too by the relative ease with which their work could be published – in chapbooks, poets' boxes, and, even before the era of cheap newspapers from the mid 1850s, in corners of the provincial press. As Burns had done. Over the course of the century it has been estimated that such newspapers printed as many as five million individual poems.[95] William Thom's first poem, signed, 'By a Serf', was published in the *Aberdeen Herald* in 1841.[96]

Just how many labouring class poets had been directly inspired to write by Burns is impossible to say, although it has been claimed that even in the early nineteenth century almost 'every village in Scotland could boast its local Burns'.[97] In the bigger places, impersonal lives found meaning through participation in self-expressive creative writing. By mid century an industrial centre like Dundee could boast several worker poets, encouraged by the patronage of the radically inclined admirer of Burns, and Scots language and Scottish history enthusiast, the Reverend George Gilfillan. Gilfillan's belief that poetical ability was a gift of God meant that he had no qualms about encouraging his 'queer, motley collection' of self-taught authors to follow in the footsteps of Burns (although never reaching the heights that Burns did), however lowly their background.[98] Rural Scotland, too, had its share of autodidact poets who acknowledged their debt to Burns, as, for example, Jane Stevenson who while herding cattle near the banks of the Garnock river in north Ayrshire 'fell in imitation of Burns ['Ye Banks and Braes o' Bonnie Doon'] to compose a few simple verses'.[99] Many saw poetry – if it could find a publisher – as a means if not of escaping poverty, of easing it.[100]

* * *

By the second half of the nineteenth century there was a ready readership for popular verse in Scotland, with working-class poets benefiting from the post-Chartist Radical-Liberal consensus, the upsurge of the provincial newspaper press after the repeal of the Stamp Duty in 1855, and the enthusiasm of proprietors and editors to print the work of plebeian poets. And even though literary patrons expected those they encouraged – not always successfully – to steer clear of contentious topics, no longer were poets with radical sympathies beyond the pale of literary respectability. Indeed, for some influential Victorian celebrants of working-class poets their writing provided evidence 'of the awakened mind of the common people of England [sic]'.[101] But Burns had been the first, and it was his influence that was the most far-reaching – although there were other role models.[102] Thus in Paisley, where 'poets were [reputed] to be counted by thousands', inspiration was provided by Tannahill and his associates, and William Motherwell, as well as Burns.[103] Whatever the origins of Scotland's efflorescence of autodidactic poetry, by January 1881 Glasgow's Mitchell Library alone had collected for its Poet's Box more than 2,200 volumes of poetry written by 1,395 writers, three-quarters of whom were 'poets of labour'. On top of this was newspaper verse.[104] In fact, so noticeable was the rise of peasant and artisan poets in Scotland, pronounced one proponent of the genre that, 'Croakers and carping critics to the contrary', it was a 'matter of national importance'.[105]

But even more direct links can be traced from Burns' poetry to that of his imitators. A compelling instance is that of our Borders farm worker Robert Davidson. His *Leaves From A Peasant's Drawer* was published in 1848, when he was around 70 years old, although many of the poems had been written earlier. Like Burns, Davidson worked as a ploughman, but as an employee rather than as a small tenant farmer, and, like others of his rank, lived with his wife and children close to edge of poverty, suffering along with other Borders' farm workers bouts of under- and unemployment.[106] The tone of the content of *Leaves* was announced in the book's dedication, '*To The Working Men of the Border*'. The poems' titles echo those of Burns: 'The Kirn Day', 'Fasten E'en', 'Lines Suggested by Incidents Following the Reform Bill', 'Wallace's Farewell', and even 'To a Red Breast'. Language and poetic form followed Burns too, as in 'Lines on the Falling Down of the Bell of Howman Kirk', which replicates 'Tam o' Shanter' exactly, even to the extent that the poem was similarly annotated, with the first stanza running:

> Twas at the solemn, silent hour
> When Mortals drop their cares and strife,
> When sleep asserts its silken power,
> And levels all the lots of life.

The framework Burns provided for a poet such as Davidson is best seen in his 'Sim and Sandy', a dramatised conversation poem that replicates Burns' Luath and Caesar in 'The Twa Dogs'. But instead of canines, Davidson's discussants are rural workers, who compare life before the process of agrarian reform – which they had both witnessed – with the present. If there is ambiguity in how Burns' 'Twa Dogs' can be read, there is none in 'Sim and Sandy'. It is direct, forceful and uncompromising, rooted in what must have been Davidson's knowledge of the enclosure process in the uplands of Roxburghshire. Despite being content with 'the station in which Providence had placed me', on this issue Davidson was clearly angered. Sim describes 'A croft converted to a sheep walk wild, / Where twenty separate harvests smiled', with the former occupants 'restless toss'd':

> Till in his breast the love of country's lost;
> He flies for shelter to far distant climes,
> Or crowded towns, to swell the tide of crimes.'

All that is left are traces, 'shapeless heaps, with hemlocks wild between' that 'mark the spot where cottages have been'.

Sandy has no doubt where the finger of blame should be pointed. It is at our 'braw new laird' who has arrived 'Wi Indian gowd' to buy the 'birken cleugh'. He was one of a breed of men who, 'By hook or crook his empty pouches fills/Returns to Scotland and buys half her hills', a reference to the habit of returnees from imperial service in the East India Company – usually scions of the landed gentry – who with the fortunes they had made in Asia purchased estates which they then set about transforming.[107]

While Davidson's debt to Burns is obvious, his devotion was not entirely slavish. In his 'On Hearing that a Monument was being erected in the Memory of Robert Burns' he lavishes praise on Scotland's 'matchless bard'. It is in stanza eleven though that is to be found what is virtually the only discordant note in the entire collection, with the lines, 'Though I adore his genius bright / I mourn his ill directed lays', a reference to Burns' celebration of drink that might 'tempt from sober paths to stray'. Dissenting congregations, to which increasing numbers of farm workers flocked in the Borders (but elsewhere and in the towns too), were sternly moral and determinedly sober.[108]

What Davidson's involvement in politics was, if any, is unknown. There are, however, cases where direct links with Burns' poetry went further than printed dissent. An example is Alexander Rodger (1784–1846), who described himself as 'an Operative Weaver of Glasgow'. Rodger was also 'an unrepentantly radical politician' who had served a prison sentence for his political views. Imitating Burns' Kilmarnock edition, the first poem in Rodger's collection was 'The Twa Weavers'. Written in the tense year of 1819, Rodger's discussants, Robin and Tammas, highlight the plight of the handloom weavers who, declares Tammas, 'starve at Tollcross', before expatiating on the many causes of the weavers' deteriorating – and desperate – working and living conditions. The poem closes with the patriotic reflection on 'Poor Britain! How sadly thou glories decline', before conceding that the weavers' prospects are 'most gloomy and black':

> Unless the BLACK Box to the flames we consign
> And begin a new score, like our fathers langsyne.[109]

Perhaps the best example of a radical poet and activist who was both influenced and inspired by Burns in the first half of the nineteenth century is the now largely overlooked Robert Nicoll – although a modest obelisk was erected in his honour near his lowland Perthshire birthplace some years after his death. Like Burns, Nicoll, who was born in 1814, died young, in 1837.[110] The son of a farm worker, and a voracious reader, he was well-versed in the scriptures, attended his local parish school, joined a circulating library, furthered his own education and, again in a manner similar to Burns, tested his ideas in debating societies in Perth and Dundee. It was in Dundee, probably in 1834, that he set up his own subscription library, and published his *Poems and Lyrics* (1836), the third section of which was sub-titled, 'Poems Chiefly in the Scottish Dialect, Illustrative of the Feelings of the Intelligent and Religious among the Working-Classes of Scotland', which contains verse which owes much to Burns in its form, subject matter and phrasing. An example of the last is 'We'll Mak' the Warld Better Yet', the third stanza of which begins with the lines, 'See yonder cooff wha becks an' bows / To yonder fool wha's ca'd a lord', an explicit reference to Burns' 'Is There for Honest Poverty'.

An ardent, uncompromising and in some respects a naïve ultra-radical and political activist who rejected compromise with the Whigs, Nicoll went on to become a successful but also very short-lived editor of the Radical newspaper, *The Leeds Times*.

Although Nicoll's life was brief, his impact was substantial, being credited in his poetry with having waged 'a glorious warfare' against the wrongs of 'an infernal system of society'.[111] In Dundee he left in his wake an active 'Republic of Letters' the impact of which was felt for many years. In radical circles he was considered second to none, not even Burns whose successor he was seen as by the 'Corn Law Rhymer' Ebenezer Elliott. Some of his poems were published posthumously in the Chartist newspaper *The Northern Star*. Indeed it is in one of these, Nicoll's 'Stanzas on the Birthday of Burns', that is to be found the kernel of the explanation for Burns' appeal to the hearts and minds of so many ordinary people in nineteenth-century Britain. From this perspective, Burns was not far short of a secular saint. The third stanza, which owes much to the lines in 'The Cotter's Saturday Night', runs:

> Before the proudest of the earth
> We stand with an uplifted brow;
> Like us, THOU wast a toil-worn man,
> And we are noble now!

It is the last line that is the key, a fly in the ointment concocted to cool the brows of those suffering at the sharp end of change in rural

Lowland Scotland, their resentment leading them towards Radicalism and Chartism.[112] A social psychological revolution was under way. Skrine's Scotland was being left behind. Burns was of major importance in effecting this.

Indeed, by the end of the 1830s, Burns was included in the pantheon of liberty-espousing radical philosophers and writers lionised by the Chartists.[113] In Scotland, though, he was positioned in the poetic vanguard, his works to be taught in the Chartist schools William Thompson, editor of Glasgow's *Chartist Circular* was then advocating.[114]

* * *

For all that it was an astounding success, as we saw in the previous chapter, the 1844 Ayr festival had had its critics. Especially piercing were some of the Chartists' barbs. No time was lost to pick over the speeches made by the principal speakers – Wilson's (again) in particular – and to recruit Burns instead for the radical cause. Ironically, notwithstanding their attractiveness to Scottish conservatives, the virtues celebrated in 'The Cotter's Saturday Night' of independent labour, and rural living, also appealed to nineteenth-century radicals.[115]

In Scotland the Reverend Patrick Brewster, Paisley's Chartist minister, led the attack.[116] The event's organisers – aristocrats and their allies – were denounced as hypocrites, honouring Burns in 1844, but spurning him during his final years in Dumfries. Do not 'feast upon your poet's grave', thundered *The Northern Star*, 'having first starved him into it'.[117] The charge was a potent one, and echoed the comments of the Chartist lecturer Julian Harney who had visited the Burns monument in Alloway the previous year. He readily acknowledged that it was a fine structure and a fitting altar to Burns. Yet, he argued, it did not reflect well on the class that had erected it. Whoever recalls Burns' deathbed appeal for five pounds, he wrote, will regard 'this cold stone pile as a monument to the meanness as well as pride, of the Scottish aristocracy'.[118] A test for the present generation of 'owners of broad acres, the titled, and the wealthy', and a mark of whether they truly repented their forefathers' treatment of Burns, would be what assistance they would provide for other poets of humble origin, such as Thom, who, like Burns, had been feted briefly (but in London) on the publication of his *Rhymes and Recollections of a Hand-Loom Weaver* in 1844. *Punch* adopted a similar stance, remarking that the genuineness of Scotland's affection for 'the dead Ploughman' could be measured 'by her tenderness towards a kindred, if lesser, spirit – the living weaver'.[119]

Scrutinised and criticised too were the festival arrangements, not least the separation of the banqueters in the great marquee and the majority of those present who remained outside in the rain.[120] 'Far better there had been no feasting than that the class from whom Burns sprung should have been excluded by the fifteen shilling ticket.' But despite the discernible anti-Scottish colouring of some of the *Star*'s comments, including its patronising preparedness to overlook for English readers the 'barbarous jargon' of Burns' language, the paper was in no doubt about Burns' importance for reformers: 'wherever the sons of freedom are gathered ... "A man's a man for a' that" [will] electrify them with the love of equality, while "Scots wha hae" will inspire them to do and dare all for liberty. The writings of Burns embrace every human heart: hence, despite his nationality, the universal homage paid to his name.'[121]

By mid century Burns' influence had extended far beyond the narrow political programme of the Chartists. With Burns' example before them, wrote Charles Kingsley, working men had 'taken courage' and 'spoken out the thought within ... in verse and prose', and in their actions.[122] Hugh Miller, still chary of Burns owing to the harmful effect his writings had had on the nation's morals, could see a positive side too. '*Robert Burns was the man who first taught the Scottish people to stand erect*' he wrote in 1856, using italics to add emphasis to his assertion. The people's 'master fault', a 'mean and creeping subservience to the great', had disappeared, they had 'lost the habitual stoop ... and all honour, say we, to the *reformer* who, more than an other, effected the change.'[123]

This was the embodiment of the growing Liberal spirit of the age about which Scottish conservatives were in despair.[124] Burns had articulated the iniquities of improvement, savaged the hypocrisy of the ruling elders within Scotland's parish states, punctured the pretensions of those whose social position depended more on social rank than social worth, and given voice to the poor and the underdog.

THREE

'Rattling the Presbyterians' cage'

The Burns centenary of 1859 and the struggle for the soul of Scotland

Hugh Miller had exaggerated the extent to which the independence-stifling bonds of paternalism had been stretched, let alone broken by the middle of the nineteenth century. But changes in the relationships between the classes were under way. By the later 1840s the skilled working classes had recovered from the attacks on collective bargaining that had culminated in Alison's breaking of the Glasgow cotton spinners' strike in 1837. Along with a newfound commitment to self-improvement, Hamish Fraser has discerned a 'powerful sense of the ability of workers to run their own affairs', and limited deference to middle-class ideology.[1] This materialised in a revival of Chartism in 1847 as well as in the form of stronger and more effective trade unions whose leaders understood the 'rules' of the capitalist game, and how to play them.[2] Notable, too, were shifts in political allegiances. Conservative domination of Scotland drew to a close after 1832, owing to Liberal advances won through the votes of the newly enfranchised urban middle classes. Before long Liberal gains would become Liberal hegemony.

What part Burns played in all of this is hard to say. What is undeniable though is that his memory was leaching deep into the Scottish body politic.

Certainly he was present in the minds of Scottish Radicals when, in August 1844 in Edinburgh's Calton Cemetery, the foundation stone was laid for a monument to Scotland's reform leaders of the 1790s. These were the men who had been sentenced to transportation after being found guilty in 1793 of sedition: Thomas Muir, Thomas Palmer, Maurice Margarot, William Skirving and Joseph Gerrald.[3] The proposal for a memorial – an obelisk – was partly motivated by a desire on the part of the campaigners, mainly Whigs, to divert attention from the 'humiliating' Tory statues to Henry Dundas, William Pitt and George IV which had been placed in prominent sites in the capital's New Town.[4] Associated, too, with the Complete Suffrage Association, the project was viewed as a means of advancing the cause of political reform in Scotland.

Telling for our purposes is that speakers at the ceremony remarked with evident pleasure, on the proximity, and sight, on Calton Hill above the cemetery, of Thomas Hamilton's monument to Burns, their brother Radical, which housed Flaxman's statue of the poet.[5] Patrick Brewster, the Chartist leader, contrasted Burns' role as a reformer with the conservative Scott, 'a man who had never shown himself favourable to the liberties of the people', a bold comment to make in Edinburgh but which in reforming circles – and beyond – was fast becoming received wisdom. Adding to the irony was the fact that Thomas Hamilton – a Tory – designer of the Burns memorial, was one of the organisers of the contemporaneous Ayr festival.[6]

But it was not many years later that the extent to which Burns had permeated Scottish society became fully apparent. The hundredth anniversary of Burns' birth, 25 January 1859 was marked by what was the first near global celebration of a poet's life and work – anywhere.

* * *

For a day, or part of it – Tuesday – large swathes of the northern portion of the world's workshop and commercial emporium closed for business. It was an astonishing occasion that united Scots at home and overseas. It has not been matched since. Other commemorative festivals, many of which focused on writers and artists, were held around the same time in Britain and Europe – Goethe in 1849, Handel, 1857, Shakespeare, 1864, and Pushkin, 1880, to name but four. As we saw in the Introduction, formalised celebrations around writers seem to have had a common function, above all in shaping and fixing collective identities, imagined and otherwise, principally that of nation, although as we will see there were other frames of reference.[7]

However, in its decentralised character, its social penetration – of classes and organisations – and the multifariousness of events, Scotland's tribute to Burns was unique. Only that for Friedrich Schiller (1759–1805), the German poet, playwright and philosopher, appears to have come anywhere near.[8]

It is difficult to convey in a few paragraphs the immensity of the 1859 jamboree. Cities vied with clachans, wrote James Ballantine, 'peer with peasant, philanthropist with patriot, philosopher with statesman, orator with poet, in honouring the memory of the Ploughman Bard'. Other witnesses confirmed Ballantine's observation. Francis Adams declared that he had 'never beheld a public demonstration at all resembling the present' – the nearest being the national jubilee of the much revered Hanoverian King George III in 1809.[9] In the coastal town of Kirkcudbright it was to 1750, and the execution of a thief, that a local reporter had to go back for a comparable turnout.[10] But what such comments obscure are the weeks of preparation, and the mounting anticipation as the day approached. Typical is the small town of Dufftown in Banffshire, Moray, where it was reported that 'Excitement, enthusiasm, gossip, and scandal were at their highest pitch for weeks, and when the day at last arrived we were afraid that it was too much for us to give anything like an adequate representation of our feelings' – although given the number of events organised and the level of participation, it is clear that the burgh more than did justice to the nation's bard.[11]

What numbers we have are impressive: of the 872 events enumerated by Ballantine, 676 were in Scotland. A further 76 were noted for England, 10 in Ireland, 48 in the colonies, 61 in the United States and one in Copenhagen. These figures, however, pale into insignificance if it is true, as has been claimed, that these account for only 5 per cent of the suppers, dinners, soirées, dances and other Burns-related festivities that actually took place.[12] Even Ballantine conceded in his voluminous *Chronicle* that he had excluded some happenings, although how many he was short is unknown. Evidence from other sources suggests that he was less likely to note the celebrations organised by the working classes, or the literally countless smaller informal gatherings held in hotels, inns, public houses, and even farm barnyards, or the bonfires and firework displays and bouts of bell ringing that were only erratically recorded. Arbroath's magistracy may have chosen to remain aloof from the centenary due to fears of disorder, but the town's inhabitants more than compensated for the lack of civic leadership by organising a variety of festivities including 'numerous' private parties.[13]

Whatever the actual numbers of individual entertainments what they cannot reveal is the generally extraordinarily high level of public participation. Even in London's Crystal Palace an estimated 15,000 people turned up to celebrate Burns – a Scot – albeit as a British poet.[14]

But it is what happened in Scotland that is our main focus here. From Coldstream in the Borders to Lerwick in Shetland and Portree in Skye and Lybster in the far north-east, communities turned out to mark the occasion. Examples abound. Thus in the modest-sized Fife burgh of Leven, the 'grand national never-to-be-forgotten demonstration in honor of "Burns"' was celebrated 'with all the pomp and pageantry which only at the time for the passing of the Reform Bill ... surpassed.'[15] In Dunfermline Burns was said to have aroused even greater passions than the cause of political reform.

What is striking, too, is the inclusiveness of the occasion. Continuing with Leven, hundreds of children were given 'fruit and confections', the burgh's trades and freemasons processed, and later, two separate dinners were attended by just under three hundred people, along with a 'tea' for eighty 'old women' and sixty 'ladies'. Of Kilmarnock, with its close connections with Burns, even more might be expected, and was duly delivered, although working-class engagement was less than hoped.[16] The day's trades demonstration in which the freemasons took pride of place was followed by a series of dinners and suppers. The biggest was in the George Hall, with others in the Commercial Inn and 'Mr George Roome's'. Additional events were organised by: the brethren of St Andrew's Lodge; John Bicket's workmen; Barclay's engineers; George Paxton; the shoemakers; the bonnet makers; the Glasgow and South Western Railway company's 'principal' employees; the Literary Association; and the Abstainers Union, who enjoyed a 'social tea'.[17] In Sanquhar, to the south, the procession was even more inclusive, ranging from the magistrates and merchants, through the various trade incorporations to shepherds, colliers, labourers and, as in several places, school children.[18]

Yet despite what was an astonishing degree of popular involvement, this most unusual of days in Scotland's history hardly merits a mention in social and political histories of the period. Much more attention has been paid to the campaign for the Wallace Monument on Abbey Craig near Stirling. The physical prominence and symbolic importance of the Wallace memorial and of Wallace as a heroic Scot and contributor to the nation's sense of itself are of course undeniable. But judged by the interest in it as measured by numbers of participants (at the laying of the foundations and in particular its inauguration), Burns' centenary leaves it a long way behind.

* * *

Although possibly partly apocryphal, the origins of the centennial may have been inspired by a Burns supper held in the Brig o' Doon hotel in Alloway in January 1858. The credit was claimed by Colin Rae Brown (1821–1897), the Greenock-born son of a sea captain but by this time the founder proprietor of the *Glasgow Daily Bulletin*. Rae Brown's recollection some years later of the genesis of the 1859 centennial was that in preparing a speech he was to give to the employees of his newspaper that he had taken out to Alloway in 1858, and under pressure to 'say something new', he struck upon the idea of a second Ayr festival. Rae Brown had been at the first, as a delegate from Greenock's Burns Club. Evidently cheered by the reception to his proposal, he then up-scaled it to become a 'Universal Centenary Celebration', and formed a committee in Glasgow to implement his scheme.[19]

There was no lack of ambition amongst the organisers. A circular letter sent to societies and individuals throughout Britain, North America and the British Empire appealed to 'Scotsmen and Scotswomen everywhere', to assist in forging a 'lasting bond of union between the inhabitants of Caledonia and those of every country and clime who . . . adopt as their creed, "A man's a man for a' that." ' Whatever the disparate readings of Burns and however he was fêted on the day, it was this – 'that glorious charter of freedom and honest independence' – that was Rae Brown's motivating principle, which we can assume applied to his fellow organisers. The circular, too, lauded Burns' 'unrivalled courage' in 'fearlessly leveling his shafts of irony against the then dominant sway of Bigotry, Hypocrisy, and Intolerance' in the Church of Scotland, another burning issue for Rae Brown. Symbolically, the knot of a liberalised brotherhood would be tied by toasting – everywhere – the poet's immortal memory at a pre-arranged time. To hasten the message and co-ordinate the tribute, telegrams were to be sent, the North American element of which had been made possible by the laying of the transatlantic telegraph cable in 1858. By this means Burns was to be an 'electric force with the power to galvanise individuals' – a 'living power' to unite the hearts of Scots, wherever they were.[20] Presumably to avoid causing offence in literary circles Scott's greatness as an author was acknowledged, but, the circular asserted, it was Burns' songs and sayings that were 'sung and cherished by countless thousands at home and abroad who knew little of Scott save the name.'[21]

This was the plan. Implementing it, however, was more difficult. Perhaps the biggest blow was that by January 1859 the transatlantic cable was out of action. While this had no effect in Scotland or on the British mainland, or indeed for communications between Burns celebrants in the United States and Canada, it meant that mutual greetings across the Atlantic had to be sent by letter.

With few exceptions the Burns clubs, freemasons lodges and associations that were approached, as well as town councils and individual employers, responded enthusiastically to the Glasgow committee's proposal (Plate 6). There was some resistance, however, to which we will return below. There were also delays caused by disputes over a number of issues, the most common being about the involvement of the working classes, and women.

Notwithstanding the emphasis on universal brotherhood in the invitations sent to likely participants, this is not quite how things transpired on the ground. With streets and buildings festooned with decorations and the involvement of the trades and other bodies in what were usually long and colourful processions, the impression was conveyed of communities united in common purpose (Plate 7). This indeed was very often how the day's events were reported afterwards. It was 'the proudest day this old city [Edinburgh] has seen for a generation', according to one witness. Military victories, political reforms, monarch's birthdays and royal marriages and births had all been celebrated but never before, 'has the enthusiasm and fervid nationality of Edinburgh been so genial, and overflowing'.[22] This, too, was what was communicated by several speakers on the occasion, with the Reverend Alex Wallace, from Glasgow, at a banquet in the Corn Exchange, asserting – to cheers – that the nationwide celebrations were 'no sectional or party gatherings, but national'. They breathed 'the spirit of an entire people'.[23] Perhaps, but the competition between classes and over the different 'frames of reference' of Burns' legacy we have noted in previous chapters was no less apparent in 1859 than it had been in the 1840s.

The banquet at which Wallace had spoken was but one of at least fifteen celebrations held in Edinburgh on the same evening, ranging in scale from those attracting audiences of well over 1,000, to the much smaller number of members of the Tam o' Shanter Club who managed to squeeze into Souter's Inn in the Canongate. The occasion in the Corn Exchange, attended by around 1,500 people, had been organised by the Total Abstinence Society (Plate 8). But apart from the promoters' plan to celebrate Burns with tea and water only, their prime motivation had been the conviction that to honour a man 'who was pre-eminently the man of the people', the admission charge should be low. This event, pointedly named the 'grand citizen banquet', was in contrast to the banquet for 700 in the Music Hall, chaired by Lord Ardmillan and attended by many of Edinburgh's leading legal figures, the city's MPs, the lord provost and town councillors, a string of academics including historians of Scotland such as Cosmo Innes, and Professor John Stuart Blackie (who on this occasion gave a toast to Sir Walter Scott), along with artists and sculptors – and Burns' grand-daughter. (Throughout the century, to have a relative of Burns – no matter how distant – in attendance at such gatherings was considered to be a major coup.) But whatever the differences in social composition, at both assemblies warmly received reference was made to that 'immortal work', 'The Cotter's Saturday Night'. Indeed at the Corn Exchange 'Great cheering' erupted when the poem was commended for its benign influence on Scotland's people.

The Total Abstainers were not the only group conscious of the incongruity of celebrations of Burns as a man of the people and their prohibitive cost for that very same audience. It was almost certainly as information became public that the function proposed for the Music Hall was to cost fifteen shillings a head, that the agitation for a working-class equivalent commenced. 'J W' from North Newington protested that the people's poet had nothing in common with 'that starched stateliness too often characteristic of men whose minds lie in their purses'. Those who could 'with most propriety' celebrate the centenary, he went on, were working men, as they alone 'can fully understand the allusions and similes to be found in so many of his poems'.[24] After some urging, a 'Working Man's Festival' was planned and subsequently held in Dunedin Hall – attracting an audience of 2,000, Edinburgh's largest. Nostalgia there was aplenty, with songs such as 'The Birks of Aberfeldy' and 'My Nannie's Awa' being sung with 'pathos and feeling'. But as Ann Rigney has observed, the commemoration was less about dwelling on the past than 'convivially enjoying the pleasures of reiteration in the present'.[25] Thus the song *'par excellence*, of the evening' was one composed for the occasion, 'Ye Sair Wrought Sons o' Daily Toil'. But there was another dimension. The audience shared through Burns the experience of the moment but, to re-iterate a theme highlighted at the beginning of this book, also dared to look to the future. It was the chorus of 'A Man's a Man' that had 'the immense assembly joining with hearty good will'. In the Music Hall by contrast it was 'Auld Lang Syne' that induced a round of communal singing by the city's elite.[26]

In exposing the social divisions that existed within Scottish society what we have just described in Edinburgh was replicated throughout much of the rest of the country. Just over the border in Carlisle the call was made for 'an entertainment to which Burns himself could have come when at his poorest estate', and in due course 'a meeting was got up, and conducted by working-men'.[27] While pleas of this nature were clearly heeded, in most places the local elite went ahead and dined and celebrated at their own separate events, often under the auspices of the local Burns club. Indeed it was unusual for there not to be a festivity of this kind. Exceptions included Kirkcaldy, where, inexplicably, 'but for the gathering up of the working classes in the theatre' there was little else to show how the townspeople felt about Burns. In neighbouring Kinghorn, too, the better attended of two meetings was that 'got up and conducted by the working men'.[28] The separation of events according to social class was ably articulated in Dumfries by John Hamilton, editor of the *Morning Star*, the main speaker at what was described as the 'town's dinner'. This was held in the sheds of a woollen manufacturing firm, Scott's of Nithsdale Mills. (Meantime the town's dignitaries and the county gentry had congregated in the fashionable George St Assembly Rooms.) Near the beginning of his address to an audience that was four times the size of that in the Assembly Rooms, Hamilton spoke of his pleasure at being 'in this rather than in another place – in your House of Commons, so to speak, rather than in your House of Lords.' And why? Because 'the topic is Burns, and Burns belonged to the people'.[29] That older certainties about class relationships were eroding – partly through and inspired by the vehicle of Burns commemoration – is revealed too in what was said by a deputation from the Nithsdale Mills gathering that interrupted the Assembly Rooms proceedings. Their purpose in coming was explained by their spokesman, 'Mr Dykes'. How pleasant it was, he remarked, for 'working men to see a meeting of what might be called the aristocracy of the town' doing homage to one who belonged to their own class.[30]

But it was in Glasgow that Burns' meaning for thousands of his countrymen – and those beyond Scotland's borders – became even clearer. As with the 1844 festival, 1859 attracted the attention of bemused visitors, mainly from England. One of these was Perth-born Charles Mackay, editor of *The Illustrated London News*, anxious to account for his countrymen's high state of excitement. After surveying and either rejecting, or judging to be of secondary importance, a series of possible explanations, the conclusion he reached was that above all else were Burns' sentiments that 'A man's a man for a' that', and 'rank was but the guinea stamp'. In what was a reinforcement of what Kingsley, Miller and Thomas Carlyle had observed some years earlier, Burns, the *News* declared, had 'held up his head among the highest in the land', and spoken to them as an equal; he stood, a 'Ploughman and Exciseman', as the 'Poet of the Scotch', 'the representative of one great democratic idea and formula'.[31]

Albeit grudgingly, this point was conceded by none other than Archibald Alison, now well into his seventh decade. He did so at what was the centennial's centrepiece occasion. This was in Glasgow's City Hall where, symbolically, 'the flags of Scotland, England, France and America drooped in mingled carelessness'. Before an audience of 800 'gentlemen', Alison ranged widely in his address, but included a section in which he acknowledged that not only had Burns been a Radical but also that he welcomed the fact, wishing indeed 'that we had more Radicals like Burns'.[32] It was an astonishing turnaround. For more than fifty years Alison and others in his circle had argued otherwise, although with increasing difficulty. Even in 1859 Alison still felt it necessary to temper what he had said by asserting that Burns was as much a patriot as a Radical; indeed, regard for Scottish nation-hood was something both men had in common, which almost certainly explains why Alison had been one of the prime movers, with Rae Brown, of the 1859 commemorations.[33] Not unlike Wilson some years earlier, Alison excused Burns' radicalism on the grounds of his poetic temperament – which tended towards liberalism – and to the febrile nature of the age in which he had been alive. Anyway, Alison judged (or more likely wished), the poems which 'we now lament', had 'long passed into oblivion'; by contrast, those upon which Burns' 'immortal flame' rested, were 'as pure as the driven snow'.[34] Lest there be any ambiguity, on display in the hall were extracts from Burns' 'most successful' poems. Written in large white letters were 'two whole verses from "The Cotter's Saturday Night"'.

But it was what Alison had said about Burns' radicalism that turned heads. The editor of the Radical-leaning London-based *Lloyd's Weekly Newspaper* commented gleefully that the distinguished sheriff 'had strained his toryism' to admit that Burns was 'not utterly contemptible', and poked fun at Alison's 'blundering' explanation for Burns' genius. More importantly, and taking into account the 1859 celebrations in their entirety, the paper in an editorial headed 'The

Poet of the People' could justifiably claim that the nation had 'spoken out its gratitude to one of its unacknowledged legislators'.[35] It was not the first time that such a role was accorded to a poet: in his *Defence of Poetry* (1819) Percy Bysshe Shelley had made just this claim for his art.[36] New, however, in that they were not confined to the Chartists, were this and other similar references that recognised Burns as an unprecedentedly powerful force in the formation of popular conscious-ness. His legacy was a substantial part of what was a fundamental challenge to the age-old social order, not only in Victorian Scotland, but elsewhere too.

* * *

In one area, however, there were only the faintest signs of challenge. Ballantine's *Chronicle* includes numerous passing references to women's involvement in centenary events. They played a useful role in the preparations, making flags and emblems in Thurso for instance, while where societies they were associated with organised centennial parties and the like, they were recruited to serve tea, cake and fruit. However, while there were several hundred (if not more) male only gatherings, Ballantine was able to find few female equivalents. One of these was held in the Perthshire village of Alyth, where forty women had 'a happy tea party' before, turning convention on its head, invit-ing in the 'gudemen'.[37] There were a few places too where no obvious distinction was made between the sexes, as in Kinglassie where both enjoyed a Burns supper and dance, while in Colinsburgh '140 persons of both sexes' attended a concert that was followed by a dance.

Women did attend many of the most prestigious demonstrations in cities and larger towns, but at these the usual pattern was for them to join in after the men (many of whom were their husbands) had dined, but seated in separate galleries. Even in smaller places the same prac-tice was adopted, as in Largo in Fife, where the committee who took charge of the festivities, resolved, 'like gallant gentlemen, to admit the ladies to share in and adorn the festive occasion'. However, the seventy or so females who were to take part waited for ninety minutes while the men had dinner, and were then served with cake and wine, and fruit. But it was just as well that they came, it seems. Cupar was not alone in reporting that the presence of females 'tended to enliven the proceedings', while in Aberdour, also in Fife, 'the ladies', who 'were beginning to get impatient', instigated the clearance of the hall and the subsequent dancing. It was more often at the men-only gatherings that the merriment was of a sedentary nature, and drink fuelled, occasionally excessively so – a situation that may have owed something to the considerably lower levels of church membership and church going amongst Scottish males.[38]

Not everyone was content with the situation just described. The second of the objections to the proposed dinner at Carlisle was that it excluded women other than those prepared to crush into the balconies and wait for the toasts to finish. In Edinburgh there were complaints that women who wished to attend the Music Hall banquet could only apply for tickets through their husbands. Protests of this kind, however, were generally ignored.

We should not place too much emphasis on the strains there were over Burns' legacy, however. The day was enveloped by a palpable sense of Scottishness. Indeed, *The Scotsman* reminded its readers, a 'chief characteristic of Burns was his Nationality . . . he was utterly and intensely, before and beyond anything, a Scotchman.' Unavoidably, given Scotland's place within the union, there was a British framework, but the firmness of its outline varied from place to place. It was virtually invisible in Alloa where the Assembly Room was awash with Scottish artefacts including a cast of Robert the Bruce's skull. One of the most striking sights in Peterhead was a hotel balcony in Broad St upon which was placed a 'female figure, intended to represent Scotland'. There was little to be heard of even the most banal unionism in the Reverend Peter Hately Waddell's soaring hymn of praise. Speaking in Alloway in terms reminiscent of the Covenanters of the seventeenth century, Hately Waddell referred to the 'ecstatic homage' which the nation was paying to Burns: Scotland, he pronounced, 'was never more in her senses than at this moment; after a slumberous dream of fifty years, incredulous admiration has awoke this day to realise the fact of her own divinity'.[39]

The idea of and commitment to Britain was just about discernible in Old Aberdeen, where the trades ball in the town house wound up with renditions of 'Auld Lang Syne' – and the National Anthem.[40] But what was symbolised in Glasgow's City Hall, where between two busts of Burns on the main table was a line of others including Wilson, Scott, Ramsay, Motherwell, Byron, Dryden, Milton, Shakespeare and Pope, was Scottish parity with the poets of England. Indeed amongst the principal guests was the Reverend Charles Rogers, who with Rae Brown had been involved in the Wallace project near Stirling, and would be with several more monuments commemorating Scottish heroes.[41] Also present was Cosmo Innes. Like Rogers he was an anti-quarian – and also a unionist. But he resisted the notion of North Britishness and sought instead to promote, through history, Scottish distinctiveness and knowledge of a past that 'had little to do with kilts or kailyards'.[42] Indeed few at any of the gatherings, whatever their social composition, would have had any quibbles with a toast given by a Mr Haig to the 'Peasantry of Scotland', again in Leven in Fife. In a speech interspersed with cheers, Haig cleverly elided class antago-nisms and instead asserted that 'There are few families who had not at some stage belonged to the noble order of the peasantry.' It was, he declared, the peasantry that had maintained Scotland's independence under Bruce and Wallace (who had been let down only by Scotland's nobles, its latter day aristocrats), and more recently manned the Highland regiments and fought at Crimea and in India – 'where you see the same indomitable spirit which influenced their fathers on the field of Bannockburn'. Haig then went on to name Scots such as Lord Clyde and Hugh Miller, successes in their respective fields, but with peasant backgrounds.[43] Like Burns, the conceit went, they represented the archetypical Scot.

*   *   *

Scotland, though, was not quite a nation united. We have already noted some of the tensions that lay beneath the protestations of Burns' universality. But what has gone almost wholly unremarked by the few people who have written about 1859 is the powerful opposition there was to the centennial, and this from what, as we saw in the previous chapter, had at the local level been the nation's most influential insti-tution: the Presbyterian churches. After the 1843 Disruption the most important of these was the Free Church.

The circular letter calling for support for the centenary had claimed that 'those base detractors [of Burns], sprung from the soil of hypoc-risy' had been defeated and sent packing at the 1844 festival. The Glasgow organising committee's optimism was misplaced.

Ministers – most of those in Scotland it was claimed – would 'refrain from taking part'. One estimate was that around 500 boycotted the proceedings. It is difficult to judge the real rate of abstention, although some of the available evidence is to be found in Ballantine's *Chronicle*. For some places – Kilmarnock, for example – explicit refer-ence is made to the absence of the clergy.[44] Cupar in Fife stood out too, as no ministers participated – nor did the burgh's provost 'on account of the immorality of Burns'.[45] More often, however, we can tell simply by looking at lists of speakers and principal guests.

It is from other sources, however, that we read of ministers preaching sermons lambasting Burns and the centenary. In Edinburgh the Reverend Dr Alexander declared himself at a loss to explain the 'infatuation that has fallen upon my country'. Others expressed their opposition in print. One of the most forceful pamphlets – *Burns' Centenary: Are Such Honours due to the Ayrshire Bard?* – conceded, as many of his detractors did, Burns' qualities as a poet (above all as the author of the praiseworthy 'The Cotter's Saturday Night'), and as a patriot. Piled against this, however – it was argued – was so much more of his less desirable work, and his 'baneful principles, his polluting sentiments, and his licentious life'. Burns was a deist, not a Christian, who had treated the Bible as a jest-book, and in much of his poetry and by the example of his life had encouraged profanity, drunkenness, and 'impurity' of various kinds. Concerned at the support the 1859 commemoration looked like attracting, including from some ministers, the pamphlet's author warned that 'flattery to the dead may work ruin to the living'. While he could understand why lovers of excitement, an ample dinner, and fine wine and jovial company should take part, he was perplexed by the attendance of 'those who profess to be enlisted on the side of Jesus'.[46] Adopting a similar line were the Reformed Presbyterians. Their *Magazine* took up where *The Witness* had left off in 1844. 'The best commemoration of Burns would be silence and shame and tears, not merely at the sad desecration of genius in its alliance with an immoral life, but at the thought of the neglect through which so little was done for him when living.' It was from this direction, too, that posters were made and stuck up in Edinburgh condemning the festival as 'Satan's revival'.[47]

The columns of the country's press, too, hummed in the heat of impassioned letter writers. 'Scotus' in the *Caledonian Mercury*, for instance, urged that instead of merriment there should be 'grave reflection upon the moral spectacle of a great genius enslaved by the passions of a carnal nature, and consecrated solely to the service of the earth'. Writing in the *Aberdeen Free Press* Alex Burnett hoped the 1859 centenary would be the last, and that a century hence 'Scotchmen' would execrate his memory, and remember Burns 'as one of the greatest villains that their land ever produced'. Meantime, he urged Scotland's clergymen on the coming Sabbath to 'bear their testimony against the festival; and that, in unmistakable language'.[48] From a slightly different perspective, and echoing the reformers of the sixteenth century and their attacks on graven images, 'Homo' from Stirling regretted the reappearance of the 'spirit which prompts the erection of statues to departed saints and martyrs'. This, which had vulgarised 'our classic hero Wallace by dishonouring him with a monument – now seeks to degrade our national bard, by dragging him through the mire of a so-called festival'.[49]

Such objections, however, were met with equally ferocious rebuttals. Atypically calm, therefore, was a lecture delivered by Robert Blackley Drummond in St Mark's Chapel, Edinburgh, on 20 January. Drummond's aim was to vindicate Burns from the charge of irreligion and to show instead that his attacks on the Calvinists of his day were not irreverent, and that 'his whole character was . . . of a man whose mind was imbued with an honest, manly and rational devoutness'.[50] However, the more typical nature of Burns' supporters' responses is captured in a reply to sermons that had been delivered by two Edinburgh ministers (one from the Church of Scotland, the other a dissenter) the week before the centenary date. The 'unmerited and uncharitable abuse' that had passed through their 'unclean lips', directed towards a man who had been dead for more than sixty years, 'Viva Voce' declared, brought 'dishonour to their sacred vocation'.[51]

That so many ministers had spoken out in opposition on the Sunday prior to the 25th was equally strongly resented, and voiced in language that reflected this. Amongst the 'shout of joy and the hymn of praise' over Burns, had been 'the sickly echo of chagrin'. James Gould, the other main chronicler of the 1859 festivities, protested that it was Burns who was the man of God, the 'friend of generous and enlightened religious faith', whose higher moral poems would be read when the sermons of 1859 had been 'torn to shreds'. Particularly emphasised was Burns' contempt for cant and hypocrisy. Whatever Burns' crimes, they were, it was alleged, not like those that 'are daily practiced by our bankers and merchants and sanctimonious elders'. Were Burns' clerical critics to look around, 'they would find many of their own class, and others holding office in the House of God, who adopt the cloak of religion to hide their iniquities – more to be pitied than ever Burns was'.[52]

Such charges were not without foundation, and amongst the insults were some pertinent observations. By their profuse 'libelous denunciations' and bigotry and intolerance, the clergy had done 'vast injury to the cause of true religion'. Burns' clerical critics had demonstrated they were out of touch with large sections of the Scottish public, above all the urban middle classes and skilled workers – precisely the people being drawn to the dissenting churches but who sought a more benign faith, one that flattered more than it challenged the believer, as Calvinism had done in less affluent times.[53] The same point was made some years later by the aforementioned Hately Waddell, who had broken with the Free Church to found a 'Church of the Future', and, as can be gathered from what has been said already, braved his critics in 1859 by delivering a powerful paean to Burns in the poet's birthplace cottage in Alloway. In a vindication of Burns' stance on religion delivered from his Glasgow base in 1867, Waddell predicted that whether or not the clergy listened, for the population at large, clerical obsessions such as holy fairs, and their 'Pharisaical oblations . . . senseless squabbles . . . [and] time serving policies' would become 'themes for this man's loudest laughter . . . and the echo of it shall be heard through succeeding generations, when the memory of their names has perished'.[54]

Looking forward we can see that Waddell had forecast correctly. In Dundee in the later 1870s the campaign for a statue of Burns had run into difficulty. In response the Burns Club put on a play, written by one of the members, J. F. Duncan. Entitled *Lights and Shadows: Or, Episodes in the Life of Robert Burns*, it attracted massive audiences for its short run. Much pleasure was derived from Burns' songs, a lively rendition of 'Tam o' Shanter' and visual effects such as a lime-light-lit tableaux of characters and scenes from the poem. But what brought the house down and led to demands for further performances were the impersonations of Burns and William Fisher; indeed 'Holy Willie' according to the *Dundee Advertiser* 'was the hero of the evening'.[55] There is deep irony therefore in the fact that albeit they were long dead, the men who were Burns' nemesis contributed indirectly and at a critical stage to the fund that would see him cast as a natinoal hero in enduring bronze.

*   *   *

In 1859, however, there were ministers from the main churches who were prepared to brave the verbal assaults of their fellow clergymen. Four of them were immortalised by Gould, who added their pictures to his memorial volumes: the Episcopalian Dean Edward Ramsay, the Roman Catholic Bishop James Gillies, the Reverend A. Wallace of the United Presbyterians and the Reverend Robert Lee of the Church of

Scotland (Plate 9). This was in Edinburgh. But scattered throughout Scotland were others who played their part – in Dundee, Dunfermline, Linlithgow, Lochaber, Mauchline and Pultenytown, Wick, to name but half a dozen locations where clergymen spoke up for Burns. Fairly representative in that he reflected the changing stance of many of the country's Presbyterians was the Reverend James Mitchell, who presided at the principal commemorative dinner in Peterhead. He had accepted the invitation, Mitchell told his audience, partly because the organisers had hoped his presence would insure that nothing was said or sung that was inconsistent with his confession. But he did so, too, as his presence represented something he had long yearned for: 'religion no longer banished from innocent enjoyment, but mingling with it', rather than being 'gloomy, sour, and ascetic', which, he allowed, it had become.[56]

The Northern Isles provide us with a telling example of the way that opinion was shifting. Shetland was thickly populated with churches, and church membership – including that of the Church of Scotland – was higher than in Orkney, or Lewis in the Outer Hebrides. After around 1840 an energetic temperance movement had got under way.[57] Yet not only was there a Burns centenary dinner in Lerwick, but it was attended by a minister, the Reverend Macfarlane who in response to a toast to 'The Clergy of all Denominations' expressed his regret at the 'absence of the brethren of his class'.[58] Formal proceedings in Kirkwall (in Orkney) were minimal, but a report that the grammar school's female pupils had been 'clamorous' for a holiday was seen by one commentator as a triumph – inspired by Burns – over the 'illiberal sectarianism' of what another observer had called a 'priest-ridden' town.[59]

The centenary year 1859 had rattled hard the cages of Scotland's Presbyterian die-hards. Some though, mainly those associated with the Reformed Presbyterian Church, still thirled to the notion of Calvinist predestination and zealous in the traditions of the Covenanters continued to growl ferociously in Burns' direction. Probably the most savage bark and certainly the most notorious was a sermon preached by the Reverend Fergus Ferguson in Dalkeith in January 1869. Ferguson's hostility to the Burns cult – which he recognised was becoming 'a great, portentous influence' – was unforgiving. He proposed that it was not Burns' birthday that should be celebrated, but his death. His life, asserted Ferguson, had been 'a gigantic failure'. Through it had run an 'evil principle', which was 'the only unity it possessed'. Burns' hypocrisy knew no bounds, painting in 'The Cotter's Saturday Night' 'a beautiful picture of a well-spent Saturday evening', to then pass his own Saturday in the public house. And worse. But Burns worship, Ferguson feared, was symptomatic of the Victorian age, an aspect of a diabolical spirit that manifested as 'creature worship', which becomes in the end devil worship.[60] For Ferguson and his audience, Burns personified the burning issue of the time, Biblical truth set against the challenges presented by geological science and evolutionary theory. If we deify man, was the thrust of his argument, we give credence to the 'impudent quackery' of those 'quidnuncs' who assure us that man was originally an ape, and that 'it is of far more importance to study rocks and fossils than to study the Word of the living God' and who would have us believe that a human being was a sublimation of the monkey.

The extremism of Ferguson – 'the crater through whose lips the unpleasant discharge was vomited' was how *The Scotsman* referred to him – was not only mocked but also confronted. Like every great poet Burns was a preacher, countered the Reverend Dr Wallace in Edinburgh's Café Royal in January 1872, before suggesting that Ferguson's listeners comprised old women 'and people of that common and coarse zeal which is blind to wit, humour, and the idea of art' and who regard Burns' 'unceremonious handling of their favourites as utter profanity'.[61]

Others went much further, not only denying that Burns had harmed religion but that he had re-made it, in Scotland. This at least is what Alexander Webster thought. We will return to Webster in a later chapter, but relevant here is what he had to say about Burns' Kilmarnock edition. We have seen hints of this already. Burns' *Poems*, Webster wrote, 'had become to the Scottish people a sacred book; a book of discipline and statute; a prayer-book; a book of spiritual songs; a text-book of moral wisdom; a volume full of inspiration and redeeming power'.[62] At the time, this was not so far from the truth.

FOUR

'A structure worthy of the Bard, of Glasgow and of Scotland'

Burns, the Burns clubs and the making of immortal memories

The year 1859 was a turning point in other ways too. By far and away the most visible, and lasting evidence of this are the life-sized or larger statues of Burns that were erected in Scotland between Glasgow's in 1877 and the start of the First World War. In all there were eleven of these – free-standing figures of Burns, on substantial pedestals, usually but not always in fairly prominent locations. The exception was at Kilmarnock where the statue of Burns was the focal point of a Scottish baronial Burns monument that included a museum. Most of the pedestals were adorned with panels generally illustrating scenes from Burns' poems. These – bas-reliefs – were pieces of artwork in their own right, and attracted almost as much attention as the statues. No substantial town that could boast any significant association with the poet was without a life-sized or larger Burns, although a handful where the links were less obvious raised them too. Civic chests were puffed with the pride of possession of a statue of the national bard. In Scotland – the mother country – the crescendo of statue construction peaked in 1896, the centenary of Burns' death. Overseas, new statues of Burns continued to be erected well into the inter-war period.[1] In Scotland by contrast, the last statues of any note were those unveiled in Montrose (1912) and Stirling (1914), although since 1945 at least two more have been acquired, in Arbroath (1959) and Kilmarnock (1995).

Ever more busts of Burns made their appearance, including one that was placed in the Wallace Monument in 1886. There was a profusion, too, of cairns, plaques, tablets and statuettes. Many were described in the annual *Burns Chronicle*, the magazine of the Burns

Federation that had been launched in 1892 – in itself another measure of the interest there was in Burns. It hints, too, at the vitality of the Burns cult, sustained by the activities of zealous editors such as Duncan McNaught.[2]

* * *

It is hard to be sure, but there is a hint that even before 1859 the suggestion had been made, in Kilmarnock, that a statue of Burns should be erected there.[3] However, even if this were true, little or nothing happened until 1872, in Glasgow.

There, the city's George Square, the management of which was taken over by the city council in 1862, was, under the direction of city's architect John Carrick, beginning to resemble something like a pantheon of heroes.[4] But it was with the appearance in June 1872 of a statue of Thomas Graham, the distinguished city of Glasgow-born chemist and Master of the Mint, that the proposal was made in the *Evening Citizen* that other Scotsmen of note should be similarly honoured: Thomas Campbell, the poet and near contemporary of Burns who had also been born in Glasgow (in 1777), Adam Smith, the philosopher and economist and University of Glasgow professor, and Burns. Burns was thought to be a particularly notable omission in 'the largest and in most respects the chief city of Scotland', and consequently one the paper's readers, John Browne, a draper, suggested that not only should a statue of Burns be raised but that it should be paid for by one shilling donations. Within ten minutes of subscriptions being called for by Browne, some 45 were forthcoming.[5] After ten days, over £42 had been collected, £269 after ten months, and, by May 1873 when the subscription fund was closed, £1,456 had been raised.[6]

Most but not all of this was subscribed locally. Responsibility for issuing subscription sheets to 'all public works' in and around Glasgow, and collecting contributions, was assumed by James Hedderwick, a stockbroker who was also the editor of the *Citizen*, and members of Glasgow's Western Burns Club. When the local well dried, the appeal was widened, in the first instance to surrounding towns such as Paisley and Hamilton. The Western had originated as the Waverley Burns Club, named after the hotel in which the first meeting was held (the new name was adopted in 1872). Founded in 1860, the Waverley was a link back to 1859 when its original members had first dined together. On the evening of 25 January 1877, with the statue having been unveiled by the English poet and Tory turned radical Liberal, Richard Monckton Milnes, 1st Baron Houghton (rather than William Gladstone, the organisers' first preference), some of them did so again as members of the Burns statue committee, basking in the praise that was forthcoming for the completed project. The brickbats would come later.

The success of the Glasgow Burns statue movement did not go unnoticed. Observers were struck by the apparent willingness of ordinary people to subscribe to it. The plaudits it had garnered roused others to replicate something like it in their own localities. Almost certainly goaded by James M'Kie (1816–1891), the Kilmarnock-born publisher and collector of all things Burns-related who had had a hand in the Glasgow preparations, a meeting of Kilmarnock's 'influential gentlemen', was convened 'to consider the practicality of erecting a statue to Burns'. This was a week prior to the Glasgow unveiling. Dundee followed days later. In Dumfries around the same time, on 2 February 1877, Robert Hamilton gave notice that at the next meeting of the town council he would draw the members' attention 'to the desirability of having a public statue of Burns in the town'.[7] Five years later it was in place. Although there was a pause until Ayr's Burns was inaugurated in 1891, this heralded another flurry of memorial construction, with new statues being erected in Aberdeen (1892), Irvine and Paisley (1896), and Leith (1898).

In the main the public's enthusiasm for the unveiling ceremonies matched that of the statue's instigators. Although, as we acknowledged in the Introduction, spectacular displays of popular sentiment of this kind were not unique to Burns, commentators were convinced that in their scale, the number of participants and the degree of public interest in them Burns-related ceremonies stood out. Take the unveiling of the Burns statue in Dundee in 1880. Such a demonstration, 'as regards its vastness or the variety of its elements', wrote one journalist, had 'never [been] witnessed in Dundee'. And little wonder, with tens of thousands of spectators watching the procession and another 20,000 or 25,000 people packed into Albert Square where the statue was being unveiled, at a time when Dundee's entire population numbered 140,000.[8] Much the same was true of Dumfries, as captured here in a description of the launch of the Burns statue there in April 1882:

As far as the eye could reach along the streets converging on the square there were only human faces to be seen, hemmed in by the houses on each side, the windows of which, and even the roofs of some of them, were filled by spectators. The vast multitude exceeded in numbers anything that we remember ever to have seen in Dumfries.[9]

Indeed, an 'ominous swaying which spoke of possible peril' during the Earl of Rosebery's speech prior to the unveiling was one reason the proceedings had to be curtailed, even though barricades had been put up to protect the platform party (Plate 10). Crowd surges were not unusual, with the best orators being capable of rousing the passions of those members of their audiences to whom they were audible and, evidently, even of those who heard little.[10] In Dumfries, however, the platform party was so crowded that not even those who were part of it could hear the speeches.[11] It is remarkable how little harm was done, other than some mild (if for those concerned, alarming) crushing. With such large numbers of closely packed people, it is not surprising that pickpocketing was a common complaint.

These, however, were relatively minor concerns. Generally, the spectacles associated with the ceremonies impressed. But not always. Paisley's Burns statue unveiling ceremony in 1896 was a serious disappointment, with no more than a thousand of the town's inhabitants turning out. Years of very public squabbling over the statue and its ultimate location, divisions amongst the promoters and on the town council – and above all the charge of sixpence to attend the unveiling in Fountain Gardens (an overly successful ploy designed to reduce numbers in what was a confined space), were the cause of what for Paisley was little short of a public relations disaster. Despite an eloquent address from the Earl of Rosebery and some excellent champagne at the subsequent dinner, overall the proceedings were judged to have been 'remarkably dull'.[12] A self-inflicted blow to civic pride, this was an aberration. Just over two years afterwards, following a considerably shorter campaign for funds than in Paisley, Leith was able to boast that it too had a Burns statue, which was unveiled by Munro Ferguson, the burgh's MP 'in the presence of a vast concourse of people, estimated at over 30,000'.[13]

That vast assemblies like this were relatively peaceable was in part the result of careful planning and sound policing, with potential flashpoints defused through prior consultation.[14] Preparation for and the marshalling of such vast numbers of participants and spectators were major logistical exercises, which had the authorities on tenterhooks for days in advance. In the authorities' favour was the fact that the freemasons and skilled tradesmen who formed the bulk of the long processions that marched slowly through the principal streets policed themselves, keen to demonstrate their respectability and rightful place in civil society. Any failure in this respect was quickly dealt with by local police forces that were always in attendance, in large numbers.

* * *

Despite the apparent ease with which the campaigners brought their projects to a successful close, behind the smooth sheen of the stone or bronze statues of Burns as they were unveiled, lay – in most cases – years of time-consuming and energy-sapping effort on the part of the sponsors. Aptly described was the experience of Dumfries' Burns statue promoters. In the words of one local commentator, they worked 'energetically and unceasingly' over a period of five years, 'in the teeth of lukewarm friends and timorous admirers, as well as faint opposition from those who thought the Poet needed no other monument than the mausoleum over the tomb'.[15]

Concealed too were the unseemly squabbles that from the time of the first Burns memorial in Dumfries could delay progress. Acrimony in Paisley, too, slowed the fund-raising process that was half-hearted from its beginnings in 1884, until it came to a complete standstill between 1890 and 1892. To complete the project there were two years of determined effort in 1894 and 1895.[16]

Funds had to be raised from private sources, not so difficult to do during periods of prosperity, but immensely challenging when economic conditions worsened either locally or nationally. Rarely were campaigners able to call on financial support from their local authority. Central government sponsorship of public memorials was largely confined to London.[17]

Sculptors too had to be identified, commissioned and worked with. Their appointments could be controversial, to say the least, and, increasingly, note was taken of their nationality, an issue that had arisen in connection with the proposed Wallace memorial near Stirling, with entries being invited only from 'native artists'.[18] Initially a measure of the success applied by the early promoters of statues in Scotland was how far they met artistic standards set in London. From the 1820s, however, indigenous sculptors began to make their mark. We shall see in chapter 6 that English sculptors, who alone were considered suitable at the beginning of the century, were by the end of it condemned by more fervent nationalists as unfit for the task. It was only Scottish sculptors who could do credit to Scotland's heroes – a sentiment that mirrored contemporaneous thinking in Ireland.[19]

There was, however, no shortage of willing sculptors. When competitions were announced, the response was usually good, as in Kilmarnock in 1877 when nine out of eleven sculptors approached agreed to submit models, encouraged no doubt by premiums of £50 and £25 to be awarded to the winner and runner up respectively.[20] A few, primarily those with a Scottish connection or who worked in Scotland, were especially keen, their enthusiasm fired by the rise in Scottish national sentiment that was evident from mid century. Throughout his career it had been the ambition of Aberdeen-born John Steell (1804–1891) 'to produce a great statue of Burns'.[21] Amelia Paton (1820–1904) too, the sculptor wife of David Octavia Hill, was a long-time admirer of Burns, and delighted to win the commission for a statue of the poet in Dumfries.[22] The ferociously nationalist poet and sculptor James Pittendrigh MacGillivray (1856–1938), who secured the commission for Irvine, reflected later how since boyhood he had 'longed to create a statue of Burns'.[23]

Statue committees often struggled to cope with the demands of the sculptors they had appointed. Not unusually they expected to be paid a proportion of the fee in advance, sometimes to buy the stone blocks or other materials from which they worked. At other times they could simply be tetchy and temperamental, understandable enough when, as happened sometimes, commissioning committees were tardy about paying – or were simply unable to pay – previously agreed fees on time. The material from which the statue would be made was an issue too: what kind of stone, or should bronze be used. Much of the casting had to be done in England, although Steell did build – evidently as a consciously patriotic act – a foundry in Edinburgh in 1849, Scotland's first in which to carry out artistic casting.[24] Enormous blocks of suitable stone for the pedestals had to be sourced. The scale and form of these was significant, the size and height of memorials instilling in the upwards-gazing viewer a sense of awe and respect for the heroic figure in question. They were designed to be highly visible, as is demonstrated in a report in the *Burns Chronicle* outlining the intentions of the promoters of the 'Highland Mary' statue at Dunoon. Positioned by the shore beneath the ruins of Dunoon Castle (near to which Mary Campbell had been born), the statue was to be constructed of 'enduring material, permanently presenting a white surface', in order to 'arrest the attention of the countless thousands who, as excursionists, travelers, and seafarers, constantly throng the familiar highway of the noble river [Clyde]'.

What then was it that motivated the men – and Burns commemoration was mainly but not entirely a male-*led* endeavour – who instigated the memorial schemes and then, often in the trying circumstances we have outlined, brought them to completion?

The question is important, as it was precisely these individuals who were responsible in the second half of the nineteenth century and first years of the twentieth for ensuring that Burns was kept firmly in the public eye across much of Lowland Scotland – literally in the form of the statues and other permanent memorials. By so doing, they harnessed the latent interest and even zeal for Burns there was in the wider community, as well as shaping it in such a way that it became one of the principal pillars of the nation's sense of itself.

On one level the answer to our questions of who and why is to be found in the great shifts that were taking place in Scotland's economic and social structures and political values over the course of the century, the central decades in particular. This is because more so than with the earlier memorials, it was from amongst Scotland's middle class that the later nineteenth-century movement to commemorate Burns drew its leaders. In fact compared to what had gone before, aristocratic involvement was slight. Even the 14th Earl of Eglinton, son of the father who had been amongst the organisers of the 1844 festival (and who had supported the idea for a statue in Glasgow as recently as 1859), turned away, declining to subscribe to the Kilmarnock monument on the grounds that he had what he called the 'bad taste', to 'neither appreciate Burns' character or poems'.[25] But Eglinton's retreat was a harbinger of what was to come, although the Earls of Glasgow and Stair – both of whom had extensive estates in the near vicinity – did agree to be patrons of a fund-raising bazaar in Kilmarnock. Support for Burns from the landed interest was maintained therefore, but it tended to be from the sidelines. Exceptional was the aforementioned Earl of Rosebery who was by far the most notable celebrant of Burns amongst men of his class, even if the 3rd Marquis of Bute was the largest single subscriber to Dumfries' Burns statue fund; the Marquis of Queensberry contributed too. Otherwise in Dumfries, it was claimed, the nobility were 'apathetic'.[26] But Rosebery was a leading Liberal, who was close to the apex of his power in the early 1880s, and an ardently patriotic Scot who recognised the importance of the historical record. Whether written, printed, spoken or sung, he pronounced, it 'stirs the blood like a trumpet'.[27] Bute too was deeply interested in Scottish history and antiquities.

The slow retreat from public participation at Burns ceremonials of the country's rural elite reflects the profound change in Scottish society that had been brought about by the leviathan that was Scotland's manufacturing economy. Accompanying this was a massive expansion of the country's towns, with Glasgow, Edinburgh, Dundee and Aberdeen housing one in five Scots by 1851. And increasingly, the middle classes – admittedly a broad categorisation, ranging from major captains of industry to lowly clerks – became the dominant force within them, accounting for one in five or six (there was significant variation between places) of the towns' occupied populations.[28] Prominent were industrialists and managers, and those in the service sector, including sizeable numbers of professionals – lawyers, bankers, accountants, clergymen and medical practitioners.

As Glasgow (with Kilmarnock) instigated the movement for statues of Burns, it makes sense to describe how that city had been transformed prior to 1859. The much-travelled James Burn, who had been born in 1802, recalled how earlier in the century a small merchant and manufacturing elite had 'ruled the roast [sic]', dividing 'the municipal places of trust and emolument among themselves, like decent respectable Tories of the "olden time".' Fifty years on, the city had spread far beyond it medieval limits, its influence extending forty miles along the river Clyde, the consequence of 'large numbers of her traders, professional men ... who have filled their flour sacks at Fortune's mill', along with merchants and others who had constructed 'princely halls, mansions, and villas' on the river's banks, all the way to Helensburgh.[29] The wealth this hints at is confirmed by what is known about middle-class incomes per head, which in Glasgow (in 1880) were not far behind those of comparable English towns and ahead of places like Birmingham, Leeds and Cardiff.

Not unexpectedly, those in industrial and manufacturing occupations accounted for 23 per cent of Scotland's wealth left behind at death, professionals for 18 per cent.[30] Incomes and wealth mattered: it is revealing that five of Scotland's better off burghs as indicated by per capita income were able to boast statues of Burns, while none of the nine worst off did. Vital too in this regard was that after 1832 political power was transferred from the Tory oligarchies of the past, to Liberals of various hues.[31] In 1868 the vote in the burghs was extended to include all male householders. That the 1870s and 1880s were decades of Liberal advance approaching hegemony in Scotland's towns and cities and parliamentary seats, as well as when the movement for Burns statuary was at its height, was by no means coincidental. Indeed, as he unveiled a statue of Burns on the Thames Embankment in August 1884, Rosebery acknowledged that Burns belonged to the class of men whose enfranchisement was at that very time the focus of parliamentary debate. It was a comment that led one observer of the occasion to remark that the 'spirit of modern Liberalism is crystalised in his [Burns'] verse'. More controversial, and inducing murmurs of dissent, was that part of Rosebery's speech in which he pronounced Burns as Scotland's greatest son; he had also coupled Burns with Knox's 'intensely democratic' preaching and dismissed Scott as the 'poet of feudalism'.[32]

The prevailing mood of spiritual enthusiasm that in so many guises was propelled by the dissenting denominations in Scotland's towns and cities seems, too, to have permeated some of the larger gatherings associated with Burns commemoration.[33] We will come to this later.

Also providing a context for large-scale Burns commemoration was the renewed sense of Scottish national consciousness that had been partly embodied in the establishment of the National Society for the Vindication of Scottish Rights in 1852. Although this was short-lived, the nationalist ethos of which it was part showed no sign of abating. In the 1880s and 1890s it became formalised into demands for Home Rule, with the Scottish Home Rule Association being formed in 1886.[34] The relationship, however, was symbiotic: Burns memorialisation was a product of the strengthening sense of nation, and should be viewed in the same light as other manifestations of the prevailing sentiment such as the foundation of the National Portrait Gallery (1882) and the creation of the office of Secretary for Scotland (1885), or indeed the emergence of neo-Jacobitism in the same decade.[35] But as we have seen in previous chapters, Burns' legacy had long before this begun to nurture the sentiments that would result in demands for greater respect for Scotland in London, and the Home Rule movement. Amongst its leading figures was Rosebery, discontented with the disdainful manner in which Scotland was governed by Westminster and who, as we have just seen, drew inspiration for his tenacious fight for better treatment for Scotland from Burns. Such was Rosebery's admiration for the poet, and so prominent was his promotion of him, that he became the first Honorary President of the Burns Federation.

Broad brushstroke explanations of this kind, however, essential as they are, only take us so far. It is only when we look more closely at the campaigns and campaigners for statues of Burns that we find the fuller answers we are looking for.

There is much to be said for Richard Finlay's assessment – referred to in the Introduction – that the Burns cult, of which the erection of statues was part, was promoted by the commercial middle classes whose rise we have just noted, with Burns being presented as an exemplar of the *laissez-faire* ideology to which they adhered. Unpacked, this meant a belief in the 'quintessentially Scottish' virtues of thrift, self-help, temperance and hard work. With the exception of temperance – sometimes a problem for those who wished to place Burns on a pedestal – they could proclaim these as Burns' values too.

And without exception those concerned at the sharp end of the Burns statue movement were either entirely self-made men who had begun life on the bottom rungs of the social ladder, or who had moved further up from the modest foothold from which they started.

The proposition is relatively easily sustained. In Kilmarnock, Archibald McKay, who was the second president of the re-formed Burns club that pressed for the statue there, was a soldier's son who had begun his working life as a piecer in a Kilmarnock woollen mill before becoming a muslin weaver until the depression of 1826 when he found employment as a trainee bookbinder. Ultimately he had his own company, and became Kilmarnock 's unofficial poet laureate. James M'Kie, mentioned earlier, was reputed to have been the illegitimate son of a carpet weaver, then became an apprentice to Hugh Crawford, a Kilmarnock publisher before setting up in business himself in 1839, marrying well, and flourishing thereafter.[36] Representing a slightly different (but also rising) trajectory was Alexander Harvey, one of the original members of Glasgow's Waverley Burns Club, and who was heavily involved in the Glasgow Burns statue movement. Harvey had begun his working life as a laboratory assistant in St Rollox chemical works before becoming a manager in Henry Menteith and Company's cotton printing and dyeing establishment before setting up his own business, Govanhaugh Dye Works.[37] Another member of the same club who was of major importance in getting Glasgow's Burns statue erected was William Wilson, whose business was in selling umbrellas and parasols. The city's *Baillie* magazine had Wilson in mind when detailing the characteristics of the city's merchant class: 'Keen, eager men of business, with their wits on the stretch ... thoroughly alive to all that affects their interest. They follow their business with untiring energy, and even in the evening of life can scarcely persuade themselves to withdraw from the whirl of traffic.'[38] Even where statues of Burns were commissioned, paid for and erected at the expense of individual benefactors, similar patterns prevailed. Stirling's Burns statue was gifted by Provost David Bayne, the son of a Muthill shopkeeper, who after an apprenticeship in the grocery trade in Glasgow moved to Stirling where he worked as a grocer's assistant before taking over the store and also branching out into property ownership. Described as shrewd and 'pawky', and speaking in 'homely Doric', Bayne's business success was attributed to his 'energy, ability, and thrift'.[39]

Finlay's proposition that the promotion of Burns also had an anti-aristocratic dimension makes sense too. With what has been described as the 'mellowing of liberalism' in the aftermath of the revolutions of 1848 and the move away from Chartist fundamentalism in favour of pragmatism on the part of many former working-class radicals, Radicalism no longer posed the threat to the established social order it had previously. Many long-held Radical tenets – liberty, anti-clericalism, opposition to privilege and aristocratic government, and a belief in collective self-help, and moral improvement – had been adopted to become popular elements within Gladstonian Liberalism.[40] Vital was Gladstone's acceptance of the need for a further extension of the suffrage as established by the Reform Act of 1832, a move premised on 'notions of social equity and political justice', and which promised full citizenship for the respectable working class.[41]

Following from this was a new-found resolve amongst men of the kind we have just described, who were now becoming more firmly established in the driving seat in the towns in which they were based, that Burns should be promoted in their interests, and image. The Burns they sought to lionise would not have been unfamiliar to the Tories' Burns, but the emphasis was different. No longer was Burns appropriated in the interests of social stability, but as a role model for a society in a state of transition.

Evidence for this is not hard to uncover. In fact the catalyst for the dinner in January 1859 from which the Waverley Club had arisen, was resentment about the arrangements for the grand banquet in Glasgow's City Hall – the crowning event for the celebrations of 1859 – chaired by Sir Archibald Alison. As was outlined in the previous chapter, alongside Alison had been several of Burns relatives, representatives of Glasgow's and central Scotland's political, legal, educational, literary and artistic and county elite, as well as a scattering of dignitaries from England including James Lowe, editor of London's *The Critic*, and Lord Houghton, mentioned above.[42]

Organised, according to one critic, by 'a job lot of weak-kneed and snobbish nobodies', the presence of this last group at the City Hall dinner had riled James Hedderwick and some of 'Saint Mungo's genuine sons . . . Glasgow's true appreciators of Burns'. The opportunity of doing 'fitting honour' to the memory of Burns, it was alleged, had been 'sacrificed to adulation of the great names of those from a distance to show us how to do that which was felt in every pulse we were perfectly competent to effect ourselves'.[43] Hinted at here is a distinctly Scottish instance of social inferiority tinged with nationalist resentment. At their rump gathering of between forty and fifty 'gentlemen' in Carrick's Royal Hotel, Hedderwick and his associates emphasised the importance of Burns' songs and poetry in binding 'Scotchmen more to Scotland, and the struggle – and triumph – of Scottish literature', 'cultivated for the most part on little oatmeal . . . and . . . [that] had the double task to perform of developing itself in the language of a neighbouring kingdom, while embalming in enduring characters its native tongue'.[44] It is deeply ironic, however, in light of the role Waverley Club members would play in the Glasgow Burns statue project, that it was in the City Hall that one of the speakers – to 'Prolonged cheering' – had expressed the hope that 'this great festival may not terminate in a mere ovation to the mighty dead', but that some 'monumental structure . . . may soon grace the metropolis of western Scotland – a structure worthy of the Bard, of Glasgow and of Scotland'.[45] North Britishness, it has been claimed, reached its zenith at this time.[46] Perhaps so, but around Burns there was little sign of it; his mid century promoters were unapologetically Scottish.

But even this sharper focus doesn't explain in full the eruption of statues of the poet that swept one by one through the towns of Lowland Scotland from the later 1870s through to the end of the century. Indeed in one respect the explanation – that Burns' sponsors were staunchly Liberal – will not do, at least not without qualification. Amongst the leading supporters of moves to memorialise Burns were some life-long Conservatives. The list includes James Hedderwick in Glasgow, and Peter Sturrock in Kilmarnock, a leading light in the Burns Club. He later became the first president of the Burns Federation. His successor in 1899, David Mackay, was also from Kilmarnock, and an active Conservative. So too was Claud Alexander MP, the main subscriber to the Kilmarnock monument and statue who also spoke at the inauguration ceremony. Even so, such men were in a minority. Edward Goodwillie's remark that it was ironic that the statue of Burns in Aberdeen unveiled in 1892 'should face the aristocratic Conservative Club', reveals in what direction the statue movement was assumed to have been travelling.[47] The distinction between the parties, however, can be too sharply drawn: after the Reform Act and the 1843 Disruption of the Scottish Church, Conservatives often found common cause with the Liberals with whom they shared interests in issues such as temperance reform, slum clearance and public health.[48] And Burns.

As an explanation for Burns promotion, party political allegiance was trumped by other factors. Freemasonry was one of these, although how important is hard to judge – not least as we saw in chapter 2, the masonic ideal of universal brotherhood through lodge membership was virtually indistinguishable from the more inclusive calls for the brotherhood of man made by non-mason followers of Burns and by the Burns clubs. Certainly freemasons continued to play prominent parts in Burns-related ceremonials, with several hundred of them participating at Kilmarnock in 1879, where the proceedings finished with R. W. Cochran-Patrick, Provincial Grand Master, pronouncing the monument fully completed 'according to the rules of masonry', and renditions of the 'Old Hundredth' psalm, the 'Masons' Anthem' and 'Rule Britannia'.[49] Ayr's Burns statue, too, in 1891, was unveiled 'with masonic honours' by Sir Archibald Campbell, Grand Master Mason of Scotland.[50] Other instances abound, such as the poems laced with masonic terminology that were turned out on 25 January each year by William Harvey 'Provincial Grand Bard of Forfarshire' in praise of 'Brother Burns'.[51] In the twentieth century a handful of masonic Burns clubs were founded, as in Kilsyth (1923) and Fisherrow (1924).

But freemasons or not, what is clear is that at the forefront of the movement was a remarkably small group of people – Burns devotees who were unstinting in their efforts to erect permanent memorials of Burns. Indeed, to secure Burns' memory in perpetuity was their purpose, articulated in 1858 as the plans for the 1859 centenary celebrations were being laid.[52] The descendants of the Covenanters in Walter Scott's *Old Mortality* are depicted as having had a special reverence for the simple graves of their fallen forefathers rather than for 'more splendid mausoleums'.[53] Burns enthusiasts in the final third of the nineteenth century, too, wanted their own statues of their own poet. By this time, it seems, Burns had been recruited in the service of the notion – partly but not wholly mythical – that in Scotland, dating back to the Covenanters if not before, there was a deep-seated commitment to civil and religious liberty, and democratic rights.[54]

Prominent amongst the enthusiasts was Colin Rae Brown, the probable instigator of the 1859 centennial celebrations. Not only was Rae Brown a freemason, he had also been one of the originators of the scheme for Scotland's most important patriotic memorial of the nineteenth century, the Wallace Monument, on Abbey Craig, near Stirling, that had been set on foot two years earlier, in 1856. Much later Rae Brown was described as a 'loyal and public spirited Scotsman', an 'untiring advocate' for the perpetuation of the memories of Wallace, Scott and Burns, and someone who should be long remembered by anyone who cherishes 'the greatness of their country's past and the names of those who contributed to its greatness'.[55]

For health reasons – he had been involved in a railway accident – Rae Brown moved to London in 1861, where in 1868 he founded the London Burns Club and afterwards involved himself in moves for a Burns statue on the Embankment. However, it is clear from reports of the various statue campaigns in Scotland that most were led by equally committed individuals without whom the projects might have moved more slowly or even come to nothing. Some of them we have mentioned already.

Glasgow's Burns statue movement owed much – at least in the initial stages of the project – to James Hedderwick.[56] One of Glasgow's most ardent Burnsians, Hedderwick – also a freemason – had been a member of the committee formed in Glasgow in July 1858 to organise the city's 1859 centenary celebrations. The attachment to Burns of the same city's William Wilson, also mentioned above, was said to be 'of the most ardent description', never seen 'to greater advantage than when consuming the national haggis . . . and washing it down with the national liquor' at Burns suppers.[57] In Kilmarnock, James M'Kie was not only credited with almost single-handedly orchestrating the campaign for a statue in Kilmarnock, but with having been 'connected with nearly every Burns movement in the West of Scotland'[58] (Plate 11). M'Kie had begun to collect Burnsiana as early as 1843, and as a publisher had from 1866 been instrumental in making available facsimile editions of Burns' works. Rae Brown wrote to M'Kie, commending him as, 'without the shadow of a doubt, the chief of literary "Scots wha hae"', having done 'yeoman service to the immortal memory of the Bard'[59] (Plate 12).

In Dundee there was the Reverend George Gilfillan of the United Presbyterian Church, and foremost of the town's 'pulpit kings'.[60] A literary polymath and nationally known critic, between 1845 and his death in 1878 Gilfillan wrote several commentaries on Burns' life and works, culminating in the hefty two-volume *National Burns* (1879–80), as well as lecturing on him in many parts of the United Kingdom.[61] Alongside him was Charles Maxwell, 'a most devoted disciple' of Burns, who seldom appeared in public 'without treating his hearers to copious . . . quotations from Burns' works'. Also prominent in Dundee were James Sturrock, and Alexander Drummond, a 'capital singer of old Scotch songs'.[62] In Dumfries, Robert Hamilton, a town councillor and 'devoted admirer of Burns', not only proposed that a statue should be erected, but, unable to muster the support of his fellow councillors, led the project from beginning to end, sometimes riding roughshod over anyone who dared challenge him, even insisting on his right to select the sculptor. In Montrose, too, it was a town councillor who in 1887 became provost, George Scott, who had been in the forefront, alongside Robert White, 'an Ayrshire man and suggester [sic] of the movement' in 1882.[63] However, Scott's unexpected death, in office, in 1890, was one of the factors that led to a delay of more than twenty years in bringing the project to fruition – thereby underlining the importance of local driving forces. In Paisley the initiative seems to have involved J. Roy Foster, conductor of the Tannahill choir and a lover of Scottish music – who turned to Burns after having successfully raised money through the choir's concerts for a statue of Paisley's poetic hero who had also died in his thirties, Robert Tannahill.[64]

* * *

None of the men concerned worked alone. Most did so as members of Burns clubs. Burns clubs, as we have seen, began to be established in the early 1800s, one of a number of increasingly numerous and influential societies of various sorts that proliferated as Scotland's new urban elites came to dominate through their associational activity the cultural life of their towns. About the importance of the clubs, Edinburgh University's Professor John Blackie (1809–1897) was in no doubt. For Blackie – a major figure in the promotion of Burns, about whom he wrote a *Life* in 1888, as well as being a radical politically and a Scottish nationalist – the clubs were 'second only to the Scotch Kirk' as a vehicle for preserving the characteristics of Scotland. The characteristics he so valued were embodied in four men: Robert the Bruce, John Knox, Walter Scott – and Robert Burns.[65] Indeed, that Scotland's history and literature became serious subjects of study owed much to the efforts of the Burns clubs in Kilmarnock, Glasgow and elsewhere in the west of Scotland in agitating and raising funds for a chair in Scottish History at Glasgow University, whose first incumbent was Robert S. Rait.[66] Aware of the provenance of his post, Rait took his responsibilities seriously and, with the University's Principal Sir Donald MacAlister, supported the Burns Federation's efforts to preserve the knowledge and use of the Scots vernacular.[67]

The nature of the clubs' membership varied from place to place, usually reflecting the economic and social character of the town or community in question. Thus in the south-west and parts of Fife, lists of founding members that survive suggest that they were not unlike those for Paisley, outlined in chapter 2, where distinctions between merchants and manufacturers (most of whom operated on a small-scale) and the better off 'fancy' weavers were less stark than in other industrial centres.[68] Small-scale textile production was also important in the north Ayrshire village of Dalry, where at least eleven of the twenty founder members of the Burns club in 1826 were handloom weavers.[69]

As a county town the economy of Dumfries was more diverse, as well as having a layer of social refinement. This is mirrored in the forty-five men who founded the Dumfries Club in 1820, who included John Syme of Ryedale, a close friend of Burns and 'Distributor of Stamps' for the county – a government sinecure. Merchants, teachers, writers, bank agents, surgeons, accountants, a bookseller, a printer, the editor of the *Dumfries Courier*, and John Staig, Collector of the Customs, were the others. Irvine's Burns Club, founded in 1826, was similar, boasting David Sillar (an early acquaintance of Burns), while the inclusion of Robert Wyllie the harbourmaster reflected the burgh's role as a port.[70] Club members tended to be well off relative to the labouring poor, but in few cases could they be described as wealthy. Presumably this and how close their members were to financial diffi-culty provide part of the explanation why Paisley's Burns Club ceased to meet after 1836. Between 1811 and 1848 Paisley suffered eight trade depressions, the worst, from 1841–3, leading to the bankruptcy of over half of Paisley's manufacturers. Judging by the fairly static numbers of Burns suppers in the 1830s, in Scotland as a whole club formation may have stalled around this time for similar reasons.[71]

However, 1859 inspired a period of renewal. Paisley's Burns Club, for instance, was revived in 1874. There was also a flurry of new foundations, such as Dumbarton's (1859), Dundee's Burns Club (1860), Bridgeton's (1870), Aberdeen's (1871 or 1872), Perth's (1873), Dumfries' Queen of the South Club (1874) and the Tam o' Shanter Club (1877), and further foundations in the following decades, as in Arbroath (1888) and Brechin (1894). In Glasgow alone there were twelve Burns clubs by 1892. Around the same time even Dumfries had six.[72]

There was little discernible difference in the social backgrounds of the members of the new or revived clubs, although over time membership of some of them does seem to have become more firmly middle class and conservative in nature, which in turn encouraged the foundation of more popular associations. Respectability, however, was always key, in intention at least.[73] Those present at the Burns Club of Kilmarnock, for example, when it was reconstituted in 1855, were: John McMillan, a druggist; the booksellers John Kellachin, Archibald McKay and James M'Kie; J. C. Paterson and William Spicer, both teachers; J. M. Ross, a student; and Daniel Frazer, an engineer. Soon afterwards a newspaper reporter, two painters, an author and a photographer joined them; almost certainly more affluent was Peter Sturrock, a civil engineer, colliery proprietor, and director of investment companies in Canada who in the later 1880s became the owner of semi-ruinous Baltersan Castle, near Maybole (Plate 13). Not dissimilar was the Waverley in Glasgow. Apart from Hedderwick, a businessman in his own right, the membership comprised works and warehouse managers, architects and artists including John Carrick, who had been apprenticed to John Bryce, brother of the better-known David Bryce, James Salmon and Alexander 'Greek' Thomson (architecture was an important profession in Glasgow, with its massive and ongoing building programme).[74] Aberdeen's Burns Club, too, with a membership of around thirty-five in the 1880s, comprised 'not a few of the leading spirits of the community – professional, literary, and commercial'.[75]

Occupations only tell us so much, however. As important, are the personalities, characteristics and motivations of the most active members. It almost goes without saying that sociability was central, the annual Burns supper with its eating and drinking and ritualistic format providing the clubs' principal *raison d'etre*. Indeed conviviality and a liberality of spirit (both literally and metaphorically), sanctioned in the name of Burns, in contrast to the solemnity, stern moralising and Sabbatarianism associated with Scotland's Presbyterian clergy, was seen by many – men in particular – as one of the major successes of what was to become the Burns cult.[76]

Initially at least, Glasgow's Waverley Club held meetings more or less monthly, with members dining together, drinking and debating, and the secretary after the November 1862 gathering noting that 'the usual flow of anecdote, reminiscence and original thought prevailed'. The members' fondness for the alcohol that accompanied their proceedings is revealed in his recommendation in June 1865 that the serious business of the meetings should be completed early on, 'before eloquence becomes generally wakened up', and when the 'disposition to yield somewhat to an opponent, is more evident'.[77] Drinking, however, was a serious matter, with the itinerary for a club outing to Linlithgow in 1878, reading: at 'High Noon', 'Inspect interior of the "Star and Garter", interview Landlord, and pronounce upon the quality of the Wine, Beer, and Spirits to be imbibed during Dinner.' At 2.10 pm the party was to repeat the process at the Golden Cross Tavern.[78] Poems, many by members – not a few of whom had poetic pretensions, but rather less in the way of poetic ability – were read, and songs sung. Further indicative of the social character of the club and perhaps of the anxieties of their class over incomes and wealth which manifested in undue concern for the symbols of their newly acquired status, was a protest by members in July 1865 that the hotel in which meetings were held had failed to provide table cloths. The same fears were betrayed in their reluctance to travel by 'ordinary' steamer to Bowling on their summer outing in 1864; they would have preferred the more 'imposing' ride by a chartered omnibus. An inordinate amount of time and effort too was spent arguing about the size of the members' photographs and whether these, for their *cartes de visite*, should be full length or seated.

Heard too, and coldly assessed, was the work of artisan poets whom members sought to promote, in the belief they shared with Gilfillan in Dundee, of the redeeming power of poetry. The Waverley Club, however, was more solidly middle class than most, and patronising too, agreeing to listen to David Wingate, Lanarkshire's self-styled 'collier poet', after being assured that he was 'of simple and unobtrusive manners', attributes no doubt that helped when afterwards he was admitted as a member. That Wingate used the proceeds from the book of poems that had so impressed Waverley Club members to attend Glasgow's Mining School, after which he rose to become a colliery manager, would have gladdened their hearts even further.[79] Club members took themselves seriously as arbiters of taste, not only in literary matters but in art and architecture too.

As has just been hinted, they felt too they had a duty to educate. In this respect they were a form of mutual improvement society. Societies for this purpose originated in Scotland and proliferated throughout Britain in the nineteenth century, although unlike the Burns clubs they tended to meet in churches or chapels.[80] Burns clubs, though, could be found in not dissimilar surroundings, with Dundee's, for example, stemming from a meeting in Lamb's Coffee House that had been called to discuss the 'propriety' of forming a mutual improvement group. What clubs like this and others in the frontline of the statue movement had in common were men who in principle and practice were committed to the idea of working-class advance and the attainment of respectability through reading and education. They were mainly but as we have seen not always Liberals. Many had sympathised with the aims but not the violence of the Chartists.[81] Typical is Dundee's Burns Club's Charles Maxwell, who although not a founder member was president in 1875 and 1876. A mill manager's son, Maxwell was a clerk and bookkeeper with James Keiller & Sons, and later general manager and a partner. He was also highly regarded as a man of letters, and as an entertaining public speaker, eventually devoting himself full-time to this. An 'ardent politician of strongly Radical type', whose 'heart and voice were always on the side of liberty and freedom', it was said of him that 'every movement for the relief or elevation of the oppressed in this or other countries secured his earnest support'.[82]

As with the Waverley, most clubs built up small libraries and collections of artefacts and organised other events during the year, ostensibly of a literary or cultural nature, usually in accordance with strict rules on format and timing. Dundee's Burns Club, for example, arranged debates and discussions on moral issues with a practical bent, like manhood suffrage, capital punishment, self denial, whether 'is the miser or the spendthrift the greatest bane of society', and if better housing would improve the morality of the working classes. They tackled, too, political subjects including monarchy versus republicanism, the British government's policy on Savoy, whether Britain had been right to enter what became known as the Crimean War, and Polish nationality. Less easy to categorise are topics like that debated in May 1861, 'The Ear Considered as a means to the Mind's Improvement', or February's discussion that had been led by William Stewart, a review of 'Mr Hart's lectures on the power of ugliness'. In addition to poetry recitals (which included surprisingly little of Burns), they read aloud extracts from a range of writers, both local and national, the justification being that 'a few thoughts from the pen of a good author is better than a deal of smattering in the shape of original composition'. Extemporising and the writing of original prose and verse – as a means of 'instruction getting' – were strongly encouraged at meetings that, at first, were held weekly for most of the year.[83] Debates, it seems, were usually conducted in good spirit, except for subjects such as religion and land nationalisation, the last named being so fraught that it was decided over two separate sessions that no vote should be taken.

What drove such men was an evangelical belief in the moral force of the printed word, and the recognition that the periodical and newspaper press had a vital part to play in the dissemination of culture and cultural values. In this regard a breakthrough had been achieved in 1855 when, following pressure from Radicals, publishers of titles aimed at lower income readers, and others, Gladstone introduced legislation that included the repeal of the newspaper tax.[84] What followed was a doubling of the number of local newspapers in Scotland by 1860, and growing circulation figures, particularly amongst the target audience.[85]

Even prior to this, in 1842, James Hedderwick had been one of the founders of the *Glasgow Citizen*, but more important from the present perspective was his mass circulation *Glasgow Evening Citizen*, which he established in 1864 and sold at a halfpenny. As we have seen, the *Citizen* was the vehicle through which he was able to launch his campaign for the Burns statue. Recognising its potential as a means of communicating with – and setting on the pathway to redemption – a new, lower class readership, in 1865 the Waverley Club had decided to support Hedderwick's venture against attempts by rival newspapers to drive it out of the market.[86] Colin Rae Brown had a similar pedigree, founding in 1856 the short-lived *Glasgow Daily Bulletin*, the city's first penny newspaper.[87]

Kilmarnock's James M'Kie, too, had established himself as a newspaper proprietor, founding the *Kilmarnock Journal* in 1846 and, in

1856, the *Kilmarnock Weekly Post*. In Dumfries, Robert Hamilton's efforts to have a Burns statue erected owed much to the support on the monument committee of William McDowall, and his publicising of the campaign facilitated by his editorship of the *Dumfries Standard*. That McDowall was also the author of a noted *History of Dumfries* points to another fairly common characteristic of the clubs – as well as of Burns enthusiasts outside the clubs – an interest in and passion for local antiquities and history. This applied to J. B. Salmond in Arbroath – who was also the editor of the *Arbroath Herald* through which organ he had urged his fellow townsmen to form a Burns club.[88] If after 1707 the grand narrative of Scottish history was harder to tell as it became enmeshed with England's, it was in the localities that Scotland's history was to be found, recorded and resumed.

*   *   *

By no means all of those interested in preserving Burns' memory belonged to Burns clubs. Indeed what is striking is how small were their core membership numbers – although most were able to attract hundreds for the livelier Burns suppers. Even so, Alloway's Burns Club, the first, was able to muster only five attendees for the supper in 1878.[89] Membership of Kilmarnock's Burns Club had dwindled by the mid 1860s to fewer than six active members and it failed to meet in 1863. Dundee's was inaugurated with only seven members, while the club secretary reported an average of nine-and-a-half attendees for 1861. Ten years later, twelve was given as the number attending regularly.[90] Numbers doubled, however, as the campaign for the town's Burns statue intensified between 1878 and 1880, that year's annual 'picnic' being the biggest in the club's history, with a party of forty-nine setting off in five 'conveyances' for reels, tea, beer and pipes at nearby Kinnaird Castle.[91] Against this, some clubs deliberately restricted their numbers – which was one reason new ones were formed, such as Paisley's Gleniffer Burns Club in 1892.[92] Even so, when in 1865 Glasgow's Western Club considered whether they should admit more, there were only forty-four members on the books – although this was more than twice as many as in 1860. For longer-established members, however, smaller numbers were far from undesirable; the inclusion of 'strangers' had a dulling effect on the proceedings as it was claimed they came to listen rather than participate.

Important, therefore, in bringing the projects to a successful conclusion, was the establishment of monument or statue committees with a wider membership. The Monument Committee in Glasgow, for example, recruited Charles Tennant of St Rollox, then the world's largest chemical works. Tennant's family connections with Burns satisfied the contemporary craving to somehow connect with the poet by association. (The Tennants of Glenconner near Tarbolton had been close friends of Burns and his father.) Charles Tennant's fondness for Burns' works (some of which he could recite by heart), and that as a boy he had attended with his father the great Reform Bill demonstration in Glasgow in 1832, would have further endeared him to many of the city's Burns enthusiasts.[93] As one of Glasgow's and the west of Scotland's leading industrialists and employers, his influence – and the example he set by supporting the campaign for the statue of Burns and in organising its inauguration – was clearly important. Later, and on the other side of the country, in Leith a similar role seems to have been played by Richard Mackie, a local coal exporter and shipowner, who was credited with providing much of the 'energy and enthusiasm' for the Burns statue project.[94]

Critical, however, was the contribution of town councillors, and town and city officials, with whom the committees necessarily worked hand in hand, even if such partnerships were not always harmonious. Some happened to be Burns club members anyway, but whatever their relationship with the clubs, town council representatives were readily persuaded to join the statue committees, where they often took leading roles. In Glasgow William Wilson, who chaired Glasgow's Monument Committee, was also a city baillie. Usefully, he had also been involved with the drawn-out campaign to secure subscriptions for the Wallace Monument near Stirling, and therefore had fund-raising experience. In Dumfries, where although the proposal for a Burns statue had been 'coldly received' by a majority of the town council, individual councillors, including the initiator Robert Hamilton and provost Thomas Ferguson Smith, provided the backbone of the statue committee.[95] Not dissimilar was the committee set up in 1886 to implement the statue proposal in Ayr, which included Burns club members such as former Liberal provost Robert Goudie as well as the current provost James Ferguson – a Conservative. In Irvine, once John Spiers' offer of the statue had been received, implementation was put in the hands of the magistrates and the Burns club.[96] Very different was Paisley, where relations between the Burns Statue Committee and a divided town council as well as a sizeable and influential body of the burgh's inhabitants were fractious, and resulted in the statue of Burns being located some distance from the prime site in County Square that the statue's promoter had wanted.[97]

* * *

Paisley excepted, it is these compact civic alliances that point us to what was the essence of the Burns statue movement. It had three inter-connected components.

The first was the ambition of Scotland's civic leaders. New civic buildings and squares and numerous schemes of improvement of the surrounding environment that emerged from the middle of the century were assertions of the emergence and authority of industrial and commercial wealth. The adoption of renaissance and neo-gothic archi-tectural styles for municipal buildings like Glasgow's city chambers, but also for the newer factories and warehouses that were to be found in even the smallest towns was a form of middle-class self-aggrandise-ment. Allied to this was a growing sense amongst the Victorian bour-geoisie that a town without some heroic statues – as well of course as the plazas in which they were located and new buildings against which they were framed – was open to the criticism that it lacked civic distinction.

Visitors were quick to point out such lacunae. In 1863 a corre-spondent to Dundee's *People's Journal*, identifiable only by the initials DYR, reported on a recent sojourn to the town. Much had impressed him, not least the flourishing docks, the bustling air of business on the High Street with its open square, as well as some fine buildings. But something was missing: statues. Compared to Glasgow, with which the writer was obviously familiar, Dundee had little in the way of public art. Even fourteen years later, when the town could boast two public statues, Thomas Couper, a manager in the Dundee, Perth and London Shipping Company acknowledged that 'there were not many beautiful things in Dundee', which needed 'statues as well as stations, pictures as well as power looms'. (It was why he was advocating one of Burns.) Until the appearance of the Burns statue in Dumfries, the editor of the *Dumfries and Galloway Standard* wrote, 'no town in Scotland ... of the same size, polish, and pretensions' had been so devoid of ornament in the form of sculptured figures. In this respect it was discreditably poverty-stricken: Dumfries would 'better merit the proud title Queen of the South if her street architecture were made more regal in its aspect'.[98] The town had the mausoleum, and some thought this sufficient. But it stood in a graveyard crowded with some

3,300 funereal monuments of various descriptions, nor was it beautiful, or 'in accordance with the character of Burns and his works', opined one local commentator, even though he was to prefer it to Hill's statue.[99]

But there was more to the Burns statue movement than simply possession of one. The manufacturing and commercial classes whose dynamism had in large part fuelled the towns' largely chaotic, unplanned expansion, anxious about anything that might disrupt the smooth flow of business, had become increasingly concerned about town and city governance and its cost. The problem in part was the masses, the labouring people who had flocked to the towns in their thousands in the first half of the century. Unknowable, prone to drunkenness, associated with rising levels of crime and liable to take collective action in workplaces or on the streets that as the experiences of the 1830s and 1840s had shown could descend into violence, they represented a threat but also a challenge for the new urban rulers.

There were various ways of tackling what was a multi-faceted dilemma. Preventative policing was one. Improvement, which included the wholesale removal of older, overcrowded buildings and their replacement by straight open streets, grand buildings and new housing, was another. In part this was about the attainment of what some historians have called cultural hegemony. What this meant in practice was the implementation of strategies designed to influence the behaviour of working people. In the case of the skilled working classes emphasis was placed by civic elites in alliance with the churches on the shared values noted earlier – in short, the creation of a common Presbyterian culture.[100] But to achieve this there was a belief that the built environment also had a part to play. This was true, for example, of the architect and Waverley Club member Alexander 'Greek' Thomson. We can assume that prior to his death in 1875 Thomson shared with his Burns club associates his conviction – as an evangelical elder of the United Presbyterian Church – of the duty of architecture to create, under God, 'works which elevate the mind of man'.[101] In this respect Thomson was part of a wider circle of urban reformers who ought to create within the towns for which they were responsible, monumental, moral and aesthetic spaces, capable of unifying the classes by engendering civic pride but also, if possible, to evoke respect.[102] Most effective as improving agents were monuments that had a commanding presence and bore 'the stamp of eternity'.[103] Through architecture and inspirational art the minds of the working

Plate 1. Burns medallion, by John Hemmings, Paisley, for Paisley Burns Club, 1807. Demand from even the modestly well off for portrait medallions was substantial. They were a fashionable means by which individuals could own an image of Burns. They could be worn on special Burns-related occasions, or displayed in the home. *Heritage Services, Renfrewshire Council*

Plate 2. Nineteenth-century Mauchline ware wooden snuff box, depicting a scene from 'Tam o' Shanter'. It was on small, personal items like this that the bawdier side of Burns oeuvre was to be seen. It was largely absent from the public memorials, including the statues. *The National Trust for Scotland*

Plate 3. (*Right*) Burns Monument, Alloway, 1820, by Thomas Hamilton. Adapted from the classical choragic model, this acknowledges Burns' Romantic and Enlightenment associations, as did the similar monument to Burns on Edinburgh's Calton Hill, also designed by Hamilton. The Alloway monument was later used as a lever by Chartists to attack Scotland's aristocracy. *Christopher A. Whatley*

Plate 4. (*Below*) 'The Cotter's Saturday Night' (Verse XII), by John Horsburgh, after John Faed RSA, Royal Association for the Promotion of Fine Arts in Scotland (1853). In the first half of the nineteenth century, Scotland's Tories promoted this poem as a model of social contentment. Images like this were commonplace, and served much the same purpose, as well as fuelling nostalgia for Scotland's rural past. *Royal Scottish Academy Collections*

Plate 5. Ayr Burns Festival, 1844. The shepherds and ploughmen in the procession preceding the festivities on the bank of the River Doon donned their caps as they passed the cottage where Burns was born, in Alloway. By paying homage to a man of their own class in this manner they were breaking with the tradition of bowing to their social superiors. *Illustrated London News*

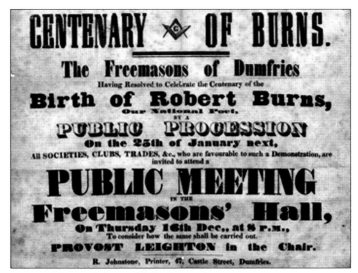

Plate 6. Invitation card, sent by the Freemasons of Dumfries, to discuss the arrangements for a public procession to be held to mark the centenary of Burns' birth, in 1859. Similar demonstrations were held throughout Scotland – as well as the rest of the UK, North America, and elsewhere. *Dumfries Museum*

Plate 7. The meticulously organised and tightly marshalled procession for the Burns centenary of 1859 in Dumfries. The number of onlookers is striking, but this was typical of hundreds of similar public demonstrations of enthusiasm for Burns that took place in other Scottish towns and villages on the same day. *Illustrated London News*

Plate 8. The 'grand citizen banquet' held in Edinburgh's sumptuously decorated Corn Exchange on 25 January 1859. Some 1,500 were present at a gathering, the price of entry to which was lower than a similar event in the Music Hall. Those wishing to pay homage to the 'man of the people' should not be debarred by cost. *Illustrated London News*

Ministers who took part in the "Burn's Centenary"

Rev.d Dr Robt Lee.
"Established Church."

Rev.d A. Wallace, D.D.
"U.P. Church."

Dean Ramsay
Church of England

Bishop Gillis.
R.C. Church.

Plate 9. (*Left*) Four Edinburgh ministers who participated in the Burns centenary celebrations of 1859. Given the hostility to Burns from the churches there had been up until this point, the involvement of clergymen marked a marked shift in religious thinking towards the poet. © *CSG CIC Glasgow Museums and Libraries Collection: The Mitchell Library, Special Collections*

Plate 10. (*Below*) Unveiling Burns statue, Dumfries, 1882. The tightly packed, seething crowd consists mainly of working men. At the insistence of the town's trades, who wanted a clear view of the proceedings, there was no high protective platform for the dignitaries. So threatening was the surge that the main speaker, the earl of Rosebery, cut short his speech. *Ewart Library, Dumfries and Galloway Council*

Plate 11. James M'Kie, the Kilmarnock publisher of new and facsimile editions of Burns' poems. M'Kie was also a Burns enthusiast and collector of his works and related material, now held in the Dick Institute, Kilmarnock. M'Kie played a part in the erection of the Glasgow Burns statue and led the campaign for one in Kilmarnock. *The Baillie*, January 1876. © *CSG CIC Glasgow Museums and Libraries Collection: The Mitchell Library, Special Collections*

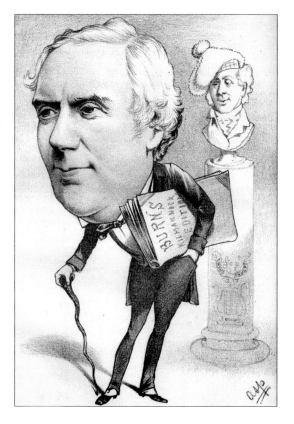

Plate 12. Cover of The People's Edition of a facsimile of Burns *Poems*, 1877. Kilmarnock's James M'Kie produced it for the unveiling of the Burns statue in Glasgow's George Square. Costing one shilling, it was a publishing masterstroke that added to the stock of Burns' works that the working classes could afford. *M'Kie Collection, Dick Institute, Kilmarnock*

Plate 13. Founding members of Kilmarnock Burns Club, 1855. It was middle-class men of this sort – professionals such as teachers, lawyers and architects, and small businessmen – who were the backbone of the Burns clubs. Their role in shaping and securing the memory of Burns was second to none. *Burns Monument Centre, Kilmarnock*

Plate 14. Unveiling Burns statue, Albert Square, Dundee, October 1880. Visible are the vast crowd, the trades' banners (including one made especially by Dundee's Burns Club), and the platform party including the lord provost and the main speaker, Frank Henderson MP. *Dundee Central Library*

Plate 15. Burns statue, George Square, Glasgow, by George Ewing, unveiled January 1877. It was the first of the post-1859 wave of Burns memorials. Controversial from the outset but much admired locally, it was one of the statues of the poet that by the end of the 1880s was judged not to have done justice to Burns' genius. Devoid of 'insight, penetration, or character' this was Burns without soul or intellect; the poet – it was alleged – was absent. *Christopher A. Whatley*

Plate 16. Engraving of William Grant Stevenson's model for the Burns Monument, Kay Park (1879), the 'most pretentious – the most colossal and imposing' – of all memorials. The statue, which followed the portrait of Burns by Alexander Nasmyth with 'fidelity', was commended by Edward Goodwillie in his 1911 compendium of the world's statues of Burns, as 'one of the finest realizations of the poet we have'. *M'Kie Collection, Dick Institute, Kilmarnock*

Plate 17. Burns statue, Dumfries, by Amelia Hill, 1882. Carved in glistening white Carrera marble, for onlookers the statue had a quasi-religious quality.
Christopher A. Whatley

Plate 18. Burns statue, Dundee, by Sir John Steell, 1880. Now recognised as a powerful piece of public sculpture, Steell's Burns was harshly judged in the two decades after its unveiling.
Christopher A. Whatley

Plate 19. Burns statue, head and shoulders, George Square, Glasgow. One early criticism of this statue was that Walter Scott (seen in the background) towered above Burns. Another was that the face was 'too sonsie and heavy looking', and lacked the nobility of a poet of Burns' standing.
Christopher A. Whatley

Plate 20. George Edwin Ewing, sculptor of the Burns statue in Glasgow's George Square. He was a controversial choice, well-known for his busts of prominent Scots but with no previous experience of life-sized statuary. *The Baillie*, April 1874. © *CSG CIC Glasgow Museums and Libraries Collection: The Mitchell Library, Special Collections*

Plate 21. (*Above*) Burns statue, upper body and head, Central Park, New York (and Dundee), 1880. Andrew Carnegie was 'distressed' that Sir John Steell had portrayed Burns 'in the form of a hump-backed simpleton', and in 1883 urged the promoters of a Burns statue in Montrose not to follow suit. *Patricia E. Whatley*

Plate 22. (*Left*) Burns statue, Montrose, 1912. One of the last of the post-1877 wave of statues to be erected. Representing Burns as the ploughman poet, it was made by William Birnie Rhind, who was awarded the commission in 1889. However, owing to the death of the main enthusiast behind the project, Provost Scott, Birnie Rhind had to assist in the fund-raising effort. Instigated in 1882, the project took thirty years to complete, at a cost of £675. *Christopher A. Whatley*

Plate 23. (*Above*) Paisley's Burns statue (1896), Fountain Gardens, in 1903. The proximity of a fountain to a statue of Burns was typical. Less so was the fact that this memorial had been erected some distance from the town centre, the location preferred by statue promoters. Despite efforts to remedy this, it remains in place. *Heritage Services, Renfrewshire Council*

Plate 24. (*Right*) Amelia Paton, the sculptor wife of David Octavia Hill, and the only female sculptor of a life-sized Burns. Her statue of Burns in Dumfries (unveiled in 1882) was much criticised, not least for what was considered to be its feminisation of Burns. Photograph by Nesbitt & Lothian, 1870s. *Royal Scottish Academy Archives*

Plate 25. Burns statue, head, Dumfries, 1882, by Amelia Paton Hill. Hill's Italian-marble Burns was described by one critic as being 'a heavy and fat figure'. The 'twinkle' in Burns' eyes, depicted here, was considered to be effeminate. *Christopher A. Whatley*

Plate 26. Sir John Steell RSA, carte de visite photograph, by John Moffat, *c.*1880s. Steell, Scotland's leading nineteenth-century sculptor, was much criticised for his statue of Burns for New York and Dundee, with slightly modified replicas also being made for London (Thames Embankment) and Dunedin, New Zealand. *Royal Scottish Academy Archives*

Plate 27. (*Above*) James Pittendrigh MacGillivray, *c.*1925–35. MacGillivray was a Scottish poet and sculptor who won the commission for the Burns statue that was unveiled in Irvine in 1896. 'Burns by an Englishman is impossible', he said, but he had little time for Scottish sculptors either. Unknown photographer. *Royal Scottish Academy Archives*

Plate 28. (*Right*) Burns statue, Irvine, by James Pittendrigh MacGillivray (1896). The first statue of Burns to break with the tradition of modelling the poet's head on Nasmyth's portrait. MacGillivray tried too to represent Burns in the round, rather than at a particular moment in his life. *Christopher A. Whatley*

Plate 29. Scott Sutherland sculpting the Burns statue for Arbroath (1958). One of the most recent Burns statues, it was unveiled in 1959, seventy years after it was first proposed. This is the most radical representation of the poet, and far removed from those in Glasgow (1877), Kilmarnock (1879), Dundee (1880) or Dumfries (1882). © *D C Thomson*

Plate 30. Burns, Dumfries, 1938. Owing to increased traffic, Amelia Paton Hill's Burns statue was moved more than once from its original location in Church Place. Others rarely shared this somewhat humiliating fate. Most of the memorials stand in their original locations. *Dumfries Museum*

Plate 31. (*Above*) Burns statue, Dundee, being cleaned (1989). There was a suggestion after the First World War that Burns should be removed from its Albert Square site and replaced by a war memorial. The statue remained in place, however, and has been cleaned from time to time by council workers, usually following pressure from Burns enthusiasts. © *D C Thomson*

Plate 32. (*Right*) Burns Night poster, 2016. Based on Nasmyth's iconic portrait of Burns, it is ironic – and a sign of the times – that this once near sacred image of the poet is now being employed by the Scottish Craft Butchers to sell haggises.

classes might be diverted from material privation, and thoughts of class war, to respectability through self-improvement.[104] The clearest evidence of this as a goal comes from a speech delivered at the unveiling ceremony for the Burns statue in Leith in 1898. Passed daily by 'large numbers of hard working men', declared councillor Richard Mackie of the town's Burns Club, the sight of Burns' face and figure would remind them that Burns' message 'to all classes of men', was that 'money-making was not the great end and aim of life' (presumably more important was work itself), while the presence of the statue would instil a sense of pride in the Port of Leith after their day's work whether as employee or businessman.[105]

The relevance of all this is that more often than not the Burns statue committees had amongst their number men who were in the forefront of urban improvement schemes in their respective towns. Glasgow of course had John Carrick, who, as one of Provost John Blackie's delegation to Paris, had been inspired by Baron Haussmann's reconstruction of Paris, and was in the process of implementing the city's Improvement Act of 1866, tearing down much of the burgh's overcrowded medieval core and building anew.[106] William Wilson was a prominent patron of the arts.[107] Similarly in Dundee, the leading figures in the campaign for the Burns statue had been behind the Improvement Act of 1871.[108] Frank Henderson, prior to the unveiling of the Burns statue in October 1880 – at which he was the main speaker – had recently been elected as one of Dundee's MPs. Beforehand, however, his principal contribution as a town councillor was as an advocate and implementer of the town's improvement scheme, so much so that the writer of his obituary claimed that 'the new city' of Dundee was his monument.[109] In Ayr provost Robert Ferguson was described as being 'too much a municipalist'.[110] Stirling's David Bayne, donor of the Burns statue, was renowned locally for his commitment to the burgh's improvement and embellishment, including the new burgh headquarters. Bayne contributed its clock tower and a stained glass window.[111] Burns and Scotland's reconstructed towns, therefore, became synonymous.

But Scotland's urban governors were not operating in a vacuum, which takes us to the third reason for the urgency with which they strove to erect statues in their public places. They were acutely aware of what was going on elsewhere, and had no wish to be left behind. Serendipitously, by the end of the 1870s an inter-urban competition had commenced, not only for status-enhancing statues but above all for statues of Burns.

To track this, we have to return again to Glasgow. There, Western Burns Club members (in particular its architect cohort) had watched with interest, and with something of a warm glow, as statues were added one by one to the city's George Square, which was 'in the way to become with judicious management the first open space in any city in the Kingdom'. In 1866 Baron Carlo Marochetti's equestrian statue of Queen Victoria was moved from St Vincent Place to sit alongside the monument to her consort, Prince Albert. Representing science was Thomas Graham, also Glasgow-born. This, as we have noted already, was the catalyst. But there was another consideration. Edinburgh had a monument to Burns – Hamilton's temple and Flaxman's sculpture on Calton Hill. But this had its critics.[112] In fact the statue, considered too large for the Regent Road 'shelter', had been taken to the University of Edinburgh before in 1861 being moved again, and was largely hidden from public view until it was placed in the new National Portrait Gallery in Queen Street in 1889.[113] There was an opportunity therefore for Glasgow to outshine its civic rival by erecting a better memorial to Scotland's greatest poet.

Burns, of course, was only one important Scot, and the Scots, it seemed to a contributor to Belfast's *Northern Whig*, were especially keen to commemorate their own countrymen. What strikes the visitor to Scotland, the correspondent wrote, was 'the multitude of monuments which stud the prominent thoroughfares of its principal towns and cities.' 'Scotchmen of historical repute' predominated, but, judging by the evidence of the nation's statuary, it was 'to the memory of Burns that the Scottish heart clings with fondest tenacity'.[114]

Why? For a town to be without a statue to respect and perpetuate the memory of Burns was first and foremost unpatriotic. This was well expressed by the editor of the *Stirling Observer* in 1913. He had observed that other than on the castle esplanade where there were memorials to Bruce and the Argyll and Sutherland Highlanders, and a figure of Wallace in the town council chambers, Stirling had 'no tribute of a similar nature to Scotsmen ... whose names are worthy of preservation in this manner': with the proposed Burns statue this 'reproach' would be wiped away.[115] This echoed sentiments expressed in Dumfries when a Burns statue was mooted there in 1877. A 'public and palpable act of homage' of this nature would claim Burns 'as our brother-townsman'. But, it was argued, this would not lose sight 'of his more general and more illustrious titles as the champion of Scottish nationality', and as the greatest poet of any age to have sprung from the body of the people.[116]

Indeed a more or less universal tribute paid at the unveiling ceremonies was to Burns' role in 'saving' Scotland's language, preserving and giving life to Scottish song, and restoring Scotland's sense of nationhood. The importance of language for contemporaries whether Liberal or Tory is to be seen in the repeated references (which we noted earlier were first made at the start of the nineteenth century) to the part played by Burns in securing 'as classic for all time the Doric tongue which, but for him, would have been doomed like other dialects to obscurity'.[117] By the end of the nineteenth century, it was still in decline – a matter of profound regret for some like Professor David Masson, the Scottish literary critic and historian – but not yet terminally so, thanks to Burns.[118] The concern, though, was that Scottish dialect was increasingly marginalised, a living language only in 'isolated uplands and rural nooks', and used in the towns by the humbler classes and even then modified by English words, idioms and pronunciation.[119] But, as we will see in chapter 5, at its best – in the hands of working-class poets, for example – it was not only powerful but also popular. References to Scotland's language still resonated with the Scottish public, and were exploited by Home Rule campaigners. Thus when the Liberal leader Lord Rosebery addressed an audience assembled in Dumfries for the Burns centenary of 1896, especially loud cheers rang out when he declared that Burns had 'hallowed Scotland and the Scottish tongue'. At a time when the Scots had been losing their place in and, it was feared, respect in the world, continued Rosebery (a mesmerising orator), Burns it was who 'seemed at this juncture to start to his feet and reassert Scotland's claim to national existence: his Scottish notes rang through the world, and he preserved the Scottish language forever'.[120]

As it had in 1859, *The Scotsman* had captured the mood of the times of which Rosebery's speech was representative. On the anniversary of Burns' birthday in January 1892 the paper declared that 'no poet ever lived who lifted the true patriotic fervour of his fellow countrymen to a holier height than Burns': he had replaced St Andrew as Scotland's patron saint.[121] There were those who frowned upon this sanctification of a flawed human being, and who, as earlier, voiced grave reservations about Burns hero worship. Nevertheless, even Aberdeen's Good Templars, who associated Burns with increased levels of drunkenness and 'unchastity' in the countryside, celebrated

Burns' birthday in 1883, commending in particular his patriotism and his 'living, growing power' as the poet of Scotland.[122] As the standard bearer of the nation through its language, Burns appealed across factions, parties and, to a large extent, social classes.[123]

As far as statues were concerned, even places with only the slightest links with Burns were determined not to be left behind, or out, a point made forcibly by Munro Ferguson MP when at the unveiling of the Burns statue in Leith in 1898 he spoke of the 'true need for a memorial here, no less than in the West, the land of Burns'.[124] Similar motives had played their part in Aberdeen.[125] By default, in Scotland, where between the Union of 1707 and the creation of the Scottish Office in 1885, there was little in the way of a tangible state, other than through institutions such as the Church and the law courts and voluntary bodies like the National Association for the Vindication of Scottish Rights, responsibility for the promotion of Scotland the nation was in the hands of the urban elites, including the Burns clubs whose member-ships they shared. Telling in this regard was the Waverley Club's members' judgment in December 1865 in the light of the financial difficulties being faced by the Wallace Monument committee, that it would be to the 'disgrace of every Scotsman' if they failed to subscribe and the monument was consequently unfinished.[126]

But to fail to respond – picking up on a theme introduced in chapter 1 – was also to risk missing out on the commercial opportunities asso-ciated with Burns, not the least of which were the aforementioned literary tourists, who as before came from England and North America, but also, increasingly as new rail routes opened up, from elsewhere in Scotland.[127] In making his case for a Burns statue for Kilmarnock, 'the manufacturing centre of Ayrshire', James M'Kie made much of Burns' association with the burgh. It was where the first edition of his poems had been printed and several of his friends had resided. No town other than Ayr had 'greater claims . . . to the honour of a monument to the Immortal Bard'.[128] But while he protested – somewhat unconvincingly (for a publisher of Burns' works) – that he had no mercenary motive in mind, he not only spelled out the economic advantages that had accrued to Ayr since the opening of the monu-ment there, including visitors all year round. Kilmarnock's merchants, he went on, could hardly shut their eyes 'to what might be seen loom-ing in the distance for the name and fame of this town if this proposal be successfully carried out'. (As it happened Ayr was redoubling its efforts to attract visitors at around the same time as the Kilmarnock statue project got under way and, helped by beach and other delights for excursionists and holiday makers, maintained its place as the leading Burns destination.[129])

Slightly different motives were at work in Dumfries, where the want of a statue had induced an unusual degree of civic angst, the burgh's inhabitants having been 'taunted' for the way Burns had been treated during his final years. The tangible sense of collective guilt was finally lifted when, 'activated by a sense of contrition', the statue was erected, a sign that the town was aware of its debt to Burns and of its 'atonement to him for the sin of past neglect'.[130] But the argument for a Burns statue had been made, too, on the grounds that owing to Burns' links with the burgh, Dumfries had been 'enriched beyond calculation, and above every other town'.

* * *

Inter-town competition was not just about ownership of any Burns statue. It was about quality too, that would reflect well on the sponsoring burgh. Leith was unable to compete with Edinburgh in terms of numbers of monuments, the burgh's MP admitted when unveiling the Burns statue there, but he declared proudly, 'she [now] has one which can hold its own by the side of the best with which the capital has adorned itself'.[131] In fact, almost from the outset, commissioning bodies had been intent on securing an original statue of the poet. The principle had been established as early as 1872 when James M'Kie had contacted James Hedderwick to enquire whether Kilmarnock might acquire a duplicate of the Glasgow statue – and so avoid the expenditure involved in holding a competition for a sculptor. He was politely but firmly rebuffed, with the advice that to 'have any attraction or value, your movement, however inexpensive, should be original'.[132] So Kilmarnock had to compete rather than collaborate. It was only overseas that replicas would do, provided they had met with critical acclaim first.[133] Consequently, sculptors who met these criteria – William Grant Stevenson, who made Kilmarnock's Burns, and George A. Lawson, Ayr's – did well through the repeat business that came their way from North America, while the same was true of Frederick W. Pomeroy, castings of whose statue of Burns for Paisley were made for Sydney, Australia, and Auckland, New Zealand.

Kilmarnock had taken Hedderwick's rebuttal to heart. Sir John Steell, arguably Scotland's leading sculptor of the period and since

1838 Her Majesty's Sculptor in Ordinary, offered the town a replica of the Burns statue he was working on in his Edinburgh studio in the spring of 1877 for New York's Central Park. This would have saved the statue committee in Kilmarnock the £75 it was to pay in premiums to sculptors who had been invited to compete for the commission. Steell's offer, however, was declined. According to provost Sturrock, the committee's chairman, 'a mere copy of another statue would hardly meet the requirements of the case', a further drawback being that Steell would provide no guarantee that this would be the only copy he would erect in the United Kingdom.[134]

Dundee's Burns statue committee, however, was less concerned and may not even have known about Steell's intentions. Justifiably or not, the Dundonians believed that Steell's previous connections with the town and Dundee's commercial links with New York were the unique keys to their acquisition of what would be an imposing bronze statue of Burns at half what it had cost the New Yorkers.[135] This, however, was the first and last of the duplications to be located in Scotland. Thereafter statue committees were at pains to identify new sculptors, managing to convince themselves that their statue was the best then in existence, even if after those inaugurated in Glasgow, Kilmarnock and Dundee, ambition had to be restrained as fund-raising became more difficult.

Dumfries was the first to suffer. Just over a third of the £3,000 hoped for was subscribed.[136] Consequently, plans for a bronze group that would have included not only Burns but also other life-sized figures representing poesy, religion and patriotism had to be scaled back to a single marble statue of the poet, carved in Italy. Initially at least, financial constraints had little effect in Ayr, where, spurred by the unveiling of Paton Hill's Burns in Dumfries, it was argued that if the town were to acquire a statue, it should be 'better than the common run of things', and be 'something on a grander scale – like the Scott Monument in Edinburgh'.[137] Although Lawson's somewhat less imposing Ayr Burns was highly regarded, there was mounting concern about the quality of Scotland's statues of the nation's poet, a problem exacerbated as monies became harder to prise from subscribers' pockets, and less than the best sculptors would work for. In Stirling David Bayne's hope that he could acquire a Burns statue for £500 was quickly dashed – if the statue was to be located in the open air and be 'worthy of the town of Stirling'.[138] By 1912, £850 was the going rate for a larger than life-sized bronze with a pedestal.

But what Bayne also discovered was that the most highly regarded sculptors had either died or already worked on Burns, and therefore had to be ruled out on the grounds that a copy would be unacceptable.[139] The Stirling commission went to the relatively little-known Albert Hodge, originally from Glasgow but based in London, who was working on a memorial for King Edward VII at Holyrood and was reputed to be capable.

FIVE

'Now's the time and now's the hour'

Keeping the lid on the Burns genie

What should be clear by now is how widespread the admiration was for Burns amongst Scotland's artisans. Recognising this, and the merit there would be in establishing a sense of common ownership of at least part of the city's public space and the values those responsible for designing it were anxious to promote, it was from this source that Glasgow's Burns statue's promoters had hoped the bulk of the necessary funds would be forthcoming.

Indeed, as we saw in the previous chapter, even before the formal campaign was launched, some monies in the form of shillings collected in warehouses and other workplaces, had begun to flow into the offices of the *Citizen* newspaper. In the months following, this continued at what was described as 'astonishing' speed.[1] Scaling up such a strategy demanded thousands of subscribers though. Accordingly, the monument committee looked expressly to the 'sons and daughters of toil' to contribute their 'democratic shilling'. A statue on this principle, it was claimed, would enable 'every Scotchman, of whatever craft and in whatever position in life, to have a claim in the nationality of the memorial to the household poet of Scotland.'[2] It would be nothing less than 'The People's own Monument to BURNS'. This was in stark contrast with the movement for the Burns monument in Edinburgh that had begun in 1819, where the smallest subscriptions – of one guinea – were twenty-one times more than the Glaswegians' single shillings.[3] Although the committee's hope that donations would continue to flow freely was disappointed and required them to recruit the provosts of Paisley, Port Glasgow and other west coast towns to garner subscriptions from their inhabitants, the committee's ambition of 'universal' (as far as possible) engagement was pretty well achieved. Eventually some £2,000 was collected. Most came from the 30,000 or so contributors from Glasgow and its hinterland, although Scots in Canada and the United States as well as St Petersburg and even Constantinople (now Istanbul) also subscribed.[4]

Similar models were followed elsewhere. The men who had gathered in Kilmarnock's George Hotel to consider how they should respond to Glasgow's initiative, were sure that Scotland had been 'moved to its core', by the unveiling of a 'truly national memorial to a truly national poet', paid for in a manner that enabled even the most humble to participate.[5] Looking in from the outside, London's *Times* thought much the same. After witnessing the scenes in Glasgow's George Square, the paper concluded that Burns personified the 'real glory of Scotland . . . the unexampled extent to which intelligence and independence have been attained by the ordinary peasantry and small farmers of the country'. Scott was 'delightful', but his were 'ideals of the past'; Burns, 'who deserved to be the poet of the working classes' represented Scotland now and for the future, embodying an ideal 'which can at all times be aimed at and approached'.[6]

To get things moving in Kilmarnock, a local versifier called on potential subscribers to 'Cast in your mite, tho' but a crown / You'll never miss't / An soon we'll see twa thoosan' poun' / On oor Burns' list.'[7] In Dundee mill managers and foreman who attended an early meeting organised by the town's Burns statue committee took away with them subscription books and sheets, with the aim of collecting contributions from their workpeople. Surviving from this initiative is a handbill headed 'A New Song on the Proposed Burns Statue in Dundee', which was also written in the vernacular. It used as a lever the indebtedness of labouring people to Burns – for the songs that had moved them to mirth and tears, and their capacity to engender joy in 'the darkness of despair', but above all Burns the man 'Who raised the head o' poverty, and lowed the might o' wrong.'[8] In Dundee, with its unusually high level of female workers, mainly in linen and jute mills and factories, there was even a hopeful nod in their direction, in the line, 'The bonny lasses in the mills they will gea what they can', followed by the rather more patronising suggestion that they should do this as 'Robby lo'ed the darlings every one.'[9]

* * *

Without detailed accounts it is impossible to say how successful such appeals were, and what proportion of the monies raised came from the working classes. Those subscription lists that survive show that hundreds of individual tradesmen contributed to the first statues. Workplace collections were also productive. These included the Glasgow and South Western Railway's workshops in Kilmarnock, along with collieries, foundries and other works in the Kilmarnock vicinity. Working men contributed too by paying to attend football matches organised in aid of the Burns statues in Kilmarnock and Dumfries.

But the shillings subscribed by eleven of Dumfries's cabmen, the fifteen shillings donated by Thornhill Young Men's Society and the two pounds two shillings and eight pence from the 'Miners of Wanlockhead' stand out amongst the single, often much larger contributions from the proprietors of small businesses and professionals who typically subscribed between ten shillings and a guinea.[10] The disappointment the statue committee felt in Dumfries that we 'did not receive so much support as we looked for from the working classes' was not unique therefore.[11]

Yet what was said when the Dundee statue was unveiled hints at another factor. The sight of such a 'concourse of horny handed sons of toil . . . holding up mottoes of staunch independence and loving humanity' would have cheered his (Burns') noble heart, according to one witness. However, the same commentator then went on to assert that no poet was 'so strictly national as Burns', for 'he wrote and sung only to the men, and *men* only of Scotland'. It was this that explained the enthusiasm manifested by 'every class of our artisans'. But the male-centric focus of the proceedings may also account for the lower level of interest evinced by the town's female weavers and spinners. Indeed Burns' laudation of drink and 'scoffin' at the clergy' seems to have met with the disapproval of some of Dundee's more respectable textile workers, mainly weavers and married women who may have imbibed the doctrine of domesticated virtue in a town where drunkenness was a particularly acute social problem and the prohibition movement unusually robust.[12] Significantly, the town's most active temperance reformer in the later nineteenth century, James Scrymgeour (father of Scotland's only Prohibition Party MP, Edwin Scrymgeour), was not only close to and popular even amongst some of the burgh's hedonistic millgirls. He had also been outspoken in his opposition to the public celebration of Burns, whom he condemned as a drunkard, a blasphemer, an infidel and a seducer.[13]

Temperance, however, was a long-standing issue for the labour movement in Scotland, and had been an early feature of Chartism.[14] It is unlikely therefore that Dundee was the only place where adulation of Burns was lukewarm amongst abstinence-supporting members of the working classes and church-going women (who in the nineteenth century had become the bedrock of Scotland's Christian community).[15] Certainly women working-class poets, many of whom (as we saw in chapter 2) admired Burns, were unsparing in their denunciations of alcohol and the child-neglect and wife-battering to which it could lead.[16] But even if working people in Dundee's textile trades had wanted to contribute, the sums they could have afforded would have been negligible. Wages in linen and jute were notoriously low, while living costs in Dundee were amongst the highest in Scotland.[17]

Paisley on the other hand – with some justification – prided itself on having bucked the trend. There, J. Roy Foster, conductor of the Tannahill Choir whose several open air concerts held on Gleniffer Braes between 1884 and 1895 had generated most of the Burns statue funds, declared that 'to a very large extent' the statue had been 'raised by the working girls of Paisley', who had not only sung in the choir but had contributed their 'programme sixpences' for the same end.[18] There were those who suggested that it was 'neither the choir nor the singing' that had drawn thousands to the open air concerts held in June on the slopes of Gleniffer Braes, hinting at less refined motives, but no one much disagreed that 'the money flowed in' from attendees from Paisley and Glasgow, and that the campaign for the statue therefore had been 'a public movement'.[19]

Even so, other than for Glasgow and to a lesser degree Kilmarnock and Paisley, it is difficult to disagree with the conclusion contemporaries reached, that it was upon the middle classes that the success of the fund-raising campaigns largely depended. But there were gradations within this category: in Dumfries it was 'tradespeople' (meaning, presumably, sole proprietors and small businessmen) rather than the 'better off' who received the lion's share of the credit.[20] But the solid middle classes too could be and were adversely affected by extraneous economic events that had apparently slowed the flow of subscriptions from labouring people in Dumfries. Indeed the backdrop to the Burns statue movement was the so-called Great Depression (1873–96), which in a sense makes it all the more remarkable that albeit more tardily than the Burns statue campaigners hoped for, monies were raised. In addition there were more immediate challenges. Dundee was hard hit as competitive pressure from Calcutta on the city's dominant jute industry mounted after 1873. Both the Dundee and Dumfries statue campaigns suffered from the catastrophic failure of the City of Glasgow Bank in 1878, and the collapse in business confidence that followed in 1879.[21] In Montrose the fishing and flax spinning industries had been buoyant when the Burns statue campaign had been initiated, but soon became depressed, leading to a loss of population – and of potential subscribers.[22] Especially important therefore for several of the campaigns, in that they could raise significant sums of money over periods of two or three days, were bazaars, organised by the statue committees who did their best to recruit influential patrons, managed by women stallholders, and patronised on weekdays by the middle classes and on Saturday afternoons by working people.[23] However, even this was not enough to meet the funding target set initially for Dumfries. At the end of 1879 only £500 of the £3,000 hoped for had been subscribed and, accordingly, ambitions had to be scaled back so that the project could be completed with a more modest £950.

If working-class subscriptions disappointed, the campaigners' hopes of working-class engagement with and their enthusiasm for the Burns statue projects did meet expectations. Organised labour in the nineteenth century, wrote the late William Walker, 'was always anxious for a place in the Liberal ascendancy' and was prepared to be 'properly deferential in the hope of securing it.'[24] With hardly an exception, invitations by the statue committees to the organised trades and friendly societies in their respective vicinities to attend at and participate in the ceremonies to lay foundation stones and to unveil the statues were warmly welcomed. In preparation for the Glasgow inauguration, representatives of several of the city's and the west of Scotland trade associations as well as Pointhouse Shipbuilding Works and the Saracen Foundry met with the statue committee to discuss the arrangements for the day, to which they gave their whole-hearted support.[25] Indeed so keen were working people to take part in such processions that they frequently travelled long distances to do so. One of the most impressive instances is that of the 700 or so of the workmen employed by a Mr Scott, the contractor for Leith's new docks, who journeyed to Kilmarnock by special train for the inauguration of the Kay Park monument and statue, accompanied by their own band, the 1st Mid-Lothian Rifles, and two pipers 'in full Highland costume'.[26]

The norm was that for weeks in advance working people threw themselves enthusiastically into the preparations. They made banners, placards and examples of the products of their particular workplaces, including, in the case of engineers, ingenious working models of steam engines and the like. The mottoes and symbols painted on the flags and banners were the same as those seen in similar demonstrations of respectable artisans elsewhere in Victorian Britain, with much emphasis on craft skill, the strength of trade unity and the virtue of mutual support. Representative of the genre was the trade flag carried by Dundee's Boiler Makers and Iron Shipbuilders which proclaimed, 'God help them who help themselves', along with four panels depicting 'Sickness', 'Relief to Widow', 'Accident' and 'Superannuation'.

It is highly likely that at least some of this material had been used on previous occasions and was brought out of store for the Burns ceremonials. Confirmation of this comes from descriptions of the procession that preceded the unveiling of Glasgow's Burns statue in 1877. The coopers and coach-makers impressed with the 'fine models' they were carrying, but described in mildly mocking terms too were their flags, that looked 'as if they had more than once done duty in the cause of Reform'; nor would it be the last time that artefacts associated with earlier reform demonstrations were seen on the streets of Glasgow.[27] But here as elsewhere what is important is that the re-used material culture of political reform was utilised again on public events associated with Robert Burns, as at the unveiling of the Dumfries Burns in 1879 where the hammermen and the smiths both bore flags dating back to 1832.[28] Burns and constitutional reform were linked again in 1886 when at the demonstration in Kilmarnock to commemorate the publication a century earlier of the first edition of Burns' poems, both the Burns statue and the Reformers' Monument that had been finished the previous year were 'adorned with evergreens and floral devices'.[29] In Dundee too – in 1884 – marchers on a mass demonstration in support of the Franchise Bill made a deliberate choice to process past the statues of the radical reformer George Kinloch as well as that of Burns, in recognition of the fact that Burns was 'the poet of the people and of liberty'.[30]

It is clear, however, that many banners and other devices were made specifically for the Burns statue unveilings and other public demonstrations held in honour of the poet. Interspersed with those described already were others that carried portraits of Burns, characters dressed to represent him, and as well-known subjects such as Tam o' Shanter and Souter Johnny. Visible too were lines in his praise such as 'Honour to Scotia's Bard', and short extracts from his poems and songs, amongst which 'A Man's a Man' was prominent.[31]

Most of the time the processions were overwhelmingly male in their composition, as were the platform parties of dignitaries. Women did begin to make an appearance though, with 150 'young girls' forming part of the procession for the commemoration of the centenary of the first edition of Burns' poems in Kilmarnock.[32] Their part in the ceremony was to place their wreaths of daisies as a votive offering at the poet's shrine. In 1896 in Dumfries female powerloom weavers formed part of a sizeable representation from Rosefield Mills, makers of woollens and tweeds. There were also some twenty dairy maids – with the sentimentalised sexism that was a hallmark of Burns commemoration in Victorian Scotland revealed in a banner purporting to represent Burns and his wife Jean Armour and inscribed 'Wilt thou be my dearie' and 'To woo a bonny lass when the kye come hame'.[33]

Although visual evidence shows they were in the minority, women were amongst the working people who formed the greatest part of the crowds who thronged to watch the unveilings. For mainly local reasons labouring class representation was less obvious in Ayr, Paisley, Aberdeen and Stirling, where those attending were more restrained (and seem to have included more middle-class women), as they were where Burns statues were inaugurated overseas. Audiences in the United States, Canada and Australia and New Zealand – often more respectable in terms of social class than in Scotland – were enthusiastic enough about Burns and his appeal to a common humanity, but their admiration for him was based in part on backward-looking sentimental attachments to the Scotland they or their forefathers had left behind.[34] In 1870s and 1880s Scotland Burns was still a force for change.

What is striking, too, about the large-scale Burns-related public commemorations of the later nineteenth century is the degree of consensus that surrounded them. We have noted already that the core values of Scotland's employing classes were not unlike those of their workers, a sense of common purpose made public by the presence in the processions of displays representing particular firms and workplaces, noted above.[35] Notwithstanding the passion with which orators on such occasions could speak for Scotland, there are few visible signs that the backcloth of the British union state against which the ceremonials were conducted was a cause of dissent, unsurprising perhaps given the strength of the commitment of patriotic Scots like Rosebery to the British Empire.[36] Thus for the laying of the foundation stone of the Burns monument in Kilmarnock in 1878, a 'Song' – drawing consciously and crudely on 'A Man's a Man' – was written and published in the local press. The penultimate stanza runs:

> And Volunteers that guard our isle
> Frae foreign foes, and a' that,
> In marshall'd raw comes one and a',
> And swell our ranks and a' that,
> And a' that, and a' that,
> Like Burns lang syne and a' that,
> Mid wars' alarms he shouldered arms,
> For Britons' rights and a' that.[37]

Indeed at formal Burns events it became increasingly common from the time of the South African (or Boer) War onwards for speakers to add their voices to the drive to recruit volunteers for the army; hesitatingly at first, by 1912 Burns was being cast in the role of recruiting sergeant.[38] Flags abounded, but it was the Union Jack that predominated, and in some cases was a central focus, being draped over more than one of the statues of Burns prior to their unveiling.

It could be argued that the consensual appearance of the demonstrations is what might be expected, given that the statue committees, working hand-in-hand with the civic authorities, had orchestrated the unveilings. But in Dumfries in 1882, where, unusually, the decoration of the burgh's buildings ands streets was left to the inhabitants, the visual messages were the same. The overwhelming impression is of a burgh proud to declare its Scottishness (the Scottish standard was flown from the Queensberry Hotel) and its affection for Burns as a friend of the people and liberty. But more often this was wrapped within a British flag – as a verse displayed in Glasgow Street made clear:

> We'll hoist the Union Jack on high,
> An' shout out three times thrice
> In memory of the brain and pen
> That wrote for liberty.[39]

The same messages were conveyed in many of the speeches. Thus in his peroration at the unveiling of the Burns statue in Aberdeen's Union Terrace in 1892, the historian and literature scholar Professor David Masson (1822–1907) claimed Burns as 'the supreme poet of Scotland by every claim to that title'. 'Scots Wha Hae' was 'the Scottish national lyric for all time' and the poetical expression of Scottish nationality. Yet (and underlining Chris Harvie's description of the song as enigmatic as regards Scottish identity) Masson went on, 'Scots Wha Hae' existed 'indestructibly' among 'the powers and forces of the present composite and united British body politic', in the service of which it would be of 'incalculable utility' as a war cry for Scottish regiments on the battlefield, their Scottish soul recovered through its singing.[40] Masson's stance, though, was in keeping with the prevailing sense in Scotland of its people's military prowess, 'a nation that bred warriors and soldiers'.[41] This was reinforced by the ubiquitous presence at Burns ceremonials of local Volunteer regiments (then in their heyday and, increasingly, recruited from the urban working classes). Where they were given, gun salutes offered aural support. Not unusual either were regimental bands which played the music to which those in the processions marched.

But to what were such loyal demonstrations being directed? Many Scots had convinced themselves that 1707 had been a union of equals. It was their duty periodically to remind England of this, and of Scotland's independence dating back to the days of Robert the Bruce. Such thinking evidently lay behind the speech of Dumfries' provost, Joseph Glover, at the luncheon that followed the laying of wreaths at Burns' grave at the mausoleum on the centenary of his death, in 1896. To cheers, Glover called Dumfries 'the shrine of Scottish independence'. Further acclamation accompanied his assertion that 'on this soil and in this climate of the free' the name of Robert Burns was 'enshrined in the hearts of the Scottish people . . . here . . . and wherever Scotsmen gather; wherever the Union Jack floats, proudly proclaiming the sovereignty of our beloved Queen'.[42]

*　*　*

Yet if patriotic speech making of this kind induced unity, there are signs, if not of dissent, that at least some of those involved had agendas which diverged somewhat from those of more politically conservative members of the organising committees. In the nineteenth century generally, artisans seized grand civic processions as a welcome opportunity to proclaim their craft skills and respectability and the extent to which they shared the values of bourgeois society. But at the same time, while nothing like a declaration of class war, the presence of working people in such numbers was also a demonstration of the prominent place in society – and potential power – of organised labour.[43] Not only does this underpin the notion of contestation over public space; it is indicative too of the limits there were to liberal bourgeois hegemony. In its form, appearance and route the procession preceding the unveiling of the statue of Burns in Glasgow in 1877 was very similar to the great Reform League march held in the city in 1866 and its predecessor prior to the Reform Act of 1832. The marchers assembled on a mud-laden Glasgow Green, the traditional mustering point for political marches and demonstrations; for centuries it had been and remained still the people's park.[44] Significantly, the carters who were, by tradition, to be at the head of the procession, behind a regimental band, were preceded by 'an advance guard' and a lorry 'built up with evergreens [a device suggesting freshness and longevity], and conspicuously flaunting the legend of the day, as it might be called, "A man's a man for a' that"'.

Even more explicit in its meaning were the good wishes expressed by the same contingent for the 'growth of the tree of liberty', the symbol used by radicals in Scotland from the time of the French Revolution.[45] The tree of liberty of course had been strongly associated with the harder-edged radicalism of the early years of the French Revolution. And even if there are serious doubts about Burns' authorship of the 'Tree of Liberty', published in 1838, it seems likely that whoever did write it (a close contemporary, Alexander Geddes, is one suggestion) was much influenced by Burns – whose commitment to liberty in a number of contexts was well-known and often celebrated, as we have seen.[46]

But context was critical. There was little sign of any breaches in the consensus over Burns in Dundee – certainly as far as its men were concerned. The town's governing elite in the 1860s and 1870s was proud of its association with political radicalism. The first public statue to be erected was that of George Kinloch (in 1872), after a struggle of almost forty years, initially in the face of Tory opposition. Like Glasgow, Dundee became staunchly Liberal, in all of its hues. At the unveiling of the Burns statue on 16 October 1880 some cat-calling of civic dignitaries who were seen to be too obviously flaunting their social standing by arriving in carriages was the only audible sign of dissent. Even the presence of 500 Orangemen whom the organisers had tried to exclude on the grounds that 'unpleasant party feeling might be manifested' was peaceable, although 'party music' was banned and they were closely watched by a contingent of plain-clothed and uniformed police.[47]

There was little restraint in the speeches. There were the usual acknowledgements of Burns' 'abhorrence of tyranny and oppression in all its forms', and his importance as a poet of Scotland's everyday life, who had 'thrown a mantle over much of the scenery of Scotland'. (Nostalgia, yes, but the countryside was also manna for mill workers, one of whom a few years beforehand had described himself as a 'caged bird'.[48]) And very much in keeping with what we have noted already, Frank Henderson MP, the main platform speaker, paid tribute to Burns' patriotism and 'Scots Wha Hae'' – 'the greatest war-ode ever penned or sung' (Plate 14).

Yet, Henderson announced, the 'true secret of his fame, and the explanation for the unbounded enthusiasm of the people for his memory' lay in 'the example and inciting them to the practices of manly independence which was so conspicuously characteristic of himself'. If Burns was a teacher, he had also been a liberator:

He shed a glory round the struggles of honest poverty. He lifted labour and set it upon a throne.

> The honest man, though e'er so poor,
> Is king o' men for a' that.

(Cheers.) He showed that nobility of soul was confined to no rank in life, but was to be found in the cottage as well as the palace . . . Under the inspiration of these two ideas with which Burns had furnished him – the essential dignity of his labour and the possible nobility of his life – the Scottish working man became transformed. (Cheers.)[49]

The millenarian quality of Henderson's address was echoed in the evening at a concert in the town's Theatre Royal organised by the Burns Club.[50] Recited before a large and highly enthusiastic audience was the radical tailor and poet James Young Geddes' evangelical ode, 'Prophet, Priest, and King', in which Burns is accorded the role of Christ's disciple:

> Now, in a common mood,
> Have said the multitude:
> 'We shall show forth his praise,
> And here his image raise
> Which shall the symbol be
> Of reverenced honesty.

'Midst all our strife and strain,
Our grasping greed of gain,
Not wholly gone are we
In base idolatry.
So shall his presence be
Within the city square
A living memory –
The scent of summer flowers,
A breath of purer air
In fever-laden hours
A solace for poor souls
Drifting to unknown goals,
A soothing influence,
A symbol to the sense
Of holier, higher things
Than Mammon's offerings.

And shall we then deride,
Expostulate, and chide,
Sneer at the people's whim,
Despite their offering,
And inly mock at him,
Their prophet, priest, and king!'[51]

Around the same time, too, Jeanie Paterson, from Springburn, near Glasgow, was writing along similar lines. Paterson's debt to Burns is obvious, in her poem 'A Brighter Dawn':

Long has the tyrant reigned supreme, but vengeance now
    awakes,
'Tis liberty we plead, for the earth's foundation shakes,
And liberty we're sure to gain, for by our toil and pains,
Have we not trammeled been, too long held in oppression[']s
    chains,
'Tis coming! Yes, tis coming, the age of liberty,
When man to man in brotherhood shall linked more strongly
    be.[52]

Even more directly associating Burns with a sense of anticipation of a better tomorrow were banners such as one of those carried during the

centennial in Dumfries in 1896: not only was it one of the most prominent, but upon it was printed the stirring line, 'Now's the Time and
Now's the Hour'. Also visible, held aloft by the employees of Dumfries
ironworks, was 'an old Chartist flag, with the inscription "Scotland
shall be free" '.[53]

It is from Dumfries too that we have the clearest indication that
working-class participation could be conditional. There the trades
announced that they would refuse to take part in the procession if the
Police Commissioners gave permission for a grandstand to be erected,
as proposed by the statue committee. (The same committee had caused
resentment earlier by organising a dinner to follow the inauguration
ceremony costing four shillings and sixpence, a prohibitive price for
ordinary Dumfriesians.) Such a structure, it was protested, 'would place
the favoured classes above the heads of other people', while a platform
right round the statue would restrict the view from 'the people'.
Reluctantly, the statue committee conceded the point and agreement
was reached that there should be a small platform for the key participants at the unveiling, and a barricade to protect it.[54] Even then the
assembled crowd was unusually noisy – another reason why Rosebery
had cut short his speech, and a sign perhaps that not all was harmonious. And despite the massive turnout in Kilmarnock in August 1886 for
the centenary of the publication there of the *Poems*, the trades were
notable by their absence, perhaps because they had not been represented
on the organising committee, choosing instead to enjoy the fact that
labour 'was virtually suspended in the town after nine o' clock'.[55]

Although we should be careful not to exaggerate its extent, the
strained consensus over Burns this evidence hints at was it seems
recognised by the statue committees, and other elite Burns sponsors.
Not unlike the apprehension that had been felt by Scotland's Tories in
the first half of the century about Burns' radicalism, was anxiety about
the greater frequency and increasingly public portrayal of Burns as a
working class hero, and his appropriation in the interest of class. By
the early 1880s socialist ideas were beginning to circulate in Scotland,
and a cause of disquiet for many middle class Scots.[56] More worrying
for the Burns promoters upon whom we focused in chapter 4, these
were being linked with and for that reason legitimised by, Burns. One
of the most telling illustrations comes from 1872 – just as the Glasgow
Burns statue movement got under way – when William Elder delivered
a lecture that was later published, in which he argued that Burns
should be admired by 'every working man ... whose hands are

hardened, whose brow is suffused with the dew drops of honest toil'. Why? Largely, Elder contended, because Burns was a Scotsman, but that while he loved Scotland, and nature, 'most of all' he loved the poor. The only hatred of which he was capable was confined to 'hypocrites and sycophants', and the poor's oppressors.[57]

Working-class poets too continued to acknowledge their debt to Burns in inspiring them to write verse that was published in the cheap newspapers and journals read by their peers. Some we have mentioned already. Janet Hamilton was one of these, a well-known and much admired poet who in 'A Plea for the Doric' (1865) was unequivocal about the importance to Scots of the vernacular (which, as we have seen in previous chapters, was feared to be in decline) and of its potency in Burns' hands:

> Juist think gif the 'Cottar's ain Saturday nicht'
> War stripped o' the Doric, we' English bedicht –
> To the leal Scottish heart it wad ne'er be the saem;
> Wi' sic truth and sic feelin' it wadnae strike hame.

Hamilton's importance here is that she may have been fairly representative of the class from which she came, and the attitudes and values of its members. She was one of a number of poets of the period from relatively humble backgrounds who deployed the 'mither tongue' as an emblem of Scottish national collective memory but also as a powerful critique of aspects of industrialisation.[58] Twentieth-century critics of nineteenth-century poets who followed in Burns' footsteps have castigated them for failing to come to terms with industrial Scotland, and instead idealising rustic life, pouring out, in Hugh MacDiarmid's words, 'an abyss of worthless rubbish unparalleled in any other European literature'.[59] The failure was MacDiarmid's, however, for having overlooked powerful evocations, written in the vernacular, of the country's new mining and manufacturing heartlands, as in Hamilton's ' A Wheen Aul' Memories' that looks back at Lanarkshire's revolutionised landscape. At Gartsherrie, for example, the location of the Baird dynasty's mammoth coal and ironworks, the former cottages have gone:

> An' the place whaur they stood I scarce ken
>   Noo ava,
> For there's roarin' o' steam an' there's reegin o' wheels,
> Men workin', an' sweatin', and swearin' like deils.

In their ability to convey the tribulations of the labouring poor, auto-didacts such as Hamilton but also the former colliery manager David Wingate (mentioned in chapter 4) were able to provide an empathetic voice for their readers.[60] Others grasped Burns' sentiments and adapted them as weapons of class war. An example is Dundee's Adam Wilson, 'The Factory Muse' who had become a mill worker at the age of twelve. His published work, which was said to have had 'an influence deep and far reaching' amongst the 'toiling thousands' of industrial Dundee, was uncompromising in its attack on the capitalist system and its inequalities.[61] The process by which Burns could be hijacked in support of what were current industrial issues like the ten hours movement, but also for socialism, is to be seen in Wilson's 'Brotherhood of Man', the second stanza of which runs:

> With meagre wage and hours too long, we'll strive now to curtail
> The working day, and have our pay set to some equal scale;
> For Labour's share in Capital's our principle and plan,
> For universal fellowship and brotherhood of man.

Even more obviously borrowed from Burns' 'A Man's a Man' is the message conveyed at the end of the poem:

> By birth and blood we are the same, though some distinguished
>   are;
> What better is the royal brow beneath its crown and star?
> All are part of those who breathed first at creation's dawn,
> In universal fellowship and brotherhood of man.

It was sentiments of this kind that may have induced the editor of the *Dumbarton Herald* in what was a carping commentary on the progress and achievement of the Glasgow Burns statue movement – headed 'The Glasgow Burns Monument Bungle' – to condemn the decision to restrict subscriptions to one shilling. Burns 'was not the mere exponent of the feelings of a class', he complained. As Burns was the national poet, the 'pounds of the rich' should have joined the 'shillings of the poor'.[62]

But it was in some of the speeches that were delivered at the unveiling ceremonies that were heard the most explicit, 'official' correctives to those who sought to represent Burns as the poet of a single class.

In the main, Liberals had few qualms about acknowledging the radicalism that was part of their pedigree, and as we saw in the previous chapter were happy to identify with Burns. They continued to do so. In Dumfries in 1896, for example, for the centenary of Burns' death the outside of the Liberal Club rooms were decorated with a portrait of Burns, a thistle and, on a yellow backing edged with rose – Rosebery's colours – the motto, 'Man to man, the warld o'er, / Shall brithers be, for a' that.'[63] Yet there was nervousness about the consequences of what some saw as the too rapid march to universal suffrage. This was especially so with those who had gone along with the franchise reforms reluctantly, conceding them as Gladstone did as a reward rather than a right, or who shared with Scotland's Lord Advocate in the 1850s and 1860s, Henry Moncreiff a distaste for the 'unmanly' secret ballot of 1872 – and the loss of patronage this entailed.[64] Thus even in the staunch Radical-Liberal stronghold of Dundee, George Gilfillan prior to his death was inclined to downplay Burns' political radicalism, preferring to promote him as the poet of the people – in the widest sense of the term.[65]

In Dundee too there was another issue that required some mediation about how Burns was to be understood. Convinced by the 1870s that low-level lawlessness was more of a problem in Dundee than in Scotland's other industrial cities, its leading citizens had good reason to focus their attentions on the moral improvement of their town's women workers – judged by many to be a major cause of the city's reputation as a sink of iniquity.[66] With this in mind the Reverend David Macrae, in his communion Sunday sermon in the Kinnaird Hall the day following the unveiling of the Burns statue, distinguished what was 'great and good and beautiful in Burns' from what he thought was bad. Into this last category fell Burns' identification of drinking and drunkenness with love and happiness, and freedom, and hospitality. It was on the streets of Dundee, through drink – 'Scotland's national sin and national shame', according to Macrae – that love turned to lust, wisdom to folly, intelligence into mental chaos and imbecility, as well as brawling, riot and brutality.[67] Professor Wilson sixty-one years earlier had imagined 'The Cotter's Saturday Night' in the hands of Radicals. For Macrae excessive drinking was creating a similarly nightmarish outcome.[68]

A similar tone, induced by concern that Burns might be misread, had been adopted three years earlier in Glasgow, by Lord Houghton. On the evening following the George Square inauguration of the Burns statue he had spoken to around 250 of Glasgow's elite gentlemen who had paid 25 shillings for what was called a 'grand banquet'. Echoing the calls for stoicism (on the part of the working classes) in the face of adversity made at the Ayr festival in 1844, Houghton asserted that it never crossed Burns' mind that there was 'anything either sorrowful or miserable in his own position' – as a hard-working ploughman. Burns, he went on, 'took his daily work just as he took his daily sustenance, and . . . sang just as happily during that work as he sang in his own emphatic and wonderful language of the common daily bread and food of the Scottish farmer'. It was recognition of this and of their shared experience that explained the veneration of Burns by 'every peasant and artisan' who had participated in the day's proceedings. Houghton drew his remarks to a close by celebrating Burns' role as a collector of Scotland's ballad literature and as a poet whose work directed the 'popular imagination in good and wholesome lines'.

So influenced, Scotland would not go into 'the violent socialistic extravagances and impossible forms of society, and which have ended in the burning of Paris', a barely concealed reference to the bloody, socialist- and republican-inspired Paris Commune of 1871, only six years previously.[69] Prudently perhaps, Houghton had kept such views to himself when he had spoken in George Square earlier in the day. Then he had emphasised the part Burns had played in the making of the enterprising Scot who, by his travels, had extended Burns' global reach. His evening address, however, had gone down equally well; at its end, it was reported, there was 'loud and prolonged cheering'.[70]

Two years later, at the unveiling of the Kilmarnock monument and statue, the main speaker the local MP Claud Alexander of Ballochmyle, a Conservative whose presence had been assured by changing the date of the inauguration to suit his diary, made his feelings on what lessons should be taken from Burns clear – and in public. 'Because Burns deprecated the incense offered to rank', maintained Alexander, 'he did not mean to imply any special merit in the absence of it. Because he showed that a man was still a man without the "guinea stamp", he did not judge that he might not equally be a man with it, or, if you like, in spite of it.' 'If it be right', Alexander continued, 'to avoid undue laudation of the upper', it is equally important to guard against 'unwholesome and extravagant adulation of the lower classes of society.'[71]

Unveiling the Burns statue in Montrose, Andrew Carnegie, too, used as his text 'A Man's a Man'. Carnegie expressed satisfaction that Britain had followed the United States in widening the franchise, giving each man the vote and 'making all citizens equal' thereby. Progressive taxation had a similar effect, 'keeping our race ever in advance in establishing the rights of man and marching steadily towards perfection'. It was with such a vision that Macrae in Dundee had ended his sermon. He had been heartened the day previous by the sight of thousands 'mustering in friendship, marching in harmony' and united in their admiration for Burns who had 'lightened their labour ... and nerved their arms in manly work' and cheered their homes. Furthermore, he declared, he had left with his faith strengthened of 'that truth and love by which conflicting interests will be reconciled, and the animosity of class to class, and nation to nation, overcome'. Without further comment Macrae then ended his sermon by reciting four lines from 'A Man's a Man'.

In his address, however, that also envisaged a world free of conflict, Carnegie was unable to resist making the point that progress towards emancipation – that had drawn on Burns' tenets – had been achieved peacefully:

> No violence, no physical force, all ... in order. Ballots not bullets; argument, not riot; all classes hand in hand co-operating as members of one family for the general weal of all law abiding classes ensures the happiness of every proper class.[72]

Such views chimed closely with leading Burnsians elsewhere. In January 1880, at the inaugural meeting of the London Burns Club, held in Rae Brown's Kensington home, Perth-born Charles Mackay spoke of his concern that Burns was being misinterpreted as commending the poor over the well off. Mackay was the former editor of the liberal, free trade supporting *Glasgow Argus*.[73] For the avoidance of any doubt – and as someone who shared with Samuel Smiles, and, as we have seen, most of his class, a belief in the virtues of self-help and independence – Mackay had felt it necessary to compose a couple of supplementary verses to 'A Man's a Man'. They are worth reporting in full:

> A man's a man', says Robert Burns,
> 'For a' that and a' that',
> But though the song be clear and strong,
> It lacks a note for a' that.
> The lout who'd shirk his daily work,
> Yet claim his wage and a' that,
> Or beg when he might earn his bread,
> Is <u>not</u> a man for a' that.

For a' that and a' that,
'Tis soul and heart and a' that
That makes the king a gentleman,
And not the crown and a' that.
And whether he be rich or poor,
The best he is for a' that
Who stands erect in self-respect,
And acts the man for a' that.

The speeches, however, were ephemeral, and, as far as is known, until their publication here, Mackay's attempts to embellish Burns had been heard only by Rae Brown's guests. What mattered were the statues – the permanent memorials to Burns. Their promoters had high hopes for them. Typical was the final section of David Masson's peroration at the unveiling of Aberdeen's Burns statue in September 1892. Standing near the town's centre:

> ... after all of us are gone, Aberdonians, old and young, will be passing and repassing it, glancing at it as they pass, and muttering to themselves, as they do now, the magical name of Robert Burns.[74]

But what Burns had the memorials secured? What messages would the statues' silent voices convey?

SIX

'Burns by an Englishman is impossible'

Burns, Scotland and socialism

As might be expected there was a palpable sense of pride in those places where memorials of Burns were erected. There was pleasure too when they seemed to serve the purposes for which they were built. Thus, on sight of the sculptor George Ewing's model for George Square in 1875 the *Glasgow Herald* declared its delight that Ewing had created 'a people's statue ... idealised as his peasant admirers would idealise him'[1] (Plate 15). Ewing had resisted the temptation of sacrificing 'true artistic feeling' to the ideal of the mob. Faithful to the well-known half-length portrait of Burns painted by Alexander Nasmyth in Edinburgh 1787 (an essential requirement, as will be seen below) and 'enriched with some traits from [Archibald] Skirving [who had also sketched Burns]', this was a Burns with which his audience would be familiar. The Kilmarnock bonnet under his right arm, and the period clothes of the small tenant farmer in which he was dressed were also instantly recognisable. Burns is portrayed in his prime, physically and as a poet – alluded to by the daisy in his left hand which had 'led him in a train of glorious thought', manifested in one of his most popular poems, 'To a Mountain Daisy'. Notwithstanding the vulgarity of what the *Herald* termed a 'little sacrifice to public taste', this was the Burns his backers had wanted to promote, or, as *The Builder* put it: 'not too lofty a conception ... [nor one] which is meretricious or commonplace on the other'.[2] Burns within touching distance, a Burns working men could emulate.

Satisfaction was expressed too with the Kilmarnock Burns two years later. The likeness to the Nasmyth portrait was 'striking and complete'. The pose of the figure was 'all that could be desired', representing better than the much smaller model had suggested it would, 'the sentiment intended' (Plate 16). As in Glasgow, Burns was dressed in the period clothes of a farmer. His standing pose – 'as if in a musing attitude' – was also similar. In one hand was a pencil and in the other a notebook. At the foot of the tree trunk upon which the poet's hand lay resting, was a daisy – 'Mountain Daisy' being the motto for the model as submitted to the statue committee by William Grant Stevenson (1849–1919). This was the theme adopted too by Henry Bain-Smith (1853–1893) for his Burns statue in Aberdeen.[3]

Carved from nine tons of pale Sicilian marble, Stevenson's statue was placed in an elevated position at the centre of the south façade of a pyramidal custom-built cenotaph designed by local architect R. S. Ingram. The ornate monument was situated in newly laid out gardens on a rise on the north-eastern edge of the town – Kay Park. Alongside was a 'magnificent' fountain adorned with five mermaids, which, like the park itself, had been donated by local benefactors. What had been constructed was, in effect, a massive reliquary, redolent with the religious connotations typical of the Gothic revival architecture of the period.[4] Kilmarnock's Monument and Statue Committee were convinced that they were gifting to the town, 'the finest Monumental Building and Statue of BURNS ever erected in Britain', a boast later inflated by advertisements for what was also a library and museum, which proclaimed Stevenson's statue as 'the finest in the world'.[5]

The numinous quality of Kilmarnock's tribute to Burns had echoes in Dumfries. After Rosebery had spoken at the unveiling of Amelia Paton Hill's Burns, carved from Italian Carrera marble, cheer after cheer 'continued to be raised by the immense crowd' who, spellbound, 'strained their eyes gazing at the statue, upon which the sun showered all its luminous splendour'[6] (Plate 17). The white marble figure, Rembrandt-like, a 'masterpiece . . . that cannot be surpassed' according to Hugh MacGregor, the statue committee treasurer, stood forth as a 'thing of life and light' against the dark backdrop of the onlookers and the surrounding buildings, a scene that, unusually for the time, was captured on camera.[7] The statue committee's defence of a marble statue rather than longer lasting bronze, however, makes for uncomfortable reading in the twenty-first century: 'It would have been a singular anomaly . . . if a dingy figure had been exhibited at the north end of Dumfries, representing Burns as a Mongolian, while at the south end, under the Mausoleum he appears truthfully as a member of the white Caucasian race' (a reference to Turnerelli's much criticised representation of Burns).[8]

In Dundee (where the unveiling ceremony was also photographed) the *Courier & Argus* proclaimed Sir John Steell's study of Burns as a 'triumph in art'. Burns was presented as a lover, farmer and poet. He gazes at the morning star as he composes, quill poised, his lyrical lament 'To Mary in Heaven', his lost love (Plate 18). This was Mary Campbell, with whom he had had a brief but intense relationship in the spring of 1786. Campbell, however, died within months of their tryst, so crushing any hopes Burns may have had of a life with her, perhaps in the West Indies where he had had plans to emigrate prior to the triumphal reception of his Kilmarnock edition. The statue, described as one of Steell's 'most successful efforts', would, the *Courier* declared, form 'one of the most attractive ornaments in the town'.[9] The national *Art Journal* (at this time) was equally effusive, commending the citizens of both New York and Dundee, 'as custodians of a statue at once lofty in conception, vigorous in design, and faithful as to execution'.[10] Aberdeen's Burns, by Henry Bain-Smith, was judged by the town's *Free Press* to be 'an excellent piece of sculpture, and a credit to the artist', and 'a distinct addition to the artistic features of Union Terrace, and to the amenity of the locality generally'.[11] Paisley's *Daily Express* gently chastised the town's citizenry for their tardiness, but expressed satisfaction that 'at last' we have a statue of Burns 'and one too, of which, as a work of art, we have reason to be proud'.[12]

But any expectation that Scotland's city fathers and their fellow Burns club memorialists might have had that they would share in the glory of the man whose memory they had been active in securing, were soon dashed. Even behind the scenes of local rejoicing at the time the statues were unveiled, were to be heard dissenting voices, and, over time, mounting criticism of the monuments themselves. Not spared either were those who had commissioned them. As in nineteenth-century Ireland, exaggerated enthusiasm for statuary that was often routine in nature betrayed a naïve admiration for artistic talent and made it difficult to establish critical distance.[13]

* * *

One has to be wary of sour grapes when disparaging comments came from outside the places where statues had been erected. A touch of civic envy seems to have been behind the caustic query raised by the *Dumbarton Herald*, grounded on the inclement weather that had marred the unveiling proceedings in Glasgow, 'as to the wisdom of honouring the dead by endangering the lives of the living'. The inaudibility of speakers was another complaint about which little could be done by inauguration ceremony organisers – the norm was to read the full speeches in the newspapers afterwards. Yet the negative reactions to Ewing's statue of Burns both before it was unveiled and in the months and years following suggests that there was something more substantial behind the sniping about the Glasgow project. We will return to the figure of Burns later, but note here the disappointment expressed that in terms both of its height and George Square location, Glasgow's Burns was on a 'par with a decent cotton yarn merchant who once on a time was to write MP after his name', a reference to Baron Marochetti's 1856 memorial of James Oswald, a reforming Liberal whose statue had recently been moved from Sandyford Place to the square to match that of the Tory Sir Robert Peel. Ewing's Burns may have been of 'heroic size', but its dimensions were almost exactly the same as the two politicians' memorials. As bad, and suggesting that Glasgow had less regard for the National Bard than for Sir Walter Scott, was that the Scott column towered above the statue of Burns which was also less grand than the equestrian memorials to Queen Victoria and Prince Albert (Plate 19).[14]

But even within Burns circles there had been reservations about Ewing's Burns. Ewing (1828–1884) had been a popular member of the Waverley Burns Club, having been elected unanimously as chairman in 1862. Examples of his work, too, had been seen and admired by club members, for instance a 'sketch in clay' of a bust of Flora Macdonald, and another he made of William Shakespeare for the Stratford playwright's tercentenary in 1864 – and it was the making of portrait busts that had established his reputation in Glasgow.[15] To be fair, Ewing had shown little interest in the Burns monument when it was first discussed by the club in August 1872 – although this might have been due to the fears he and other club members had that they would be called upon to fund-raise or even contribute to its cost directly.[16] Nevertheless his appointment as sculptor for the project had aroused bitter resentment, at the root of which, somewhat surprisingly, was James Hedderwick.

Despite being one of Glasgow's most prominent Burns enthusiasts, henceforth (after Ewing was awarded the commission) Hedderwick distanced himself from the statue movement. Piqued perhaps by the fact that the committee he had invited to join him may have had views at variance with his own, and possibly upset by a remark made in jest by Ewing about the newspaper proprietor's motives (more readers and sales income), the egoistical Hedderwick had objected to the decision of the statue committee not to hold a competition for the commission, and the nepotism this implied. The committee included several Waverley club members. Amongst them was Ewing's patron, Baillie William Wilson, who now assumed responsibility for fund-raising.[17] There was some concern too about Ewing's experience – in busts and marble statues, but nothing in bronze, although he was considered to be one of Glasgow's leading living sculptors (Plate 20).[18] Indeed this was the main justification given for his appointment (in most respects a 'made in Glasgow' movement, it was fitting that a 'local' artist – Ewing had been born in Birmingham, England – was appointed as sculptor).[19] Burdened by his own ambition to succeed, and the expectation that he was to produce 'the most complete [statue] of Burns in existence', he made slow progress, a delay for which he was publicly rebuked in some quarters.[20] Yet, as we saw at the start of this chapter, he also had his admirers. Even so, only days prior to the statue's inauguration – and conceding that the newspapers 'speak well of it as a work of art' – a correspondent of James M'Kie expressed doubts about the extent to which it represented Burns, judging that the face was 'too sonsie and heavy looking', more fitting perhaps as a likeness of the eighteenth-century writer Dr Samuel Johnson.[21]

In Dundee too there were revealing mutterings about the town's Burns statue. One local journalist evidently solicited opinions from the public within days of its unveiling. Most were critical – the statue was too low and lacked dignity, Burns' body was twisted and the cravat round his neck was too thick, elements that would elicit the comment some years later that while Burns 'was not a model of grace . . . there is no ground for believing that he was a hunchback' (Plate 21). From a somewhat different perspective but almost as damning was the observation made by one female wag that, 'thae legs could hae made him a grand partner in a fowersome reel'.[22] This set of largely negative comments was followed by others soon after, although in private correspondence rather than publicly. This was in 1885, when Andrew Carnegie, on being approached to subscribe to the Montrose Burns statue fund agreed to do so but urged the committee not to purchase a replica of the statue in New York (which Dundee had done). This he had found distressing. Indeed he had yet to see a satisfactory statue of Burns, but Steell's depiction of the poet seated, he concluded, was 'an outrage' and he would have no part in encouraging further versions of such a monstrosity.[23] Montrose's Burns, by Edinburgh's William Birnie Rhind (1853–1933), when it was eventually finished – and as we saw in chapter 5, unveiled by Carnegie – stood tall (Plate 22).

Similarly downbeat was the verdict of many of those who came to see Dumfries' Burns – a statue that some rancorous townspeople had thought unnecessary anyway, being prepared only to credit its promoters with having secured a day's holiday and a temporary influx of visitors.[24] From the outset there had been some belittling of the statue. It was made of marble rather than bronze. The carving of the working collie dog poorly represented Luath, from Burns' duologue, 'The Twa Dogs'. More seriously, the pedestal was too low for a statue of Burns that stood nine feet high. One consequence of this was that instead of inducing awe the monument became an object of ridicule. Sooner than elsewhere it was subject to minor acts of vandalism, as in September 1894 when 'a crown of heather was placed around the poet's brow' and red garters were added to his legs.[25] Although its supporters argued (with little conviction) that the nearness to eye level of the figure was an advantage, allowing spectators to examine it in detail, within five years the statue committee, under duress, had agreed to raise the pedestal by three feet. Nowhere else was the same mistake made, and certainly not Irvine where Burns was placed upon a pedestal of red Aberdeen granite standing twelve feet high.[26] Aberdeen's was even loftier.

But at least in Dumfries the statue in its central location of Church Place could be seen. Elsewhere this was not always the case. We know that Victorian sponsors of public statuary were convinced of its didactic virtues. Yet of Stevenson's Burns at Kilmarnock the art historian Edward Pinnington asked rhetorically, if it was to have its desired moral influence, would it 'not have found a better place amongst the people', rather than in a park some distance from the town centre. This was a proposition that had been put to – and rejected by – the statue committee as early as the autumn of 1877. Winning the argument were those who wanted Burns – like the Wallace monument on Stirling's Abbey Craig – to be set 'enthroned upon a hill'. Such a location for Burns would symbolise his high god-like status and immortality, and in addition be in sight of so many of the places with which he was associated locally and nearby. One of these was Mossgiel farm, 'in which the Muse of Coila consecrated her poet with . . . prophetic truth', and that many of his admirers held to be little short of sacred.[27] But Kilmarnock was not the only site under scrutiny. Why in Irvine was James Pittendrigh MacGillivray's statue of Burns – of which Pinnington very much approved – banished to Irvine Moor, 'away from humanity, from the men and women the poet loved, of whom and to whom he sang?'[28] (As in Kilmarnock there had been considerable local debate about the most appropriate location – and although a town centre site was rejected, even decades later there were hopes that the statue might be moved there.)[29] Pinnington might have said something similar about F. W. Pomeroy's Burns monument in Paisley, some way distant from the High Street throng in secluded Fountain Gardens. The prime site in the town centre, Dunn Square, was reserved for Thomas and Sir Peter Coats, thread manufacturers and major employers in Paisley. The opportunity had gone, almost certainly forever, 'A Burns Worker' wrote to the *Paisley Daily Express*, 'to adorn our principal square, and . . . honour our great national bard . . . not only to the present, but to future generations.'[30] Hopes that the Gardens would become 'the Valhalla of Paisley' failed to materialise (Plate 23).

*　*　*

But it was the memorials themselves that were the focus of most adverse comment. This was led in September 1889 by the *Glasgow Herald*, which published a series of articles headed 'Monument Building' – in reality a critique of the country's Burns statues. With Burns now supplanting in the eyes of some of his admirers Saint Andrew as Scotland's patron saint, his memorials had to be fit for their elevating purpose. The *Herald*'s writer was withering in his conclusions, and was soon followed by an equally damning critique published in *The Scotsman*. As indicators of public taste, judgment and wisdom the statues of Burns erected so far were inadequate, and little wonder, having been commissioned by 'small bodies of irresponsible men who usually know as much about sculpture as they do about the courses of the stars'. Indeed it was the patrons and town councils – ignorant, the *Herald*'s critic alleged, of artistic worth and about what could be achieved by Scottish sculpture, and conservative in their commissions – upon whose shoulders the responsibility for what had been constructed lay. But they were not wholly to blame. Four of the five large statues of Burns surveyed were the work of Scottish sculptors who, it was asserted, had failed in their duty to both the poet and the nation. What Scotland possessed was a series of statues of Burns that were 'painfully suggestive of incapacity'. It was a 'lamentable fact', trumpeted the *Herald*'s critic, that there was no statue 'of even approximately co-ordinate quality with his genius'; instead were statuesque caricatures.[31] *The Scotsman* more or less concurred: even if all the decent qualities of the statues then erected were thrown together into a composite statue, 'the result . . . would not be satisfying'.[32] The *Herald* was slightly more optimistic, and hoped that of the three statues then being planned, for Ayr, Paisley and Montrose respectively, at least one would be a monument worthy of Burns, and that harmonised 'in artistic merit with his position in Scottish literature'.

What impact this indictment of the product of the Burns statue movement had in Montrose is hard to say, as the campaign had run into the ground. The promoters of the statue in Ayr, however, not only took note but also acted by recruiting (within days of the appearance of the *Herald* articles) the English sculptor Hamo Thornycroft, a member of the Royal Academy, to advise them on the choice of sculptor.[33] The prolific Edinburgh-born sculptor George A. Lawson (1832–1904) was the man chosen. Paisley followed suit, and asked the celebrated London sculptor Thomas Brock to judge the competition there. This resulted in the appointment of London-born F. W. Pomeroy (1826–1924), a naturalist sculptor and a leading light in the Arts and Crafts movement.[34]

Brutal as it was, the *Herald* series was but the precursor of what by the mid 1890s had become a torrent of criticism. That some of this found an outlet in the Burns Federation's annual *Burns Chronicle* is perhaps surprising but it is indicative too of the dissatisfaction about the disparity between Burns' standing in Scotland and how he was being memorialised. To Burns, wrote a contributor using the pseudonym 'An Art Student', 'we are indebted . . . for elevating in us that manly and independent spirit which other nations acknowledge to be the outstanding characteristic of Scotsmen'. Yet, regrettably, 'in most of the statues of Burns, the art has not equaled the enthusiasm'.[35] He conceded the difficulty that sculptors of Burns had faced hitherto, which in part was due to restrictions on creativity imposed by the Victorian demand for portrait sculpture. As was outlined in the Introduction, the urge to see rather than imagine Scotland's heroic dead was paramount and by no means confined to Burns. This was in keeping with the European aesthetic predilection at the time for realism. Verity was key, and the reason why, in the weeks immediately prior to the unveiling of Paisley's Burns statue, a panel for the pedestal in which Tam o' Shanter was dressed in a kilt had to be hastily re-designed with Tam attired in the more authentic (for a Lowland Scot) knee breeches. Mirthful commentators ensured that Paisley's reputation in its efforts to commemorate Burns plummeted to a new low.[36]

But woe betide the sculptor of Burns who strayed from the Nasmyth image.[37] It was what commissioning committees, the general public and journalists insisted upon and expected – as we have seen. In itself, conformity to Nasmyth need not have been a problem. The 'Art Student' noted the 'fidelity' with which Stevenson had followed Nasmyth's portrait for his Kilmarnock Burns. He praised too the 'dignified and graceful' pose of the body, and concurred with those who had judged this to be 'one of the best realisations of the Poet that has yet been attempted'. Ayr's Burns, by George Lawson, who earned admiration elsewhere for his diligence in searching out 'the facts of the portraiture of Burns' – and who also relied heavily on Nasmyth – was considered to be acceptable too.[38] Upon others, however, the 'Art Student' frowned, the main failing being the 'heaviness in some of the figures which is inconsistent with the vigorous and active temperament of the Poet'. This was true, he argued, of Ewing's Burns, although he was prepared to defend it on the grounds that it showed 'a quiet reserve of power, and a pensiveness truly representative of one phase at least of the Poet's character'. But he could find few redeeming features in Paton Hill's 'heavy fat figure' of Burns in Dumfries. Betraying attitudes that would today be denounced as sexist, he described as 'woman-like' the array of accessories that formed part of the group – the daisy, the mouse and the 'carefully brushed collie' (Plate 24). Nor did he have much time for the 'effeminate twinkle' of an eye (of Burns) that should have been glowing (Plate 25). Dumfries, he concluded acidly, 'has yet to get a statue of Burns'.[39]

Also the subject of critical tirades was Steell's Burns in Dundee. This was not only because of the statue's shortcomings already alluded to, but also as it had failed to do justice to its creator who had been too old at the time of the commission 'to infuse much energy' into a work that was out of proportion and artificial in its composition. Steell was in his seventies (Plate 26). The statue had its admirers, but most opinion was negative, not only about its form but more so the subject matter. Steell was condemned for continuing to hold onto and give credence to the 'old and exploded' myth of Highland Mary and for portraying Burns in such a setting, thereby obscuring the poet's, 'worth, dignity, power, and greatness'.[40] There was certainly little obvious connection between Steell's depiction of a seated Burns, the statue's 'concentrated sentimentality', and the lofty ideals that had been enunciated and cheered at the inauguration ceremony. Pinnington's quip that 'Dundee would lose nothing if its Burns sat on the Sidlaw hills' was harsh, but his observation that 'of an ideal Burns it emits not a whisper' was apt for the time. As the *Glasgow Herald* had commented almost a decade earlier, Steell's memorial was far from being 'a fitting embodiment of the manly, independent, great-hearted and liberty-loving Burns'. Such was the penalty paid by Dundee's Burns statue sponsors for accepting a statue that had been commissioned for a very different purpose, namely to mirror Steell's statue of Sir Walter Scott – seated – in New York's Central Park. This was a copy of what the sculptor in his younger days had designed for the Scott Monument in Edinburgh in 1846. But even for Dundee's ardent Burns lover and former Radical Charles Maxwell, this seemed not to matter, his commitment to urban embellishment trumping all else. Steell's, he was convinced, 'was the most life-like statue of Burns within the British isles'.[41] And it was in Dundee.

There was a similar kind of disconnect between Ewing's Burns in Glasgow, paid for largely by the working classes and acclaimed by them on the day of its inauguration, but offering, 'no clear word to the city worker'; it was Burns 'uninspired, phlegmatic and dull, and gives out scant inspiration'.[42] But as with Henry Bain-Smith in Aberdeen – who also depicted the poet addressing a mountain daisy – Ewing was credited with having thought deeply about his subject.

But what both these instances reveal is something of a division between the art establishment in Scotland and the Burns-loving public: had there been a popular contest, Lawson's Burns in Ayr would have been voted the best statue of Burns yet erected, opined Edward Goodwillie in his classic survey published in 1911.[43] Lawson's success as a sculptor of Burns came late in the day, however, and it was after his death in 1904 when the first of five copies of his Burns for destinations abroad was unveiled – in Melbourne, Australia. By this time another Scottish artist was being crowned with the mantle of the best at Burns: James Pittendrigh MacGillivray (Plate 27).[44]

It was MacGillivray, a poet and early Scottish nationalist activist as well as a sculptor, who had broken the link with Nasmyth. At the turn of the 1890s he was emerging as an artist of note, but had failed to win the Ayr competition. Consequently, however, he was approached by John Spiers – an Irvine man who had flourished in business in Glasgow – to make a Burns statue from his unsuccessful model for his native burgh. It was MacGillivray's first major commission.[45] The antecedents had not impressed him: he had seen most and they were all contemptible. In Dundee he had found 'a Methodist like person writhing in the throes of an address to Mary in heaven'; he fled from Bain-Smith's in Aberdeen; Lawson's Burns in Ayr 'neither in mood nor physique would . . . do'; Paton Hill's in Dumfries lacked character. Glasgow's was worse, Ewing's Burns suggesting 'a great heavy innkeeper, publican type of man' – a bourgeois Burns – an 'utter libel' that he wished the city's Burns club would remove and 'put fire in it by melting the whole metal desecrated by such a shape'. But MacGillivray's ire was expressed most pointedly in the direction of Flaxman and Pomeroy. Flaxman had produced a 'rigid, mummy looking statue' without the 'faintest idea' of the 'man of molten metal' he was dealing with. Pomeroy's Burns resembled 'a Sussex peasant leaning on his plough with an extravagance of pose which might be styled French' – recognition of Pomeroy's place in the French-influenced naturalistic New Sculpture movement of the later nineteenth century. MacGillivray's assessment chimed with that of the Glasgow art dealer and Burns enthusiast W. Craibe Angus, for whom the Pomeroy's statue 'was not Burns at all', but instead a 'Cockney masher' who 'never knew the toil of the fields'.[46] Other than the Kilmarnock bonnet, which, uniquely, Pomeroy depicts Burns wearing rather than carrying, there was – Craibe Angus alleged – little else that identified this Burns with Scotland (or even with Burns – who was unrecognisable), although there was a thistle in the group, partly hidden, deliberately, as Pomeroy had wanted to proclaim Burns as a poet of humanity first and Scotland second.[47] Where, Craibe Angus demanded, was Burns 'the man of letters, the song-writer, the heralder of the brotherhood of man'? For the proto-nationalist MacGillivray, much influenced by and a contributor to the Celtic Revival in Scotland that at just this time was, under the leadership of Patrick Geddes, flourishing in anticipation of a 'Scottish Renaissance', this would not do.

There was a related issue. Both Flaxman and Pomeroy were English, and in MacGillivray's view, 'Burns by an Englishman is impossible'. Flaxman's in particular was 'a very good example of the futility of employing an alien artist in a case of national character'.[48] This echoed a strand of opinion heard earlier in the century in relation to the Burns monument on Calton Hill. A *Scotsman* letter writer in 1831 had complained that the 'tame subdued Grecian temple' proposed to be built in an 'obscure corner' of Calton Hill was an inappropriate way of commemorating Burns. Instead of erecting copies of 'mutilated fragments of Athenian buildings', the correspondent asked rhetorically, was there no 'native architect who will . . . give us something original, something Scottish, something that will tell its meaning'.[49] Although running against the grain of the Greek revival fostered by

Scotland's gentlemanly elite – inheritors of Enlightenment taste – there were, he believed, two men who fitted the bill. One was John Greenshields (1792–1835), a mason sculptor who had been admired and patronised by Walter Scott (and who had designed the statue of Scott for the column in Glasgow's George Square).[50] The other was the self-taught sculptor James Thom (1802–50) whose grey stone statues of characters from Tam o' Shanter to be housed in the Alloway monument had very recently caught the public's attention – and been praised for their attention to detail, and realism, an antidote perhaps to the classicism of the monument itself. This 'extraordinary person', one critic waxed lyrically, 'hitherto known as a stone mason, a cutter of slabs into head-stones in country church-yards – has ... started forth, meteor-like, as a master, in the highest department of sculpture'.[51] There was another advantage: Thom, who carved from blocks of sandstone directly, would do so at a lower cost. Thom did secure a Burns commission, apparently, but in Newark, New Jersey, where he settled after leaving Scotland in pursuit of monies owed to him.[52] In the land of their birth, largely self-taught mason sculptors like Thom struggled to find statuary work, to the extent that in Perth in 1854, William Anderson, of Perth Marble Works, carved a statue of Burns at his own expense, and set it in a niche above his house in County Place – and then gifted it to the town council.[53] It now stands above the entrance to the aptly named Robert Burns Lounge bar.

MacGillivray, however, had little faith either in the ability of his Scottish sculptor contemporaries. He accused them of having imported from elsewhere ideas and practices about sculpture – as well as architecture, painting and poetry. They had disregarded what was natural to Scotland, 'their old CELTIC art in ornament and gravestones and crosses', a view current in the 1890s about the richness of Scotland's history and culture and their importance for the nation's future.[54]

Without the shackles that might have been imposed by a more conservative commissioning committee, for his Irvine Burns MacGillivray had a relatively free hand. Which meant he could take the bold step of dispensing with Nasmyth to create what one critic called a 'new Burns' (Plate 28). But with his conviction that 'the world spirit of Scotland was not born till Burns touched its eyes', MacGillivray was acutely conscious of the challenge he faced. The more he read about the poet, and thought about him, he wrote, 'the more difficult of embodiment it [the statue] seemed to become.' Unlike the previous statues which Pinnington and others had criticised for representing a single mood or character (concentration being 'fatal to breadth'), somehow he had to capture Burns the ploughman, the advocate of the rights and dignity of man, the lover, the humourist, the wielder of the 'flaying knife' of satire, and as a man with the most tender of hearts: 'so many stirring and superficially conflicting characteristics' in the man who personified the 'soul' of Scotland, the 'world spirit' of which 'was not really born till Burns touched its eyes'. By the mid 1920s, just prior to the formation of the National Party of Scotland (1927), MacGillivray was promoting Burns as 'social revolution incarnate', a 'potential Mussolini, with, in the browbeaten Scotland of his day, little stuff out of which to make black shirts'.[55]

Did MacGillivray at Irvine reach the high bar he had set himself? If Pinnington had doubts as to the wisdom of departing from accepted notions of what Burns looked like, he had few reservations about the figure MacGillivray produced, which he judged to be strong and dignified. Other reviewers purred in admiration. If the 'best test of the native quality of a Scottish sculptor' was a statue of Burns, MacGillivray had passed with flying colours. MacGillivray according to *The Sketch* had been 'the first to grasp the character as a whole, as a ploughman and a poet', and to embody Burns in the abstract. With his Burns but also his other work, MacGillivray had not only 'interpreted ... Scottish subjects in a Scottish way', but put Scotland 'upon her throne again'.[56] In this respect MacGillivray's achievement was in keeping with the dominant Scottish zeitgeist of the later nineteenth century and the first years of the twentieth century – the main manifestation of which was pressure for Home Rule.[57]

* * *

The search for fitting memorials was but one sign of the enthusiasm there was for Burns, which showed no sign of slackening as the hundredth anniversary of his death in 1796 approached. Burns club numbers are one indication of this. Those affiliated to the Burns Federation rose from an initial eight (in Scotland) in 1885 to over 200 by 1911. If we take the list of clubs and societies on the Federation's roll in 1926, it appears that the peak period – ever – for new club formation in Scotland was between 1900 and 1914 when some forty-eight new clubs were founded (around two dozen on the list dated from the 1890s, slightly fewer from the 1880s).[58] There were many more – although exactly how many is hard to say – that were unaffiliated.[59] Wilhelm Meister – who we first encountered in the Introduction

– was struck in 1891 not only by the fact that new clubs were still being inaugurated but that whereas 'in former years, they were chiefly confined to the towns of Britain', now, 'many of the outlying mining and agricultural districts rejoice in possession of them'.

Much the most important event the Federation fronted were the centenary celebrations of 1896, although of greater lasting significance was the Federation's role – in the vanguard of which was Rosebery – in campaigning for the preservation of Ayr's Auld Brig.[60] Famously, this had featured in Burns' poem 'The Brigs o' Ayr', in which the fifteenth-century bridge had forecast (correctly as it happened) that it would long outlast the new one, opened in 1788, which in time would become a 'shapeless cairn'. For Scotsmen and admirers of Burns, it was asserted, this bridge stood as 'the finest monument . . . to his memory', and one of the most iconic locations associated with Burns that in 1923 was scheduled as an Ancient Monument.[61] This, however, was simply one of the more spectacular achievements of the Federation and its affiliated clubs which had embarked on what was in effect a nationwide effort to secure Burns' memory by restoring buildings, erecting cairns and tombstones and placing plaques and tablets in places with even the slightest Burns link – as well as for distant relatives and friends, and characters who had appeared in his poems.[62] Hardly a year went by in the first decades of the twentieth century without yet another marker of this kind being laid down – so adding to the itinerary of visitors who continued to flock to Scotland in search of Burns. Articles could serve the same end, with the *Burns Chronicle* in 1898 publishing a piece on 'Glenbervie: The Fatherland of Burns'. The 'Mecca' for 'pilgrims to the northern "Land of Burns" was the churchyard where were buried the remains of previous generations of Burneses, Burns' father's ancestors.[63] Within their communities the clubs were active too, as in Dundee where the Burns Club not only put on annual concerts for the public but also donated a silver cup for which local football clubs competed, raising £1,000 between 1883 and 1889 for local charities.[64]

The centenary of the poet's death in July 1896 was celebrated on a more restricted scale than in 1859, but in those places where efforts were made to do Burns justice the results were equally impressive. Dumfries, as 'the guardian of the mausoleum' in which Burns' remains were preserved, was the hub, not only for Scotland but the world. There, Burns fervour was unabated, with the procession on the day itself being even more 'gigantic' than in 1882 (for the unveiling of the statue) or 1859.[65] But there were large-scale celebrations in other places too: notably Ayr, Kilmarnock, Dundee and Haddington.[66] In Perth, where in the open air on the North Inch a concert was staged on a scale 'never before attempted in this district of the country', as many as 15,000 people took part. At this the Scottish standard was the focal point of the decorations, while of the songs of Burns that were sung by a choir comprising six hundred voices, those that stood out were 'A Man's a Man' and 'Scots Wha Hae', the singers being 'thoroughly carried away with the sentiments of the Scottish National Anthem'.[67] The Burns Federation was gratified too by the Burns Exhibition held over the summer months in Glasgow, the biggest ever of Burns memorabilia, 'signal proof' of the nation's affection for Burns and 'one of the greatest tributes ever paid to the memory of the poet'.[68] The exhibition was opened with a rousing patriotic speech by William Wallace, later to be the editor of the *Glasgow Herald*, in which he declared that Scotland had not only never 'knuckled down to England' but had only been 'conquered' by Scotsmen – John Knox and Robert Burns.[69]

The year 1896 was also the target date for some more Burns memorials. In July MacGillivray's Burns statue was unveiled in Irvine, after an address from Alfred Austin, the Poet Laureate. A fortnight later the statue of Highland Mary in Dunoon that had been promoted by Colin Rae Brown was inaugurated, the main speech having been made by Lord Kelvin. Paisley's Burns came later (in September), its inauguration delayed by the struggles to find a suitable location even though the statue and the pedestal had been ready some months beforehand.

Statues, however, were on the way out, with more pragmatic Burns enthusiasts arguing that there were more appropriate ways of commemorating the peasant poet. Although they had been lone voices and had fallen on deaf ears, arguments along these lines had been articulated earlier. For example, instead of the 'cold statue' that was proposed for Kilmarnock in January 1877, more in keeping with 'this utilitarian age' and to ameliorate the 'evil' condition of the town would be a hospital, a Burns bursary or a Burns Christian institute.[70] Others – equally ardent followers of Burns – took the view that statues were but the 'visible sign of an inward and invisible faith' (in Burns), the responsibility of the clubs being to promulgate his lessons and to encourage, missionary-like, the study of his works and the 'realization of his prophecies'.[71] This was the Burns cult in religious guise.

The outcome of the pressure for alternative monuments was what became the National Burns Memorial at Mossgeil near Mauchline, hitherto altogether neglected as a memory site despite Burns' many intimate connections with the district. Spearheaded by the Glasgow Mauchline Society, in the eyes of the Burns Federation this was the outstanding consequence of the 1896 centennial, the foundation stone of which was laid in accordance with masonic rites. Accompanying the turreted tower (which was to house various Burns relics along with local antiquities), was a group of cottages, provided rent free – but only for 'persons who have been respectable and deserving'.[72] An estimated £100,000 had been spent on statues, busts and similar memorials. Favoured therefore was the socially beneficial nature of the Mauchline memorial which after the First World War was replicated elsewhere, primarily through the provision of Robert Burns beds and cots in several hospitals both north and south of the border.[73] (The National Health Service lay some way in the future.) In Mauchline this was supplemented in 1924 by the provision of accommodation for 'deserving' old people in the house of Nanse Tinnock – proprietor of the inn that appears in Burns' 'The Holy Fair'. It was here that Burns had drunk and caroused, and discussed politics. Part of the same package, initiated by the Glasgow and District Burns Association, was a section of the restored house in which Burns had lived with Jean Armour, and an adjoining property that had belonged to Dr John M'Kenzie, with whom Burns had been acquainted.[74]

The £4,410 collected for Mauchline was less than the £5,000 hoped for but it was sufficient even if the facility's inauguration in May 1898 was two years late.[75] Although £4,410 was more than had been subscribed for any other Burns monument, noticeable is how hard the promoters had had to work to raise money from 900 subscribers; a modest return for the 55,000 letters and circulars that were sent out, and 5,000 personal calls. Only £80 came from overseas (and only a single pound from the USA), slightly less than the £90 (two per cent of the total) contributed by the duke of Hamilton and the rest of the Scottish nobility. Glasgow and the west of Scotland – including the proprietors of many of the region's major industrial corporations – along with fifty-five Burns clubs provided the vast bulk of the funding. Progress with the Burns statue in Montrose, almost the last in Scotland to be funded by private subscriptions, was even slower. By the end of 1898 fewer than forty of the town's 13,000 or so inhabitants had contributed.[76] It was left to the sculptor, William Birnie Rhind, to agitate to get the campaign for subscriptions re-started (the first had fallen into abeyance ten years earlier). In the absence of local people willing to become involved in fund-raising, Rhind had an uphill struggle, and in 1911, short of money, had to ask the statue committee for an advance of £100.[77]

We should be wary of reading too much into Montrose's difficulties. Even Rosebery had initially declined to support the proposal, on the grounds that he knew of no 'special circumstances in Burns' career that makes it a matter of public moment that a statue of the poet should be erected in Montrose.'[78] What is significant, however, is that along with some late donations, including £100 from the Dundee jute magnate James Caird, it was the burgh's Burns Club that saw the project to completion. It was becoming increasingly apparent that it was upon the clubs' shoulders that responsibility for maintaining Burns' memory and his reputation lay, something they pursued vigorously after 1918 – although as we will see in the next chapter there was criticism in some quarters of the nature of that commemoration.

Defending Burns' reputation is something the Federation and its members took seriously. Indicative is the response of the Burns Federation and of Burns club members to the less than flattering assessment of the poet by William E. Henley, the conservative English poet and critic, who in 1896 published the four-volume edition of Burns' works he had compiled with Thomas F. Henderson. Henley had not failed to recognise Burns' worth as a poet, or his intelligence. Burns' love of Scotland, too, he acknowledged, which 'could scarce have been the Scotland she is, had he not been'. But there was much, too, that was grudging: Burns was not a 'miracle' but 'a local poet', the 'last of a school' – the Scottish Vernacular – in which Allan Ramsay had also been a pupil; his work on Scottish song was made easy by the rich inheritance of 'many nameless singers' he was able to draw from, while some of his own productions, asserted Henley, were not even as good. Apart from patronising Burns, Henley's greatest offence was to condemn the poet's pride ('of Lucifer'), his Jacobinism, his 'lack of chivalry' towards women and above all his drinking, to which Henley attributed Burns' early death. Burns, he concluded, had strengths, 'but the weaknesses were greater'.[79] The reaction to Henley's verdict, which piqued his critics as it was delivered in the year of the centenary celebrations, was intense, unforgiving, and enduring, particularly amongst the Burns clubs, although beyond this circle Burns still mattered sufficiently for others too to take umbrage at what was considered to be a slur upon Scotland.[80]

*　*　*

Amongst the general population Burns could still draw large crowds. The impression given, however, is that more came to spectate and enjoy the associated pleasures of a day out and less to participate in what had been quasi-religious experiences for those most closely involved in Glasgow in 1877, Dundee in 1880 or Dumfries in 1882. There had always been a marketable dimension to Burns commemoration, but this became even more pronounced later in the century. But perhaps a better indicator of changing priorities was the barbed contrast made by one Paisley newspaper of the audience of 'a few hundreds' for the inauguration of the Burns statue in Fountain Gardens and a football match played around the same time that had been 'attended by thousands', and generated gate money of almost £100.[81] But this was just one instance of the newfound 'mania' for football and other organised sports that gave shape to and strengthened local and workplace identities, and also reflected a change in and lightening of social attitudes.[82] The extent to which this had happened in relation to Burns is seen in the 'Burnsettes' competition that was run by Dundee's *People's Journal*. With a circulation of over 220,000 copies the *Journal* was the best-selling weekly outside London.[83] Whereas for most of the nineteenth century newspaper competitions held under the auspices of Burns required entrants to submit their carefully crafted, usually solemn and overly sentimental poems, the *People's Journal* offered cash prizes, busts of Burns and Burns ash-trays to readers who could identify Burns poems from picture clues.[84] Not only was the *Journal* straying from its roots as a champion of the working classes under its ex-Chartist editor William Latto; in its pages too Burns was becoming fun.

As we have seen, searching questions were being asked about the utility of the statues and similar monuments, as well as their significance for the general public after the immediate excitement surrounding their first appearance died down. For their intended meaning to survive in the longer-run, memorials such as statues require what James Coleman has called 'recurring acts of commemoration'.[85] Without these, he argues, they could become symbols without meaning, their stone or bronze voices conveying very different messages to those originally intended. Re-consecration did happen, annually, on or around 25 January. (The Glasgow and District Burns Association is rightly proud today to have paid homage at the George Square Burns every year since 1877.[86]) By and large, however, the more ardent members of the Burns clubs who conducted the ceremonies did so with reverence but little of the attention from the public that had marked the statues' unveiling. Even in Kilmarnock for the 150th anniversary of Burns' birth in 1909 only 500 people assembled at the Kay Park monument, while in Dumfries and elsewhere where similar memorials had been erected, the later ceremonies were low-key affairs, involving mainly town provosts and town councils, Burns clubs and invited dignitaries. Even some of the clubs struggled to survive, Arbroath's for example doing little between 1901 and its revival in 1909. A proposal, made in 1890, for a Burns statue was quietly shelved.[87]

* * *

The cooling off of ardour (as distinct from affection) for Burns amongst the general public that this suggests may not be so difficult to explain. Social attitudes were changing. Working people – women as well as men – were becoming more confident, and assertive. If the skilled working classes had led the way in this regard, the rest were not so far behind, with Dundee's maidservants – generally considered to be the meekest and most deferential group of employees – having come out on strike as early as 1872.[88] But in many industries and across much of Lowland Scotland the labouring classes were increasingly militant, and forming more effective, and aggressive, trade unions. Their legal status was enhanced in 1906 with the Trade Disputes Act that granted unions immunity from damages as a result of strikes. The numbers of these mushroomed on Clydeside, the country's manufacturing heartland, in the years immediately preceding the First World War. But no part of Scotland was immune from the upheavals and challenges to the prevailing order. In the north and west too, relationships between the people and their landlords had become more confrontational, with the revolt of the crofting communities from 1882 forcing concessions in the shape of tenure rights as early as 1886 with the Crofters Holdings (Scotland) Act.

Impoverishment continued to be endemic, but for skilled workers especially real wages and living standards were rising from the 1880s.[89] The introduction of old age pensions in 1908 and the National Insurance Act of 1911 went some way towards ameliorating the indignity of poverty that Burns had deplored and resisted. But higher incomes for many and shorter hours for some meant there was more opportunity for consumer spending. With the country's stricter Sabbatarians being forced onto the back foot, Sundays – the single day most but by no means all working people were free from the demands of the workplace – became the occasion of a growing range of activities other than church attendance and reading. The pace of secularisation was slow, and resisted by the Free Church and the Church of Scotland, but the direction of travel was clear.[90]

As citizens too, by the end of the nineteenth century the status of working people had improved markedly in comparison to what it had been prior to the watershed Reform Act of 1832 and its successors. The Scottish electorate, a tiny fraction of the adult population before 1832, had with the 1884 Reform Act been extended to include all male householders. Although women were excluded from the provisions of the Act, they had been campaigning for female suffrage from 1867, and were increasingly active in both local politics and the national political parties.[91] One of these was the Scottish Labour Party, formed in 1888, many of whose members joined its successor the Independent Labour Party (ILP), in 1893.

The point in relation to Burns is this. He represented certain fundamental principles and ideals that had, as we have seen, stirred tens of thousands of his countrymen (and women). But his was a quest for liberty and a vision of greater social equality, not a party political manifesto.[92] Anything more specific related to the circumstances in which Burns had been alive in the early 1790s, that is, during the repressive government of William Pitt at a time of grave national crisis. By the end of the nineteenth century, with working people on the cusp of what Selina Todd has defined as the people's century, poems and songs were not enough.[93] The need now was for practical steps – on electoral reform, welfare provision including housing, and worker rights. And agitating for these were pressure groups and parties that had made it their business to incorporate as members and supporters ordinary people who previously had been excluded from the political process.

In turn the parties hijacked Burns for their own purposes, identifying him with policies on which, necessarily, he had had nothing to say. As might be expected, the 150th anniversary of his birth in 1909 was widely celebrated, although in smaller numbers than the two earlier centenaries. The vast majority of the speeches reported in the press sung Burns' praises in familiar terms, a recurrent trope being his role in sustaining national pride. Altogether new, however, were assertions like that made at Edinburgh's Balfour Burns Club, that Burns' conception of independence was such that he 'did not wish to see . . . State pensioners' or 'doles from other people'. This of course pleased an audience of Edinburgh's leading Conservatives and Unionists. In stark contrast, in nearby Melbourne Place, at a meeting held under the auspices of the ILP, William Stewart, editor of the *Clarion* and *Labour Leader*, was applauded after asserting that 'no movement in the world had more right to claim Robert Burns or to hold a celebration than the Socialist movement'. Burns would not only have been at the front of such a movement today, but, he counselled those present, Burns should be used 'to the utmost possible advantage' as long as a socialist movement was necessary.[94]

Burns' influence was waning but, as we have just seen, it would be wrong to suggest that he had none. Amongst socialists, including some of the early Labour leaders, he had a great deal, and there were those who wanted him to have more. Alexander Webster, author of *Burns and the Kirk: A Review of What the Poet Did for the Religious and Social Regeneration of the Scottish People* (1888), acknowledged that social reform was under way, and credited Burns with lifting ordinary people out of 'abject servility'. Indeed for Webster, Burns had been a prophet, 'as remarkable in kind as an Isaiah', a comparison on a par with Scottish socialists at the time who proclaimed Christ as a social reformer and drew on the New Testament for their moral map and political ideals.[95] Even so, what incensed Webster was that many of the wrongs that Burns had condemned in poems such as 'The Twa Dogs' were still in evidence: 'the cup of landlord iniquity is full, and can no longer be carried by the tenant folk', he raged; 'the hour has come for strenuous efforts for complete deliverance'. Land-based social inequality, however – and the demand for land reform that dated back to the Chartist era and intensified from the 1880s – was not confined to the countryside.[96] The 'graphic passage' in the 'Twa Dogs' describing the 'poor tenant bodies, scant o' cash' was in Webster's eyes equally applicable to city tenants. Their 'deliverance' too demanded action on the part of the state, namely the abolition of landlordism and 'the planning of house-building and owning in the hands of the community'.[97]

Calls to action of this nature, however, were at odds with what appeared to be happening in the Burns clubs. There had long been critics of the Burns cult, and its association with drink-warmed brotherhood that from early days had been part and parcel of the annual Burns commemorations. (Even from within there was some concern about this. A visionary proposal was made in 1891 that the clubs should do more than sup together to celebrate Burns' birthday, and instead create an order to be called 'The Knight Templars of Humanity', to put into practice 'the poet's dream and man's hope' of global brotherhood.[98]) Immediately prior to the 1859 centenary the *Reformed Presbyterian Magazine* had forecast that by the day's end 'the name of the poet will have echoed from the lips of many a roaring chorus of hiccupping Bacchanals'.[99] By the later years of the nineteenth century observations of this kind were not confined to evangelical churchmen. Nor were the charges without foundation, the greater levity of many of the annual Burns suppers, for example, being underlined by the agreement amongst members of Glasgow's Waverley Club in 1880 of the need for 'a funny man to do the oratory'. Admittedly much later, but symptomatic of what was a hollowing out process of Burns' legacy was the restiveness reported amongst London Burns Club members towards the end of Pittendrigh MacGillivray's 'very fine', heart-felt but distinctly humourless Immortal Memory in 1925.[100]

Writing in 1891, Robert Williams Buchanan, who in his youth had met and been inspired by Robert Owen, Louis Blanc and other early socialists, acknowledged that Burns had been 'a great man and a great poet' and, as we saw in chapter 2, applauded Burns for his role in reducing in Scotland the influence of the 'unco guid'. Buchanan had little time, however, for Burns' bacchanalianism or the drink culture that surrounded his memory. In the heart of Scotland, Buchanan was sure, 'there lies a well of pure and abiding gratitude to Robert Burns', but he doubted 'if those who love the poet best and study his works most tenderly are those who stand before his shrine in the public house', or who celebrate his birthday, 'fill their glasses, hiccup "Auld Langsyne" and cry in chorus: "Robin was a rovin' boy"'.[101] Others were even more antagonistic, arguing that the measure of a great poet was not 'the number of people who make his name a rallying call for convivial gatherings', and pointing to the 'huge discrepancy' between Burns' 'highest' poetical works and 'the filth which soils the pages of the Kilmarnock edition'.[102] Henley too had his say, alleging that on 25 January 'a great mob assembles, all over Scotland, to drink whisky, and eat haggis, and make speeches in the Idol's praise'.

In the opinion of some Burnsians who were inclined to defend the Burns supper tradition as an honourable one, there was little point in denying the facts.[103] Notwithstanding the charitable and other useful work done by Dundee's club, for example, the minute books of the period do contain more than isolated references to the quality of the whisky at club functions, and disorderly members. In October 1890 the committee acceded to a request from 'Mr Lumsden the Scottish comedian' that the club act as patrons for his forthcoming concert in Kinnaird Hall.[104] Elsewhere it was the destination of and arrangements for the annual outing – often to Burns country – that took up much time; minute books suggest that Burns himself was little discussed.[105]

The Federation, however, protested and numerous letters were sent to the press from outraged Burns club members countering the charges and pointing to the existence of non-abstainers amongst their ranks, and the educational and charitable work the clubs performed; Greenock's in particular was hailed as being particularly virtuous – with good reason.[106] Yet it was the reality of concerns about what the clubs had become that lay behind the decision by members of Dundee's literary elite in 1896 to establish a Burns Society. At the initial meeting to discuss its formation, Andrew Stewart expressed the hope that the new organisation, if established, would disassociate 'the worship of Burns from haggis and whisky'. Those present were at pains to distance themselves from the existing clubs, not least by their decision to include females (one of whom, Mrs R. A. Watson, spoke at the first conversazione), although ironically the topics for discussion and debate and the earnest character of the proceedings were not unlike those of the Burns clubs in their earlier years. There was, however, greater emphasis on Scottish history and literature including poets such as Robert Henryson and William Dunbar, Alexander Wedderburn and Robert Tannahill, as well as English, American and Irish writers.[107]

The sharpest criticism though came from the pens of writers such as Webster. He was far from being alone, however, in condemning the sentimental turn of the Burns cult. The increasingly commonly used terms 'Robbie' and 'Bobbie' Burns were indicative of the trend that at the popular level was dragging Burns into the kail-yard enclosure, and what has been termed 'tartanry'.[108] Deplored by radically inclined Scots was the softening of the hard edge of Burns' social critique that this terminology and the 'Jack the lad' image of Burns from which it derived represented. They feared, too, that the calls for action they attributed to him would lose their purchase. It is this to which Webster alluded when he wrote that we should 'hang our heads in shame' when 'A Man's a Man' is sung. We sing it, he went on, and 'expect the Millennium'. For too long the song had served as 'a pot house sentiment ... [and] made the motto a thing of cant'; rather, he urged, 'we must make it the watchword of cross-bearers, the rallying call of men determined to end the conditions that degrade humanity'. In Dundee, where amongst many locals great pride was taken in the town's Radical past, a versifier in 1889 affected to address Burns on his Albert Square pedestal when drawing attention to 'the people [the magistracy and other members of what was about to become, by royal warrant, a *city* elite] that shout 'The rank is but the guinea stamp', but whose souls were 'athirst for trumpery titles'.[109]

Even more explicit was Dundee-born James Young Geddes, whose work we noted in chapter 5. Geddes was another artisan poet in the mould of Robert Davidson whose critique of Scottish landlordism owed much to Burns, with other poetic influences being Arthur Hugh Clough and Walt Whitman.[110] With the highland land question still fresh in the public mind, and only partly resolved by the legislation of 1886, in his 'Memory of Burns', delivered at a Burns 'anniversary concert' in Alyth in January 1890, Young urged his fellow celebrants to 'Go mark in every Highland glen / The ruined homesteads of her sons . . . Exiled by pleasure's myrmidons'. Then, inspired by Burns, to keep alive his memory until Scotland's peasantry were restored, to 'find again on Scottish sward / A recompense for honest toil.'[111] For Young, Burns' songs were still 'bugles calling', agents of change: 'Do not speak with maudlin feeling / Of the coming brotherhood', he urged his fellow celebrants of Burns at a supper in January 1891, but 'fall in line' and be 'Midst the marshaled hosts of freedom, / Waging war with tyranny'.[112]

SEVEN

'King of sentimental doggerel'

Twentieth-century Burns, and Burns now

It was not long before Burns was recruited to engage with another kind of tyranny. The threat of war that had rumbled across Europe during the summer of 1914 became real for Great Britain early in August as hostilities with Germany were declared.

For the many thousands of Scots and others who had pinned their hopes on and found succour and purpose in Burns' vision of universal brotherhood as encapsulated in the final stanza of 'A Man's a Man', the outbreak of war came as a jarring disappointment. Andrew Carnegie, who had been due to unveil the Burns statue in Stirling in September, pulled out to return to the United States. Almost exactly two years earlier – in Montrose – he had waxed eloquently on the theme of world peace, and of 'the prophecy of Burns, to the fulfillment of which we are steadily marching'.[1] By August 1914, and in view of 'the impending destruction of the greatest number of civilised beings ever sacrificed in the history of the world', Carnegie admitted that he was struggling for words and could have said little that was useful.[2] Later in the war, efforts would be made to reclaim Burns for the peace movement, but to little avail. The poet of humanity, whose universally applicable values from 1859 onwards had crossed oceans and on occasion served to obscure national differences, was harnessed for very different purposes.

* * *

As the First World War intensified, Burns and his bugle songs were conscripted in service of the British state. Even as early as the Stirling unveiling, the mood was changing. Baillie Thomson, in accepting Burns' statue on behalf of the burgh, noted the proximity of

Bannockburn and spoke of the 'agonies' of those in the past but of the present too, and the men who 'had gone under on the plains of Europe in the cause of liberty against despotism'. The hopes encapsulated in 'A Man's a Man' he acknowledged were now deferred, although he looked to a better future. Those looking on were heartened by the presence amongst the onlookers of a group of Ayrshire men from the Royal Scots Fusiliers who at the end of the formal proceedings 'broke out into song', singing 'The Star of Robbie Burns', and 'Ye Banks and Braes' before ending with a rousing rendition of 'It's a Long Way to Tipperary'. And at a reception afterwards in the Golden Lion Hotel, in stark contrast to the lines from Burns' 'Address to the Unco' Guid' the statue's sculptor Albert H. Hodge (1875–1918) had carved on the pedestal ('Then gently scan your brother man, / Still gentler sister woman'), he condemned the damage wreaked on Rheims cathedral by the Germans: 'the day of reckoning', he concluded to loud applause, 'would not be long delayed'.[3]

Even in these first weeks of conflict Burns was again (as he had been during the South African war) exploited in the guise of warrior poet. The University of Glasgow's Professor Robert S. Rait had acknowledged that Burns was not 'distinctively' a martial poet, but argued that he could express 'in immortal words both the memories and the battles of the past and the determination which wins the battles of the present'. 'Scots Wha Hae' was clearly the song he had in mind, which before long became 'the battle-cry of the nation'.[4] Any ambiguity about Burns' loyalty to Britain during the early years of the conflict with revolutionary France from 1792 when he was in Dumfries was conveniently forgotten: by 1915 Burns was the noblest of British patriots. In fact not only was he presented as a militarist but also as ardently anti-German. In January 1915 the *People's Journal* invited its readers to submit 'Burns' Telegrams to the Kaiser'. Not surprisingly the many entries submitted were 'unanimous in one direction'. None, it was reported, had a 'good word to say for Germany's War Lord', whose dastardly conduct some entrants thought would cause him to be spurned even by the Devil.[5] The winner of the ten shillings prize was a Mrs D. Campbell from Melrose, whose play on 'To a Haggis' illustrates the general tone:

> Deil tak' yer ugly squirmin' face,
> Great savage o' the sausage race;
> Sune may yer carcase fin a place
>   In some au'd midden.

Others were even more direct, another writer addressing the Kaiser as 'ye auld Hun', who should be 'placed afore a gun / And blawn tae Hell'.

It was testimony to Burns' iconic status and the power it was assumed he had to influence behaviour, that his work was plundered, extrapolated and shaped to serve the war effort and to galvanise Britain's anxious citizenry over the following three years.

By the time the war ended, Burns had become not quite a figure of fun, but the Scottish poet who had provided in verse so many models for popular pastiche. Perhaps, to build upon a suggestion of Richard Price, the generation that had lived through and too often died during the conflict was the last that was truly alive to Burns' importance as an historical agent.[6] For writers in the inter-war years – like George Blake and Lewis Grassic Gibbon – Burns had become 'the past incarnate', by this time associated with melancholy, nostalgia and loss. He had always been difficult to pin down, given the plurality of his poetic voices. But with so many competing interests seeking sustenance from his work, his essence was in danger of being drained. Criticism of Burns' morals and other alleged weaknesses by Henley and others had induced an angry response from the Burns clubs, but the result was a neutered Burns. As the militant socialist and between 1929 and 1931 the ILP's MP for Maryhill, John S. Clarke wrote in *Forward*, 'Enthusiastic defenders . . . [in] their attempts to remove the blemishes from his moral character . . . have removed a trifle too much.' If the process continues, he went on, 'posterity will be presented with an emasculated and filleted dummy, labelled "Burns", as truly grotesque as the clay-footed, drunken caricature offered to us by malicious slanderers'.[7] This was in spite of the publication in 1925 of a series of articles in the *Glasgow Herald* by Sir James Crichton-Browne, one of the country's most eminent psychiatrists and neurologists, in which he denied that Burns had died from drink – the cause alleged by 'sermonisers' on Burns' life from the time of James Currie onwards.[8] That instead the cause of Burns' death appeared to have been rheumatism contracted in childhood, and heart failure, was joyously greeted by Burnsians, relieved that their hero was no longer tainted by the charge of alcoholism.

New Burns clubs were founded during the war, while in the six years from 1920 over thirty more appeared. They included the 'Bonny Jean' ladies Burns Club in the mining village of Glencraig, Fife, the coal producing districts of which county saw the emergence of several other Burns clubs during and soon after the First World War.[9] In this part of Scotland their appearance and the area's strong support for the Labour Party during the 1920s (and in 1935 West Fife returned the country's first Communist MP) seems hardly to be coincidental.[10]

As this suggests, many on the left – people like Pittendrigh MacGillivray and Clarke – stuck by Burns. The Co-operative movement used him in advertisements designed to show that anti-capitalism in Scotland had a long – and reputable – pedigree.[11] In 1945 the Communist John R. Campbell expressed the hope that the example of Burns' life and his legacy of song and verse would inspire his countrymen to 'continue the fight' against hypocrisy and privilege until a new and better social order had been put in place. In this respect he would take his place 'in the procession of Great Scottish Rebels who have striven to make the lot of the common people a happier one'.[12]

Campbell's stance, however, and those before him who had claimed Burns for socialism, was very far removed from that of the Burns Federation. In 1925 the *Burns Chronicle*'s stalwart editor Duncan McNaught protested that in the whole of Burns' writings, there was not a 'single line that expresses the slightest sympathy with the doctrines of . . . Bolshevism, Communism and Socialism which are now so loudly proclaimed from the housetops'.[13] The Federation, a string of its spokesmen protested, was strictly apolitical. It was a claim that sat uneasily with the Federation's President Sir Joseph Dobbie's assurance to this effect in January 1929 that in the same speech was followed by the comment that any policy the Federation adopted should be 'constitutional', and conform with what Burns had written:

> Be Britain still to Britain true,
> Among oursels united!
> For never but by British hands
> Maun British wrangs be righted!

While Dobbie was also able to assert that 'every member of a Burns Club was a Scottish Nationalist' his none too subtle appropriation of Burns for Unionism was in keeping with the political mood in Scotland in the 1920s and 1930s where electoral support for the Conservatives grew strongly, more so than for Labour, and in contrast to the crashing fortunes of the divided Liberals.[14]

* * *

Even although the standard that had once drawn marchers to demonstrate for Burns was now tattered and torn, he continued to attract adherents to the clubbable aspects of the cult – preponderantly in the Lowlands. Although celebrants of Burns had long incorporated symbolism such as bagpipes and tartan in their processions – thereby claiming him as a poet for Scotland – there were still no Burns clubs in Inverness-shire or in the far north or the Gaelic speaking islands of the west. Even so, in 1931 the Federation's President Sir Joseph Dobbie could with much justification speak of the recent 'extraordinary' increase in club membership: twenty-six new clubs were founded in one year alone, 1929, and twenty-two the following year. A significant growth area was amongst women, and of exclusively female Burns clubs – a development that Dobbie employed to counter the charge that the Burns 'movement' was merely convivial (presumably on the assumption that the presence of 'ladies' would curb the 'boozing' culture with which the clubs were associated).[15] The move to include women, however, was neither universal nor always enthusiastic: Arbroath's Burns Club decided to take the plunge, so to speak, in 1925, but within months their decision to invite females to the annual Burns supper was rescinded.[16]

In most respects the clubs were carrying on as they had in the previous century, celebrating Burns' birthday every January and, where appropriate, securing additional memory sites – not only relating to Burns but for other patriotic figures in Scottish history. These included Wallace, who shared a memorial with Burns that was unveiled in Leglen Wood near Auchincruive in September 1929.[17] Irvine Burns Club also erected a memorial to mark the site where Wallace's army had camped during the wars of independence, while in 1931 the Federation's president urged delegates to the annual conference to back the movement to oppose building works proposed for the field of Bannockburn. In some places the focus was on restoring plaques and other memorials that had fallen into decay. Improvements at Burns' birthplace cottage in Alloway were lobbied for by Ayrshire's Association of Burns clubs, with the suffragette attack of 1914 having aroused concerns about the risk of fire to the property and its contents.[18] From 1928 and during most of the 1930s much time and effort was devoted to restoring the mausoleum in Dumfries, where Turnerelli's much-criticised marble carving of Burns was disintegrating. In 1935 a sculptor was appointed after what was considered to be a weak competition – Joseph Hermon

Cawthra (1886–1971), from Yorkshire and best known for his war memorials and bas-relief work. Although fund-raising was slow at first (£3,000 was sought), in part owing to the Wall St stock market crash of 1929 and the Depression of the 1930s, the decision of Dumfries' Burns Club to pledge their copy of the Kilmarnock edition for the balance had the desired effect of sparking a flood of donations (including £300 from 'Ladies from Alloa', just over six shillings from Castle Kennedy WRI, and much the same 'Collected on a bus at Annan'). The mausoleum was refurbished (with the red sandstone structure being painted white), complete with a new statue of Burns – 'on better lines, and avoiding or rectifying any manifest artistic defects'.[19]

Not to be overlooked either, was the work done by the Federation and its affiliated clubs in resuscitating and encouraging the use of the Scottish language, or what was called the vernacular or the Scottish Doric. So called 'vernacular circles' were established in Edinburgh and Glasgow (and London). These along with some of the clubs took their role seriously and included in their syllabuses talks on older Scottish poetry and local history and customs. The Federation encouraged members to support the work of the Scottish Dialects Committee (founded in 1908) that in turn spawned the Scottish National Dictionary Association, formed in 1928, and took a leading role in taking the project forward during and immediately after the Second World War.[20] For many years some clubs – Bridgeton since 1878–9 – sponsored competitions in the schools, of which well over 200 (or around 15,000 children) in the early 1930s participated by drawing sketches, writing essays and reciting poetry; indeed, this – heightening an awareness of Burns as well as greater understanding of Scotland's history, literature, art and music amongst young people – was one of the Federation's key objects.

In the light of this, the criticisms of Burns, and of the Burns cult, that were made in the 1920s and 1930s seem rather harsh. In his search for the essence of Scottish life as it was at this time the novelist George Blake was convinced that the 'average' Scot was overly sentimental, with Burns devotion being 'an uncritical indulgence of the emotions, a thoroughly uncultured . . . and amusing species of Freemasonry'. But he also thought it harmless.[21] The vitriol was thrown by the journalist and nationalist poet 'Hugh MacDiarmid' (otherwise Christopher M. Grieve), in prose essays and verse that reflected MacDiarmid's contempt for most Scottish cultural production during the nineteenth century. In relation to Burns, most often quoted are lines from his *A Drunk Man Looks at the Thistle*, published in 1926:

> No' wan in fifty kens a wurd
>   Burns wrote
> But misapplied is 'abody's property,
> And gin there was his like alive
>   The day
> They'd be the last a kennin' haund
>   to gi'e –
>
> Croose London Scotties wi' their
>   braw shirt fronts
> And a' their fancy freen's, rejoicin'
> That similah gatherings in
>   Timbuctoo,
> Bagdad – and hell, nae doot – are
>   voicin'
>
> Burns' sentiments o' universal love,
> In pidgin' English or in wild-fowl
>   Scots,
> And toastin' ane what's nocht to
>   them but an
> Excuse for faitherin' Genius wi
>   their thochts.

Many present day commentators have taken a similar line.[22] From being the 'model' for new national cultures (inspired by Ossian and Burns in the later eighteenth century, as we saw earlier), Scotland by the 1920s and 1930s had 'declined into a parody of national culture', a parody 'signaled by Burns Suppers' and the 'fake romantic "tushery"' that had displaced the best of Walter Scott's historical novels.[23] 'Puirrabbieburnsism' was but one of a number of 'isms' coined by the playwright James Bridie that had combined to generate a caricatured and sentimentalised Scottish nation.[24] To be sure, this is what the Burns legacy was becoming. But it was not yet universal and, as we have seen in earlier chapters, it was not always thus. Indeed MacDiarmid had witnessed this personally when as a young man in Wales in 1911 he had met and seen in the Labour leader James Keir

Hardie's effortless quoting of Burns, the political utility of Burns' poetry.[25]

MacDiarmid's self-assurance that spilled over into arrogance is partly reflected in the title given him by Alan Riach: 'Demolition Man'.[26] His opinions on what constituted the Scottish vernacular were extreme to say the least, as was his call for a Scottish nationalism 'with a pronounced Sinn Fein element'; one of the catalysts for the National Party of Scotland which he helped found in 1928, was the Irish struggle for independence.[27] MacDiarmid's vision was of a Scottish nation reborn through the adoption, use and adaptation of the older Scottish tongue – what he termed 'synthetic' Scots.[28] Thus his attacks on Burns were largely concerned with his poetic worth (although MacDiarmid also called credited Burns as 'the most powerful lyric poet the world has ever seen'), and the 'debased' language in which he wrote (there was too much English in it), which left him, in MacDiarmid's eyes, far behind predecessors like Sir David Lindsay, Dunbar and Henryson and other exponents of what he called 'Braid Scots'.[29] As we have seen in the extracts from the 'Drunk Man', however, much of MacDiarmid's ire was directed towards the Burns clubs whose primary function he claimed was social – for a few hours each year only – rather than cultural. The crowning toast of the ubiquitous Burns suppers, the Immortal Memory, offered nothing of value 'save for purposes of satire'.[30] The clubs' efforts to do more – as for example the London Vernacular Circle of the London Burns Club – he derided as aiding and abetting the literature of the kailyard, and for promoting low literary standards.[31]

According to J. C. Ewing, first editor of the second series of the Federation's *Chronicle*, that more than half (54 per cent) of the clubs affiliated to the Federation had failed to buy even one copy of the journal certainly points to a lack of engagement with, and little serious interest in, Burns. In this regard MacDiarmid's description of the Burns clubs as wanting in their knowledge of Burns and the critical abilities (of their members – 'hordes of mediocrities') to assess his literary worth, may in some instances be justified. However, it was disrespectful of the many Burnsians who had a genuine regard for a man beloved by countless Scots and whose antiquarian squirrelling away of documents and artefacts makes it possible today to understand a cult that, for all its foibles, as a strand in Scotland's modern history has been at least as important as the Scottish Renaissance.[32] Having said that, what largely impressionistic evidence we have from the clubs themselves suggests that in many the earnestness of the nineteenth century continued to dissipate.[33]

But whatever the egotistical MacDiarmid's reservations about Burns' place in the pantheon of Scottish poets, he was acutely aware – perhaps even envious, given the pitiful initial sales of his 'Drunk Man' – of Burns' popularity. 'A Man's a Man' may have been 'unspeakable', but MacDiarmid in 1959 had to acknowledge its success, and Burns' 'tremendous' influence.[34] As we have seen, MacDiarmid's ally Pittendrigh MacGillivray was convinced that Burns in the 1920s was still worth recruiting for the cause of nationalist socialism. Even at the end of the decade the English travel writer and *Daily Express* journalist H. V. Morton in his *In Search of Scotland* felt justified in describing Burns as 'a warm, living force ... part of daily life' of the nation, although like MacDiarmid he recognised that while Burns was commonly quoted, few had read him.[35] But in his observation that there was no English poet whose songs had 'curled up like an old dog on the hearthstone', Morton also confirmed that the Burns who had survived attempts in Victorian Scotland to dampen the fieriest parts of his legacy was in grave danger of becoming the poet of the fireside.

With the virtual collapse of the Home Rule movement during the Great War, another of the causes for which his name and legacy had been evoked sank from view. As we have seen, the new nationalists of the 1920s had less time for him, and anyway nationalism in Scotland was very much a minority cause, tainted as it was by association with European fascism.[36] Albeit that MacDiarmid's denunciations of followers of Burns were not without foundation, the fact is he was a cultural elitist who patronised his fellow Scots. A Communist Party member again from 1956, he admitted to feeling more comfortable with audiences in the Soviet Union and its satellite states where Burns' identification with the poor and the oppressed, and social justice and peace, drew him close to socialist hearts.[37] MacDiarmid's disparaging comments about his countrymen, though, did not go unchallenged. Professor John Morrison at Greenock Burns Club in January 1935 issued a spirited rejoinder to MacDiarmid and his associates, declaring that the leaders of 'what calls itself the Scottish renaissance are a coterie standing substantially in isolation from the Scottish people as a whole, whom they apparently despise'.[38] True. Yet discernible more widely was a growing complacency amongst the Burns fraternity about his place in Scottish society and the nation's history. Dobbie, the aforementioned Federation President, who in other contexts could be a stickler for hard evidence, adduced none to back his assertion that it was 'Burns and those whom he had inspired' who had created the revolutionary public sentiment that had led to the enfranchisement of women in Britain in 1928.[39]

And whilst the Federation and Burns club members had been happy with Crichton-Browne's revisionism, there was a public furore over the publication in September 1930 – in serial form in the *Daily Record and Mail* – of Catherine Carswell's *The Life of Burns*. In this, Glasgow-born Carswell had not only maintained that Burns had fathered the infant whose remains had been found buried in Mary Campbell's grave, but, in a wish 'to draw aside the veil of adulation that surrounded Burns', had conceptualised him as sexual man.[40] The biography made Carswell a household name – with the debate over the biography making newspaper headlines over a period of weeks – but also enemies. The full force of the Burns Federation was trained on her, while rather more ominously, she received in the post, anonymously, a bullet, with the request she use it to 'leave the world a better, brighter, cleaner place'.[41] Even years later she was never quite forgiven, with one of her obituary writers arguing that her book would have earned higher praise had she 'disliked Burnsians less' and if it had been less splenetic.[42] (She would have done better too if she had stuck to the evidence, according to one recent Burns scholar whose assessment was that Carswell had actually written a 'brilliant novel', but that as a biography it was 'gripped by a Modernist sexual hysteria, of the kind that . . . only a thoroughly bourgeois person could produce'.[43])

The puritan reaction Carswell's biography provoked was nothing new in the context of Burns. Indeed even a century after those ministers who 'came out' for Burns in 1859, there seem still to have been churchmen who considered him unworthy of a place in God's house. Specifically this meant St Giles' Kirk in Edinburgh, where the Burns Federation had unsuccessfully petitioned for a plaque for him to be placed (although the Cathedral Board protested that it was lack of space that was the problem).[44] However, the 1960s saw a further sharp decline in the membership and influence of the Church of Scotland, and, correspondingly, a self-conscious move on the part of the kirk towards a policy of what has been called 'niceness' – with the church reflecting rather than shaping public opinion.[45] A visible consequence was the fitting of a stained glass window in St Giles in 1985, commemorating Burns, and celebrating love, life, the brotherhood of man and man and nature.[46]

*   *   *

What this mild kerfuffle exposed, however, was an ongoing tetchiness in Burns Federation circles. Slights were perceived where none was intended. To question was to offend, as Ian McIntyre, the author of *Dirt and Deity*, a biography of Burns, discovered in 1996 when he tried, unsuccessfully, to procure a lock of Burns' hair in order to use DNA analysis to ascertain if he had fathered the infant in Greenock's cemetery, where the remains of Mary Campbell also lay.[47] While women are less marginalised by the clubs, those that still adhere to the male-only tradition can rile against any suggestion of chauvinism, or that they are somehow behind the times.[48]

By the end of the twentieth century few would have disagreed that Burns' principal role was as a 'cultural portal' for the country's tourist industry, a conduit through which the Scottish diaspora could continue to connect with the mother country.[49] Indeed in this capacity Burns is arguably more important than he has ever been: in a poll conducted at National Trust for Scotland properties in the spring of 2016 he was voted the country's 'Great Scot', and hailed as a leading ambassador for Scotland.[50] Burns' global reach and influence, impressive enough in the nineteenth century, spread further and deeper during the twentieth century, and has survived the collapse of the USSR, engaged tens of thousands in China and become part of the United Nations' call for brotherhood, compassion and tolerance.[51] Although the basis of the calculation is uncertain, it has been estimated that some 900,000 Burns suppers are held around the world every year – in over eighty different countries.[52] In de-industrialised Scotland culture and heritage have become commodities (much more so than in the past – although as we have seen Burns had long been commoditised), and had a major role to play in the process of economic regeneration, especially at the local level.[53] The Scottish Executive and later the Scottish Government identified him as a key economic asset, with the capacity to generate millions of pounds of spending power (a recent estimate put this at £160 million).[54] With the wholehearted blessing of the then First Minister Alex Salmond, Burns was used to spearhead the *Homecoming Scotland* initiative in 2009, an international tourism campaign that coincided with the celebrations to mark the 250th anniversary of Burns' birth. In many ways it was a remarkable year, with a host of activities organised to tie in with the anniversary, including new and enhanced websites, art exhibitions and festivals, and symposia and conferences both popular and academic. New commemorative coins and stamps were issued (as they had been for the bicentenary of 1996), while the Burns 'brand' was re-energised by whisky and shortbread manufacturers. The crowning achievement was the production by the US drinks giant Coca Cola of a special limited edition bottle featuring Robert Burns – the first ever designated to one country and a single individual.[55] Burns sells.

At the same time, and capitalising on the fascination – and lure – of Burns, the ambitious and expensive (£21 million) National Trust for Scotland's Robert Burns Birthplace Museum project was under way, building on the success of the Burns National Heritage Park that had been created in 1996 from the several monuments, including Burns' cottage, associated with the poet in Alloway.[56] Visitor numbers have risen from around a quarter of a million annually in the mid 2000s, to well over 300,000 since the new museum was opened (late in 2010), with an all-time peak of over 400,000 in 2011–12.[57]

* * *

Much of what has just been described was aimed at visitors to Scotland. What Burns meant to his fellow Scots is harder to say. The bicentenary year, 1959, was marked as previous anniversary dates had been. Exhibitions abounded and numerous Burns clubs held special dinners. Over 20,000 people 'thronged' to Alloway, taking advantage of free entry to the Burns cottage. As 25 January was a Sunday, the BBC broadcast a sermon from Alloway's new church, while the bell of the old kirk was also rung – after decades of silence. In douce Ayr, around 1,000 people listened as Grigori Ioanisyan, from the Russian embassy in London, waxed lyrically on Russia's long-standing admiration for Burns, and announced that Moscow radio was that very day broadcasting across the USSR a programme on Burns made by Emrys Hughes, the Labour MP for South Ayrshire and the son-in-law of Keir Hardie.[58] Yet there was nothing like the large-scale public involvement of the past; crowds assembled around the various monuments, for example, but in relatively small numbers. In stark contrast to 1859, churches were the main venue in many places, and clergymen were often the main speakers. Only one new statue was unveiled, in Arbroath, after a campaign that had lasted – intermittently – for seventy years (Plate 29). Messages from the event, held on 24 January – in the burgh's Old Church, which held the entire audience – were mixed, and demonstrate how readily Burns could be packaged to suit most political ideologies, in this instance at the same time.[59] Commissioned by the Burns Club, the statue, by Scott

Sutherland (1910–1984), was draped in the Saltire flag and the Lion Rampant. Standing erect with bulky legs slightly apart, hands clasped just below his waist, Burns is less like a poet than in any previous stone or bronze incarnation. Burns in Arbroath is a freedom fighter (a depiction that might have owed something to the fact that Sutherland had designed the Commando war memorial that was unveiled near Spean Bridge in 1952), an heir perhaps of the signatories of the Declaration of Arbroath in 1320. The burgh's provost in his speech referred to the Stone of Destiny that eight years earlier had been deposited in Arbroath Abbey after being taken from Westminster Abbey: both it and the statue, he declared, were 'representative of the soul and aspirations of a nation'. His hope was that the statue would remind onlookers of Burns and 'that love of humanity . . . democratic freedom and . . . individual responsibility which has characterised our nation and which he immortalized in verse'. Yet it was a representative of one of the county's oldest aristocratic dynasties, the Earl of Airlie, who performed the unveiling part of the ceremony, after two verses of 'God save the Queen' had been sung.[60]

It was that same Queen, Elizabeth II, in front of whom Sheena Wellington, the singer of Scottish traditional music, sang 'A Man's a Man' at the opening of the Scottish Parliament in Edinburgh in 1999. That Burns was sung by Wellington – and received rapturously – on such a momentous occasion in Scotland's history, with the democratic sentiments of the song referenced in the then First Minister Donald Dewar's speech that followed, is surely indicative that, for some Scots, Burns is more than simply a sufficiently well-known Scottish cultural icon to legitimise a genial evening out in what is invariably a wet, gloomy and wind-chilled late January.

Dewar's remarks were tasteful and eloquently put, patriotic but non-partisan. Subsequently though there has been something of a resurgence of the practice we noticed in the years immediately preceding the First World War – the impressment by politicians both left and right, unionist and (especially) nationalist, of Burns.[61] This last had not gone down well in Bo'ness in 1960 where the second annual Burns supper of the '200 Burns Club' had ended in fisticuffs involving some of the country's literary giants, including Norman MacCaig and MacDiarmid, then in his late sixties. It is not clear what incited the outbreak of disorder, although the comment of one attendee that there was 'too much talk about Scottish Nationalism and not about Burns' provides a pointer in the proximate direction of the likely cause.[62] In general, however,

Nationalists were helped by the repeated assertions about Burns' stance on the Union of 1707, and his likely attitude when the opportunity came to break it that had been made over the years by SNP loyalists such as Paul Scott.[63] More significant, in that it had many more readers, was the Scottish *Sun* newspaper's conflation in January 1995 of Burns, Scottish independence and support for the SNP. What had largely been an academic question became more immediately relevant as the referendum on Scottish independence in September 2014 approached. Predictably, Salmond, effectively the leader of the Yes (for independence) campaign (and, to be fair, reasonably knowledgeable about Burns), was sure that the poet would have been in favour.[64] So too was Scotland's Makar since 2011, Liz Lochhead.[65] Academics, who should have known better, but doubtless delighted to be asked, threw their professional caution to the wind, and also joined the fray.[66] Burns, Scotland's elastic symbol, was near to snapping.

Even if Burns would have voted in the affirmative to the question of 'Should Scotland be an independent country?' did anybody much care? Not, it would seem, in Burns' own Dumfries and Galloway, where there was a 65.7 per cent vote to remain within the UK (against 34.3 per cent Yes), one of the country's strongest demonstrations of support for the Union. There were other signs too that for Scots in Scotland Burns was no longer the clarion caller he had been. Until the National Trust's intervention for instance, the Burns cottage had 'continued to deteriorate into a state of increasingly shabby dampness'.[67] The National Monument in Mauchline as well as other memorials that had once roused the passions of those who fought for them, celebrated when they were inaugurated or who afterwards visited in hushed droves, were similarly ignored. Plans for a Burns International Festival in 1996, to mark the bicentenary of Burns' death, fell apart as the three Ayrshire councils involved squabbled, leading to delays in getting the fund-raising effort under way, the withdrawal of star performers such as Dame Kiri Te Kanawa and Billy Connolly – and the flight of the festival director from his wife and family in Mauchline to a new partner in Essex.[68] Plans for a worldwide Burns supper – along the lines of that of 1859 but this time linked by satellite – also had to be abandoned. The organisers did manage to commission another Burns statue (by Alexander Stoddart), however. This was unveiled in Kilmarnock – at the town cross – alongside that of Burns' publisher John Wilson. The numbers spectating, though, were a fraction of those in 1879.[69] With television and radio now beaming Burns into Scotland's living rooms – more often than not during the Burns supper season, including in the shape of the actor John Cairney, 'Burns' himself (in a six-part STV series in 1968, following his triumph in Tom Wright's play *There Was a Man* in 1965), there was less need for people to pay homage to Burns in person.[70]

Although the broadcast material was mixed in quality and often less challenging than some would have wished (audience numbers were the broadcasters' priority), the coverage helped keep Burns in the public eye. So too does the Robert Burns World Federation from its base in Kilmarnock, through the publication of the venerable but now refreshed *Burns Chronicle*, a quarterly newsletter, and host of events, including competitions for children, and the annual Robert Burns Humanitarian Award. In a poll that asked Scots who the country's most important historical figure was, conducted by the publishers of *Who's Who in Scotland* in 1999, Burns came top, ahead of Wallace and Bruce.[71] This reflects in part the fact that paperback editions of this long-dead poet's work have continued to sell in airport and railway bookstalls alongside popular fiction and footballers' life (and wife) stories. CDs of his songs by Wellington, Eddi Reader and others have a large audience too, while there are quite extraordinary viewing figures for YouTube renditions of 'My Love is like a Red Red Rose' and 'Auld Lang Syne'.[72] Newspaper editors continue to recognise that a new Burns story – dressed up as a sensational revelation, usually in the weeks immediately prior to the Burns supper season – will attract readers and a flurry of letter writing, depending on how controversial the article. At the forefront has been Glasgow's *Herald* newspaper, which to its credit sponsored for many years the University of Strathclyde's Centre for Scottish Cultural Studies' annual Burns conference series that began in 1990, now the responsibility of the city's older university. Freelancing columnists have also not been slow in recognising the opportunity the approach of Burns Night provides to stir up controversy. An instance is Michael Fry's blast at Burns (in January 2009 – the 250th anniversary, and therefore a canny choice of date on which to intervene), in which he pronounced him a 'drunken, misogynistic, racist philanderer', unfit to be a national hero and certainly not someone whose example could be useful at a time of economic crisis, as was being argued at the time by Scotland's First Minister.[73] Fry's intervention, though, was of minor consequence compared to the fury that had erupted the previous summer when the BBC television journalist Jeremy Paxman had described Burns – in passing in an introduction to a new edition of

Chambers Dictionary – 'as the king of sentimental doggerel'.[74] 'GET STUFFED, PAXO', was the banner headline of the Scottish edition of the establishment *Daily Telegraph*, which ran a piece in which Alan Cochrane and others, including an 'outraged' Alexander McCall Smith, rose in Burns' defence.[75]

However, the testiness that lies just beneath the skin of many Burns aficionados had erupted volcano-like more than a decade earlier when a relatively young Burns scholar, Patrick Hogg, announced that he had discovered a number of 'lost' poems by Burns, written in the 1790s and published in the *Morning Chronicle* and the *Edinburgh Gazetteer*.[76] So subversive was their content during a period of acute anxiety on the part of the British state, then at war with revolutionary France, that had Burns (as a government official – in the excise department) been identified as their author, he could well have been hanged.[77] More of the poems were published, backed by additional research carried out by Hogg and his collaborator Andrew Noble, in the *Canongate Burns*, in 2001. While there were those who welcomed the addition to Burns' oeuvre, at conferences and symposia, in the columns of the press and in learned articles the authenticity of the forty or more poems was hotly – and often intemperately – debated, with Hogg's 'discoveries' even being likened to the forged Hitler diaries that had been part-published in 1983. On both sides of the argument was serious underpinning investigation (the most forensic of which was conclusive in demonstrating that Burns had certainly not written them all – and that the author of one was probably the man who in 1793 had also written the very un-Burns-like *A Voyage to the Moon Strongly Recommended to all Lovers of Real Freedom*).[78] But, for many, at stake was the issue first raised more than two centuries earlier. This was about ownership, and whether or not – and to what extent – Burns had been a radical. That the quality of the poems newly attributed to him was generally reckoned to be poor (and would certainly not have satisfied the self-critical, word-precise Burns) was beside the point.

What these incidents highlighted was that, despite popularisation and commercialisation, Burns retained the capacity to ignite passions. 'Burnomania', or better, 'Burnsmania', has survived into the twenty-first century. But far less universally than in the past, other than amongst the Burns clubs, some of which are impressively buoyant. Equally striking was the relative narrowness of the constituency from which contributors to these heated and intense arguments were drawn. Prominent were academics. Scholarly interest in Burns had declined after the Second World War, the reputations of Romantic writers whose work was intensely national being tarnished by its association with 'the toxic stock of Nazi *volkisch* ideology and celebration'. In favour were writers of the imagination, vision and transcendence – like Wordsworth and William Blake.[79] Other factors accounting for Burns' disappearance from the ranks of the great British poets into which he had been firmly set in the nineteenth century, included the reduced status of literary Scots (and the alleged difficulties of his language), the prominence of the Burns cult itself, the absence of new critical approaches to Burns' work, charges of provincialism and his classification as a labouring class poet.

Not only have literary academics risen to Burns' defence in the past two to three decades, they have also begun to take him seriously as a subject of study – although to be fair some Scottish literature special-ists had long done so. As is the way amongst academics, there have been charges of careerism, the commodification of Burns, and of his being fetishised in conferences and books and essays.[80] Perhaps, but the formation of the international Global Burns Network project was indicative of more honourable intent. The establishment of the University of Glasgow's Centre for Robert Burns Studies around the same time, in 2007, and dedicated to 'the development of research, scholarship and teaching in the area of Robert Burns, his cultural period and related literature', is suggestive of something more compre-hensive, far removed from the 'wha's like us' school of Scottish self-satisfaction, and of lasting value. Indeed those involved are currently employed on a new multi-volume edition of Burns works in their entirety, along with other related publishing projects, some of which have already appeared in print.[81] Another memorial that promises to be every bit as important as those we have discussed in this book.

* * *

We began with a description of the unveiling of a statue. In the years since 1877 Burns statues have been the sites of intense fervour and exhilaration. They have also endured ignominy. Over time they have been neglected and defaced, and become depositaries of urban grime and, in more recent times, pit stops for town-dwelling gulls. The foun-tains that often sat alongside them, spouting fresh water for thirsty townspeople as their spirits were refreshed by gazing on Burns, have mainly been removed. The statues themselves in some places have been threatened with removal, although other than in Dumfries and

Leith stout resistance, mainly from local Burns clubs, has kept them firmly in place (Plate 30).

Although most of them can now be considered as important works of public art, silent witnesses to the centrality of Burns' place in Scotland's history until relatively recently, mainly they go unnoticed. The hopes expressed by their sponsors, that they would speak for all time to those who cared to look and listen, were in vain. True, as we saw in the previous chapter, the more zealous members of some Burns clubs, with civic support, place wreaths and other floral devices on and around them on 25 January each year. There are periodic agitations to have them cleaned and restored (Plate 31). Yet illustrative of the ebbed tide of popular engagement with Burns – of his having become a shadow (albeit a looming one) rather than a tangible force – was a ceremony I watched on an overcast afternoon in August 2012, on Montrose's Mid Links, to mark the centenary of the unveiling of the Burns statue there. The occasion was dignified, and in a low-key fashion, moving. Fittingly, Montrose Burns Club organised it and provided most of the speakers. But it was club members too who comprised most of the audience of no more than thirty or so. The few non-aligned spectators silently dispersed, a little underwhelmed and hardly noticed, after the town's band had played 'Auld Lang Syne'. All that fund-raising energy over the best part of three decades that had been expended by the club and the sculptor William Birnie Rhind at the turn of the twentieth century, not to mention his artistic endeavour, had come to this. But the extent to which things had turned was even more vividly illustrated in January 2016, when Nasmyth's Burns, for so long the icon of Burns worshippers, was employed by the Scottish Craft Butchers to advertise their haggises (Plate 32).

*   *   *

In January 1875 Walter Alexander, secretary of Glasgow Western Burns Club received a letter from John Finlay, in which was enclosed a poem, 'The Vanished Wood o' Craigielea'. Finlay, now forgotten, was ill and intimated this might be the last poem he wrote. But in his epistle he also commented on the statue of Burns then being prepared by George Ewing. Finlay had no objection to honouring the 'Immortal Bard', but even the most lasting statue, he argued, would be 'a frail memorial in comparison with the enduring nature of his works'. Finlay's prediction therefore was that 'instead of our monument preserving the name and memory of Burns, the Works of the great Bard will keep alive <u>the memory of the monument</u>'.[82]

The ailing Finlay was right. Despite all that has been said of Burns, and attributed to him, and notwithstanding the plundering of his legacy by competing and incompatible interests, it is Burns' poems and songs that remain. The sentiments expressed in the last couplet from the poem Burns had written on the tombstone he had erected in Edinburgh's Canongate graveyard to honour his fellow poet Robert Fergusson are as applicable in his own case:

> But dear to fame thy Song immortal lives,
> A nobler monument than Art can show.

Enigmatic perhaps, but owned by no one, Burns' works speak to us all, or at least to those who choose to read or listen.

Notes

Introduction

1 Ann Rigney, 'Embodied Communities: Commemorating Robert Burns, 1859', *Representations*, 115 (Summer 2011), p. 78; see too, Leith Davis, 'The Robert Burns 1859 Centenary: Mapping Transatlantic (Dis)location', in Sharon Alker, Leith Davis and Holly Faith Nelson (eds), *Robert Burns and Transatlantic Culture* (Farnham, 2012), pp. 191–2.

2 See James Ballantine, *Chronicle of the Hundredth Birthday of Robert Burns* (Edinburgh and London, 1859).

3 Edward J. Cowan, 'William Wallace: "The Choice of the Estates"', in Edward J. Cowan (ed.), *The Wallace Book* (East Linton, 2007), pp. 9–25.

4 Graeme Morton, *William Wallace: A National Tale* (Edinburgh, 2014 edn), pp. 144–7.

5 Stuart Kelly, *Scott-Land: The Man Who Invented a Nation* (Edinburgh, 2010).

6 For a list see J. A. M., 'The World-wide memorials to Robert Burns', *Burns Chronicle and Club Directory*, 98 (1989), pp. 77–82. Hereafter the annual *Chronicle* will be abbreviated to *BC*, with the year of publication, whether for the first, second or third series.

7 Ann Rigney, *The Afterlives of Walter Scott: Memory on the Move* (Oxford, 2012), p. 178.

8 See, for example, Henry V. Morton, *In Search of Scotland* (London, 1929, 1930 edn), p. 267.

9 William Robertson Turnbull, *The Heritage of Burns* (Haddington, 1896), pp. 3–4, 410.

10 *Otago Daily Times*, 12 May 1913.

11 Thomas Keith, 'Burns Statues in North America, A Survey', in G. Ross Roy (ed.), *Robert Burns & America: A Symposium* (Columbia, SC, 2001), pp. 23–33.

12 Christine MacLeod, *Heroes of Invention: Technology, Liberalism and British Identity, 1750–1914* (Cambridge, 2007), p. 24.

13 See, for example, Avner Ben-Amos, *Funerals, Politics and Memory in Modern France, 1789–1996* (Oxford, 2000).

14 Ray McKenzie, *Public Sculpture of Glasgow* (Liverpool, 2002), p. xiii.

15 *Scotsman*, 26 February 1949.

16 Tanja Bueltmann, *Clubbing Together: Ethnicity, Civility and Formal Sociability in the Scottish Diaspora to 1930* (Liverpool, 2014), pp. 176–9, 226.

17 Clark McGinn, 'Vehement Celebrations: The Global Celebration of the Burns Supper since 1801', in Murray Pittock (ed.), *Robert Burns in Global Culture* (Lewisburg, PA, 2011), pp. 189–203.

18 See Duncan Macmillan, *Scottish Art 1460–1990* (Edinburgh, 1990), chapter 9 especially.

19 Nicholas Roe, 'Authenticating Robert Burns', *Essays in Criticism*, 46 (1996), pp. 205–6; *The Times*, 18 December 1854.

20 John Erskine, 'Scotia's jewel: Robert Burns and Ulster, 1786–c.1830', in Frank Ferguson and Andrew R. Holmes (eds), *Revising Robert Burns and Ulster: Literature, Religion and Politics, c.1770–1920* (Dublin, 2009), pp. 15–16.

21 Ranald MacInnes, 'Robert Burns, Antiquarianism and Alloway Kirk: The Perception and Reception of Literary Place-making and the "Historic" Monument', *Architectural Heritage*, 24 (2013), p. 10; Nicola Watson, *Literary Tourism and Nineteenth-Century Culture* (Basingstoke, 2009), pp. 72–7.

22 *Scotsman*, 31 July 1819.

23 William McDowall, *History of Dumfries* (Edinburgh, 1867), pp. 732–3.

24 Michael A. Penman, 'Robert Bruce's Bones: Reputations, Politics and Identities in Nineteenth-Century Scotland', *International Review of Scottish Studies*, 34 (2009), p. 35.

25 Samantha Matthews, *Poetical Remains: Poets' Graves, Bodies and Books in the Nineteenth Century* (Oxford, 2004), pp. 72–4.

26 Mitchell Library [ML], MS 52890, James Gould, *Poems, Letters and Speeches Relating to the Centenary*, Vol. I, 1859–1882, handwritten introduction, n.d.

27 For a comprehensive account, see James A. Mackay, *Burnsiana* (Alloway, 1988).

28 Elizabeth Ewing, 'This "Burns–Relic" Business: The Decline and Fall of Hero-Worship', *BC* (1943), p. 11.

29 *John Hemming 1771–1851* (Paisley, 1977).

30 Pauline A. Mackay, 'Objects of Desire: Robert Burns the "Man's Man" and Material Culture', *Anglistik*, 23, 2 (2012), pp. 27–39.

31 Mackay, *Burnsiana*, p. 120; see, too, Murray Pittock and Christopher A. Whatley, 'Poems and Festivals, Art and Artefact and the Commemoration of Robert Burns, *c.*1844–*c.*1896', *Scottish Historical Review*, XCIII, 1, 236 (April 2014), pp. 56–79.

32 Ewing, ' "Burns-Relic" Business', p. 17.

33 Henry L. Fulton, *Dr John Moore, 1729–1802: A Life in Medicine, Travel, and Revolution* (Newark, NJ, 2015), p. 445.

34 Rhona Brown, ' "Guid black prent": Robert Burns and the Contemporary Scottish and American Periodical Press', in Alker et al. (eds), *Robert Burns*, pp. 80–1.

35 G. Ross Roy, ' "The Mair They Talk, I'm Kend the Better": Poems About Robert Burns to 1859', in Kenneth Simpson (ed.), *Love & Liberty, Robert Burns: A Bicentenary Celebration* (East Linton, 1997), p. 53.

36 Erskine, 'Scotia's jewel', pp. 27–29.

37 J. G. (ed.), *The Bibliography of Robert Burns, with Biographical and Bibliographical Notes, and Sketches of Burns Clubs, Monuments and Statues* (Kilmarnock, 1881), pp. 5–6.

38 See Basil C. Skinner, *Burns: Authentic Likenesses* (Edinburgh and London, 1967).

39 University of St Andrews, Special Collections, PLFR/1/A/1, Journal of the Rev. James Macdonald, 1796.

40 Ian McIntyre, *Dirt & Deity: A Life of Robert Burns* (London, 1995), pp. 397–9.

41 John Davies (ed.), *Apostle to Burns: The Diaries of William Grierson* (Edinburgh, 1981), p. 63.

42 Gerard Carruthers, 'Burns and Publishing', in Gerard Carruthers (ed.), *The Edinburgh Companion to Robert Burns* (Edinburgh, 2009), pp. 6–19.

43 See Jonathan Rose, *The Intellectual Life of the British Working Classes* (New Haven and London, 2002; 2010 edn), pp. 1–11.

44 Paul Barnaby and Tom Hubbard, 'The International Reception

and Literary Impact of Scottish Literature of the Period 1707–1918', in Susan Manning, Brown, Thomas Clancy Owen and Murray Pittock (eds), *The Edinburgh History of Scottish Literature, Volume Two: Enlightenment, Britain and Empire* (1707–1918), p. 39.

45 Murray Pittock, '"A Long Farewell to All My Greatness": The History of the Reputation of Robert Burns', in Pittock (ed.), *Robert Burns*, p. 28.

46 *Report of the Meeting Held to Celebrate the Centenary of the Birthday of Robert Burns, at the Revere House, Boston, January 25, 1859* (Boston, MA, 1859), p. 7.

47 James Coleman, *Remembering the Past in Nineteenth-Century Scotland: Commemoration, Nationality and Memory* (Edinburgh, 2014), p. 17.

48 *Scotsman*, 26 January 1877.

49 See Ferenc M. Szasz, *Abraham Lincoln and Robert Burns: Connected Lives and Legends* (Illinois, 2008).

50 Michael Fry, *A Higher World: Scotland 1707–1815* (Edinburgh, 2014), pp. 349–57; and T. Christopher Smout, *A Century of the Scottish People, 1830–1950* (London, 1986), pp. 19, 237, 246, 256.

51 Michael Lynch, *Scotland: A New History* (London, 1991), p. 357.

52 James D. Young, *The Rousing of the Scottish Working Class* (London, 1979), p. 65.

53 Christopher Harvie, *A Floating Commonwealth: Politics, Culture, and Technology on Britain's Atlantic Coast, 1860–1930* (Oxford, 2008), p. 38.

54 David Torrance, *The Scottish Secretaries* (Edinburgh, 2006), pp. 248–69.

55 William Knox (ed.), *Scottish Labour Leaders, 1918–1939: A Biographical Dictionary* (Edinburgh, 1984), pp. 37, 52.

56 Richard J. Finlay, 'The Burns Cult and Scottish Identity in the Nineteenth and Twentieth Centuries', in Simpson (ed.), *Love & Liberty*, p. 74; Isobel Lindsay, 'Scotland and Burns', *Perspectives*, 20 (Winter 2008–9), pp. 11–13.

57 In the British context see Paul A. Pickering and Alex Tyrrell (eds), *Contested Sites: Commemoration, Memorial and Popular Politics in Nineteenth-Century Britain* (Aldershot, 2004).

58 MacLeod, *Heroes*, chapters 6 and 10.

59 Alex Tyrrell, 'The Earl of Eglinton, Scottish Conservatism, and the National Association for the Vindication of Scottish Rights', *Historical Journal*, 53, 1 (2010), p. 94.

60 Kenneth G. Simpson, *The Protean Scot: The Crisis of Identity in Eighteenth-Century Scottish Literature* (Aberdeen, 1985).

61 Carol McGuirk, 'Writing Scotland: Robert Burns', in Susan Manning et al. (eds), *The Edinburgh History of Scottish Literature, Volume Two: Enlightenment, Britain and Empire (1707–1918)* (Edinburgh, 2007), p. 169.

62 David Hutchison, 'Burns, The Elastic Symbol: Press Treatment of Burns's Anniversary, 1995 and 1996', in Simpson (ed.), *Love & Liberty*, pp. 79–86.

63 George Rosie, 'Museumry and the Heritage Industry', in Ian Donnachie and Christopher Whatley (eds), *The Manufacture of Scottish History* (Edinburgh, 1992), p. 168.

64 Roland Quinault, 'The Cult of the Centenary, c.1784–1914', *Historical Research*, 71 (1998), pp. 303–23; Eric Hobsbawm, 'Introduction', in Eric Hobsbawm and Terence Ranger (eds), *The Invention of Tradition* (Cambridge, 2010 edn), pp. 1–14.

65 See Ann Rigney, 'Plenitude, Scarcity and the Circulation of Cultural Memory', *Journal of European Studies*, 25, 1 (2005), pp. 209–26.

66 For an exploration of this dualism, largely through literature and literary figures, see Matthew Campbell, Jacqueline M. Labbe and Sally Shuttleworth's 'Introduction' to their book of essays, *Memory and Memorials: Literary and Cultural Perspectives* (London and New York, 2000).

67 Thomas M. Devine, *Independence or Union: Scotland's Past and Scotland's Present* (2015), pp. 80–1, 89.

68 John Wolfe, *Great Deaths: Grieving, Religion, and Nationhood in Victorian and Edwardian Britain* (Oxford, 2000), pp. 4–5.

69 Michael Eaude, *Catalonia: A Cultural History* (Oxford, 2007), p. 61.

70 Lindsay Paterson, *The Autonomy of Modern Scotland* (Edinburgh, 1994), pp. 59–60; they continue to be, as in Jamie Maxwell, 'Still "Yes"', *Scottish Review of Books*, 11, 3 (2016), p. 18.

71 *Glasgow Herald*, 27 January 1877.

72 See Marcus C. Levitt, *Russian Literary Politics and the Pushkin Celebration of 1880* (New York, 1989), pp. 83–4.

73 Levitt, *Russian Literary Politics*, p. 4.

74 A. Tvardovsky (ed.), *Alexander Pushkin: Selected Works in Two Volumes, Volume One, Poetry* (Moscow, 1974), p. 14.

75 Marilyn Butler, 'Burns and Politics', in Robert Crawford (ed.), *Robert Burns and Cultural Authority* (Edinburgh, 1997), p. 111; Cairns Craig, 'National Literature and Cultural Capital in Scotland and Ireland', in Liam McIlvanney and Ray Ryan (eds), *Ireland and Scotland: Culture and Society, 1700–2000* (Dublin, 2005), pp. 41, 46–7.

76 Colin Kidd, *Union and Unionisms: Political Thought in Scotland, 1500–1900* (Cambridge, 2008), pp. 23–4.

77 Billy Kay, *The Mither Tongue* (Edinburgh and London, 2006), pp. 105–38.

78 Paula Murphy, *Nineteenth-Century Irish Sculpture, Native Genius Reaffirmed* (London, 2010), pp. 225–46.

79 Johnny Rodger, *The Hero Building: An Architecture of Scottish National Identity* (Farnham, 2015), pp. 78–85.

80 Archibald Alison, *Miscellaneous Essays* (Philadelphia, PA, 1845 edn), pp. 73–84.

81 *Scotsman*, 28 September 1833.

82 Marinell Ash, *The Strange Death of Scottish History* (Edinburgh, 1980), pp. 10–11.

83 Cairns Craig, 'Nineteenth-Century Scottish Thought', in Manning et al. (eds), *Edinburgh History*, pp. 267–76.

84 For a useful summary of the debate see Richard A. Marsden, *Cosmo Innes and the Defence of Scotland's Past c.1825–1875* (Farnham, 2014), pp. 3–19.

85 Kidd, *Union*, pp. 29–30.

86 Michael Fry, *Patronage and Principle: A Political History of Modern Scotland* (Aberdeen, 1978), pp. 208–9.

87 Morton, *Wallace*, pp. 174–96.

88 John Morrison, *Painting the Nation: Identity and Nationalism in Scottish Painting, 1800–1920* (Edinburgh, 2003), p. 14.

89 Nuala Johnson, 'Cast in Stone: Monuments, Geography and Nationalism', *Environment and Planning D: Society and Space*, 13 (1995), p. 57.

90 For a helpful discussion of these issues, see Richard Cronshaw, 'History and Memorialization', in Berger and Niven (eds), *Writing the History of Memory*, pp. 219–37.

91 Paul A. Pickering and Alex Tyrrell, 'The Public Memorial of

Reform: Commemoration and Contestation', in Pickering and Tyrrell (eds), *Contested Sites*, p. 2.

92 Stefan Berger and Bill Niven, 'Writing the History of National Memory', in Stefan Berger and Bill Niven (eds), *Writing the History of Memory* (London and New York, 2014), pp. 140–6.

93 Benedict Read, *Victorian Sculpture* (New Haven and London, 1984), p. 85.

94 Rigney, *Afterlives*, pp. 172–3.

95 *Scotsman*, 28 September 1863.

96 DI, MC, Section XIII, 26, Burnsiana, Vol. III, Collected and compiled by Walter Paterson, 1894, pp. 64–5, letter, Wilhelm Meister to the *Weekly Chronicle*, 24 Jan. 1891.

97 Graeme Morton, 'What if? The Significance of Scotland's Missing Nationalism in the Nineteenth Century', in Dauvit Broun, Richard J. Finlay and Michael Lynch (eds), *Image and Identity: The Making and Re-Making of Scotland Through the Ages* (Edinburgh, 1998), p. 167; Eric Hobsbawm, 'Mass-Producing Traditions: Europe, 1870–1914', in Hobsbawm and Ranger (eds), *Invention*, pp. 263–307.

98 Rigney, *Afterlives*, p. 172.

99 Tanja Bueltmann, Andrew Hinson and Graeme Morton, *The Scottish Diaspora* (Edinburgh, 2013), p. 262.

100 *Glasgow Herald*, 12 July 1890.

101 The wider issue of the male-centric nature of Scottish culture is addressed in Lynn Abrams, Eleanor Gordon, Deborah Simonton and Eileen J. Leo (eds), *Gender in Scottish History since 1700* (Edinburgh, 2006).

102 Leah Leneman, *A Guid Cause: The Women's Suffrage Movement in Scotland* (Aberdeen, 1991), pp. 204, 206.

103 Reverend William Peebles, *Burnomania: The Celebrity of Burns Considered In a Discourse Addressed to All Real Christians of Every Denomination* (Edinburgh, 1811).

104 Callum G. Brown, *Religion and Society in Scotland since 1707* (Edinburgh, 1997), pp. 69–74.

105 Carruthers, 'Burns and Publishing', pp. 12–13; Patrick Scott, 'The First Publication of "Holy Willie's Prayer"', *Scottish Literary Review*, 7, 1 (Spring/Summer 2015), pp. 6–12.

106 Steve Bruce, *Scottish Gods: Religion in Modern Scotland* (Edinburgh, 2014), pp. 1–2.

107 *The Witness*, 7 August 1844.

108 Alexander Webster, *Burns and the Kirk: A Review of What the Poet Did for the Religious and Social Regeneration of the Scottish People* (Aberdeen, Glasgow and Edinburgh, 1888), pp. 12–13.

Chapter 1

1 Edward Cowan and Mike Paterson, *Folk in Print: Scotland's Chapbook Heritage 1750–1850* (Edinburgh, 2007), pp. 11–40.
2 DI, MC, XIII, 24, Newspaper Cuttings, 1868–87, p. 82.
3 William McDowall, *History of Dumfries* (Edinburgh, 1867), p. 731; *Scotsman*, 8 February 1817; *Otago Daily Times*, 20 January 1968.
4 Fiona A. Black, 'Tracing the Transatlantic Bard's Availability', in Alker et al. (eds), *Robert Burns*, pp. 55–69.
5 *Hibernian Journal*, 3 August 1796.
6 *Hull Packet*, 28 February 1804.
7 National Library of Scotland [NLS], MS.8499A, Extracts, Diary of John Smith, 1812–54.
8 Davies, *Apostle*, p. 259.
9 Davies, *Apostle*, p. 275.
10 John Galt, *Autobiography* (London, 1833, 2 vols), Vol. II, pp. 281–2.
11 National Trust for Scotland [NTS] Burns Birthplace Museum [RBBM], Minutes, Monument to Robert Burns, 1814–41. I am grateful to David Hopes for providing me with transcripts of this material.
12 Johnny Rodger, 'The Burnsian Constructs', in Johnny Rodger and Gerard Carruthers (eds), *Fickle Man: Robert Burns in the 21st Century* (Dingwall, 2009), p. 61.
13 NTS, RBBM, Minutes, Monument to Robert Burns, 1814–44.
14 Nigel Leask, ' "Their Groves o' Sweet Myrtles": Robert Burns and the Scottish Colonial Experience', in Pittock (ed.), *Robert Burns*, 180–1.
15 *Scotsman*, 17 August 1831.
16 *Caledonian Mercury*, 29 April 1819.
17 *Caledonian Mercury*, 10 June 1819.
18 Edward Goodwillie, *The World's Memorials of Robert Burns* (Detroit, MI, 1911), 37–9.
19 Bob Harris and Charles McKean, The *Scottish Town in the Age of Enlightenment, 1740–1820* (Edinburgh, 2014), p. 362.

20 Dumfries Museum, DUMFM: 1965: 648, Minutes of Meeting Respecting Burns Mausoleum.

21 NTS, RBBM, Minutes of the Burns Monument Committee, 1814–45, 24 March 1814.

22 *Caledonian Mercury*, 29 April 1819.

23 *Dumfries Courier*, 7 June 1814; *Scotsman*, 8 February 1817.

24 Bueltmann, *Clubbing Together*, p. 31.

25 *Liverpool Mercury*, 28 October 1814.

26 *Scotsman*, 22 September 1831, 22 June 1833.

27 Colin Kidd, 'Burns and Politics', in Carruthers (ed.), *Edinburgh Companion*, p. 72.

28 National Records of Scotland, Buccleuch MSS, GD 224/653/4, Rev. H. Duncan to duke of Buccleuch, 20 December 1813, Buccleuch to Duncan, 30 Dec. 1813.

29 *The Autobiography of William Jerdan, with his Literary, Political, and Social Reminiscences and Correspondence* (London, 1852, 4 vols), Vol. II, p. 113.

30 'Scotus', 'Remarks on the Nationality of the Scots', *Kilmarnock Mirror and Literary Gleaner*, 1 (1819), p. 279.

31 *Scotsman*, 27 January 1827; see, too, Thomas M. Devine, *Scotland's Empire 1600–1815* (London, 2004), pp. 250–70.

32 *Caledonian Mercury*, 29 April 1819; 'An Indian Officer', *Pilgrimage to the Shrine of Burns During the Festival with the Gathering of the Doon and other Poetical Pieces* (Edinburgh, 1846), p. 9.

33 See Susan Manning, 'Robert Burns's Transatlantic Afterlives', in Alker, et al. (eds), *Robert Burns*, pp. 152–9.

34 On the 'clannishness' of the Scots see Douglas J. Hamilton, *Scotland, the Caribbean and the Atlantic World, 1750–1820* (Manchester, 2005) and, for the 'near diaspora', Bueltmann, *Clubbing Together*, pp. 27–59.

35 Szasz, *Abraham Lincoln*, pp. 31–2.

36 Harris and McKean, *Scottish Towns*, pp. 114–15, 123–4.

37 Christopher A. Whatley, 'Robert Burns, Memorialization, and the "Heart Beatings" of Victorian Scotland', in Pittock (ed.), *Robert Burns*, p. 211.

38 I am grateful to Robin Usher for providing me with transcripts of the correspondence (1818–19) between Turnerelli and William Grierson in Dumfries.

39 See Nigel Leask, 'Burns and the Poetics of Abolition', in Carruthers (ed.), *Edinburgh Companion*, pp. 47–60.

40 Watson, *Literary Tourism*, p. 68.

41 Davies, *Apostle*, p. 261.

42 'Scotus', 'Remarks', p. 274.

43 Cairns Craig, 'The Making of a Scottish Literary Canon', in Bill Bell (ed.), *The History of the Book in Scotland, Volume 3: Ambition and Industry, 1800–1880* (Edinburgh, 2007), pp. 266–7.

44 Colin Kidd, *Subverting Scotland's Past: Scottish Whig Historians and the Creation of an Anglo-British Identity, 1689–c.1830* (Cambridge, 1993).

45 George Davie, *The Democratic Intellect* (Edinburgh, 1991 [1961]), pp. 3–25; Paul H. Scott, ' "The Last Purely Scotch Age" ', in Douglas Gifford (ed.), *The History of Scottish Literature, Volume 3: Nineteenth Century* (Aberdeen, 1988), pp. 13–21.

46 'Scotus', 'Remarks', p. 275.

47 Ian G. Brown, 'Modern Rome and Ancient Caledonia: the Union and the Politics of Scottish Culture', in Andrew Hook (ed.), *The History of Scottish Literature, Volume 2: 1660–1800* (Aberdeen, 1987), pp. 33–48.

48 MacInnes, 'Robert Burns', pp. 5–11.

49 Sir Walter Scott, *The Letters of Malachi Malagrowther* (Edinburgh, 1981); Kidd, *Subverting Scotland's Past*, p. 266.

50 Craig, 'Making of a Scottish Literary Canon', pp. 267–8.

51 Fulton, *Dr John Moore*, pp. 448–9.

52 *Journal of Henry Cockburn* (Edinburgh, 1874), Vol. II, pp. 89, 295–6.

53 Kidd, *Subverting Scotland's Past*, p. 251.

54 Kidd, *Subverting Scotland's Past*, pp. 2–4.

55 J. Derrick McClure, *Language, Poetry and Nationhood: Scots as a Poetic Language from 1878 to the Present* (East Linton, 2000), p. 10.

56 Kilmarnock Burns Monument Centre, Sec IX, 51, Transcription of the minutes of Kilmarnock Burns Club, 1808–59.

57 Kirsteen McCue, 'Burns's Songs and Poetic Craft', in Carruthers (ed.), *Edinburgh Companion*, pp. 77–85.

58 Celeste Langan, 'Scotch Drink & Irish Harps: Mediations of the National Air', in Phyllis Weliver (ed.), *The Figure of Music in Nineteenth-Century British Poetry* (Farnham, 2005), pp. 25–49.

59 Dumfries Museum, DUMFM: 1965: 648, Report of a Meeting of Friends and Admirers of Robert Burns in London, Free Masons Hall, Saturday 25 May 1816.

60 See John Prebble, *The King's Jaunt: George IV in Scotland, 1822* (London, 1988).

61 Alex Tyrrell, 'Paternalism, Public Memory and National Identity in Early Victorian Scotland: the Robert Burns Festival at Ayr in 1844', *History*, 90, 1 (2005), pp. 49–50.

62 Andrew Noble, 'Introduction', in Andrew Noble and Patrick S. Hogg (eds), *The Canongate Burns* (Edinburgh, 2001), pp. xlvi–lxxxviii.

63 ML, Currie Correspondence [CC], Envelope 5 (1), James Currie to John Syme, 1 September 1796. I am grateful to Dr Rhona Brown, University of Glasgow, for this reference.

64 James Currie, *The Works of Robert Burns, With a Criticism on His Writings, To Which are Prefixed Some Observations on The Scottish Peasantry* (London, 1801, 2nd edn), p. 9; ML, CC, Envelope 16 (3), George Thomson to James Currie, 8 September 1799.

65 Robert H. Cromek, *Reliques of Robert Burns, Consisting Chiefly of Original Letters, Poems and Critical Observations on Scottish Songs* (London, 1808), pp. vi–xi.

66 John Wilson, 'On the Genius and Character of Burns', in John Wilson and Robert Chambers, *The Land of Burns, A Series of Landscapes and Portraits, Illustrative of the Life and Writings of the Scottish Poet* (Glasgow, 1840), pp. ci, cxviii–ix.

67 Bob Harris, *The French Revolution and the Scottish People* (London, 2008), pp. 174–83.

68 *Hull Packet*, 28 February 1804.

69 *Caledonian Mercury*, 3 February 1825.

70 Robert Brown, *Paisley Burns Clubs 1805–1893* (Paisley, 1893), pp. 144, 266.

71 See Charles J. Esdale, 'The French Revolutionary and Napoleonic Wars, 1793–1815', in Edward M. Spiers, Jeremy M. Crang and Matthew J. Strickland (eds), *A Military History of Scotland* (Edinburgh, 2012), pp. 407–35.

72 *Autobiography of William Jerdan*, Vol. II, p. 119.

73 Noble, 'Introduction', p. x; see, too, Andrew Noble, 'Versions of Scottish Pastoral: the Literati and the Tradition 1780–1830', in T. Markus (ed.), *Order in Space and Society: Architectural Form and its Context in the Scottish Enlightenment* (Edinburgh: Mainstream, 1982), pp. 263–311.

74 Thomas M. Devine, *The Transformation of Rural Scotland: Social Change in the Agrarian Economy, 1660–1815* (Edinburgh, 1994), p. 165.

75 Malcolm Gray, 'The Social Impact of Agrarian Change in the Rural Lowlands', in Thomas M. Devine and Rosalind Mitchison (eds), *People and Society in Scotland, Volume I, 1760–1830* (Edinburgh, 1988), pp. 59–62.

76 Devine, *Transformation*, p. 160.

77 Michael Michie, *An Enlightenment Tory in Victorian Scotland: The Career of Sir Archibald Alison* (East Linton, 1997), pp. 13–49.

78 Stana Nenadic, 'Political Reform and the "Ordering" of Middle-Class Protest', in Thomas M. Devine (ed.), *Conflict and Stability in Scottish Society, 1700–1850* (Edinburgh, 1990), pp. 68–76; Harris, *Scottish People*, pp. 80–6.

79 Herbert J. C. Grierson (ed.), *The Letters of Sir Walter Scott, 1819–21* (London, 1934), pp. 1–3, 16–18, 29–33, 38–47.

80 Christopher A. Whatley, *Scottish Society 1707–1830: Beyond Jacobitism, Towards Industrialisation* (Manchester, 2000), p. 287.

81 *Journal of Henry Cockburn, Being a Continuation of the Memorials of his Time, 1831–1854* (2 vols, Edinburgh, 1874), Vol. II, pp. 2–6; Gordon Pentland, 'The Debate on Scottish Parliamentary Reform, 1830–1832', *Scottish Historical Review*, 85, 1 (April 2006), p. 112.

82 Whatley, *Scottish Society*, pp. 307–27.

83 Duncan Kelly, 'The Art and Science of Politics in Blackwood's Edinburgh Magazine', in Robert Morrison and Daniel S. Roberts (eds), *Romanticism and Blackwood's Magazine* (Houndmills, 2013), p. 138.

84 Nigel Leask, ' "The Shadow Line": James Currie's "Life of Burns" and British Romanticism', in Claire Lamont and Michel Rossington (eds), *Romanticism's Debatable Lands* (London, 2007), p. 73.

85 Noble, 'Introduction', p. liii.

86 Carruthers, 'Burns and Publishing', p. 13.

87 Lawrance J. Saunders, *Scottish Democracy, 1815–40* (London, 1950), p. 52; and see, too, contemporaneous local histories such as Andrew Mercer, *The History of Dunfermline* (Dunfermline, 1828), pp. 192–3.

88 James Tait, *Two Centuries of Border Church Life* (Kelso, 1889), p. 144.

89 Emerus, 'The Radical's Saturday Night', *Blackwood's Edinburgh Magazine*, 6, 33 (December 1819), pp. 257–62.

90 Christopher A. Whatley, '"Zealous in the Defence of the Protestant Religion and Liberty": The Making of Whig Scotland, *c.*1688 – *c.*1746', in Allan I. Macinnes, Kieran German and Lesley Graham (eds), *Living with Jacobitism, 1690–1788* (London, 2014), pp. 55–70.

91 Wilson, 'On the Genius and Character of Burns', p. xxx.

92 Goodwillie, *World's Memorials*, pp. 38–9.

93 See, for example, University of St Andrews Special Collections, CH5/274/1, Records of the Free Presbytery of St Andrews, Vol. 1, 1843–62, 15 July 1844.

94 David Eastwood, 'The Age of Uncertainty: Britain in the Early Nineteenth Century', *Transactions of the Royal Historical Society*, Vol. VIII (1998), pp. 110–15.

95 Alan B. Campbell, *The Lanarkshire Miners: A Social History of their Trade Unions, 1775–1874* (Edinburgh, 1979), pp. 247–53; Young, *Rousing*, pp. 81–8.

96 ML, Glasgow, Burns Collection, No. 52910, MS 55/4, Resumé of an address delivered [by Colin Rae Brown] to members of the London Burns Club, 25 January 1882.

97 DI, MC, XI, 2, Burnsiania Scraps, 2E, *Guide to the Burns Festival, 1844.*

98 Davis, 'Robert Burns 1859 Centenary', p. 189.

99 DI, MC, VIII, 28c, Andrew Park, *Festival in Honour of the Memory of Our National Poet, Robert Burns* (Glasgow, 1844), p. 3.

100 John Strawhorn, *The History of Ayr* (Edinburgh, 1989), p. 175.

101 Tyrrell, 'Paternalism', p. 44.

102 James Coleman, 'Unionist-Nationalism in Stone? The National Wallace Monument and the Hazards of Commemoration in Victorian Scotland', in Cowan (ed.), *Wallace*, pp. 158, 161.

103 Whatley, 'Robert Burns', p. 217.

104 Park, *Festival*, p. 14.

105 DI, MC, XI, Burnsiana Scraps, 2E, Guide to the Burns Festival, 1844.

106 Saunders, *Scottish Democracy*, pp. 69–72; David McClure (ed.), *Ayrshire in the Age of Improvement* (Ayr, 2002), pp. 126–7.

107 John MacQueen, *A letter to His Grace the Duke of Hamilton and Brandon, Lord Lieutenant of Lanarkshire, Detailing the Events of the Late Rebellion in the West of Scotland, With Observations on the Present Alarming State of That and Other Parts of the Empire* (Glasgow, 1820), p. 39.

108 Strawhorn, *History*, pp. 153–8.
109 Alexander Fenton, *Scottish Country Life* (East Linton, 1999), pp. 72, 227.
110 John Rule, *The Labouring Classes and Early Industrial England, 1750–1850* (London, 1986), pp. 360–3.
111 Reported in the *Dundee Warder*, 23 July 1844.
112 *Scotsman*, 10 August 1844.
113 *The Witness*, 7 August 1844.
114 Tyrrell, 'Paternalism', p. 57.
115 *Pilgrimage*, pp. 5–6.
116 Quoted in Davis, 'Robert Burns 1859 Centenary', p. 191.
117 *Punch*, Vol. 7, 1844, p. 81.
118 DI, MC, XI, 2E, Guide.
119 See *The Illustrated London News*, 10 August 1844, for a full report.
120 Brown, *Religion and Society*, p. 79.
121 John Burnett, 'The Banner of Liberty: Symbols and the Celebration of the 1832 Reform Bill in Scotland', *Review of Scottish Culture*, 21 (2009), p. 92.
122 Charles Mackay, *Forty Years' Recollections of Life, Literary and Public Affairs* (London, 1877, 2 vols), Vol. I, p. 259.
123 *Pilgrimage*, pp. 9–11.
124 *The Witness*, 7 and 10 August 1844.
125 DI, MC, Sec III, 249.
126 Smout, *Century*, pp. 192–4.

Chapter 2

1 Jonathan Rose, *The Intellectual Life of the British Working Classes* (New Haven and London, 2002, 2010 edn), p. 9.
2 Harris and McKean, *Scottish Town*, pp. 378–94.
3 John de Lancey Ferguson (ed.), *The Letters of Robert Burns* (Oxford, 1931, 2 vols), Vo. I, p. 320, Vol. II, pp. 89–90.
4 William McDowall, *Burns in Dumfriesshire: A Sketch of the Last Eight Years of the Poet's Life* (Edinburgh, 1881), p. 30.
5 Robert Heron, *A Memoir of the Life of the Late Robert Burns* (Edinburgh, 1797), p. 17.
6 Valentine Bold, *James Hogg: A Bard of Nature's Making* (Oxford, 2007), pp. 203–53.
7 Rose, *Intellectual Life*, p. 16.

8 Norman Murray, *The Scottish Hand Loom Weavers, 1790–1850: A Social History* (Edinburgh, 1978), pp. 152–3, 168–76; Tony Clarke and Tony Dickson, 'Class and Class Consciousness in Early Industrial Capitalism: Paisley 1770–1850', in Tony Dickson (ed.), *Capital and Class in Scotland* (Edinburgh, 1982), p. 27.

9 Alexander B. Grosart (ed.), *The Poems and Literary Prose of Alexander Wilson, The American Ornithologist* (Paisley, 1876, 2 vols), Vol. I, pp. xxiii, xxxvii.

10 See Tom Leonard (ed.), *Radical Renfrew: Poetry from the French Revolution to the First World War* (Edinburgh, 1990); Douglas Dunn, 'Auld Breeks and Daft Days', in Robert Crawford (ed.), ' "*Heaven-Taught Fergusson*": *Robert Burns's Favourite Scottish Poet* (East Linton, 2003), p. 46.

11 Liam McIlvanney, *Burns the Radical: Poetry and Politics in Late Eighteenth-Century Scotland* (East Linton, 2002), pp. 103–7.

12 Brown, 'Guid Black Prent', pp. 76–7.

13 Leask, ' "The Shadow Line" ', p. 64.

14 Bob Harris, *The Scottish People and the French Revolution* (London, 2008), p. 165.

15 Bold, *James Hogg*, pp. 215–16.

16 Florence S. Boos (ed.), *Working-Class Women Poets in Victorian Britain: An Anthology* (Toronto, 2008), pp. 47–50.

17 Vivien Dunstan, 'Glimpses into a Town's Reading Habits in Enlightenment Scotland: Analyzing the Borrowings of Gray Library, Haddington, 1732–1816', *Journal of Scottish Historical Studies*, 26, 1–2 (2006), pp. 50, 55.

18 *Kilmarnock Standard*, 7 April 1877.

19 Christopher A. Whatley, ' "It Is Said That Burns Was a Radical": Contest, Concession, and the Political Legacy of Robert Burns, ca.1796–1859', *Journal of British Studies*, 50, 3 (July 2011), p. 659.

20 Kidd, 'Burns and Politics', p. 72, and see n. 48.

21 William Donaldson, 'Popular Literature: The Press, the People, and the Vernacular Revival', in Gifford (ed.), *History of Scottish Literature*, p. 203.

22 Cowan and Paterson, *Folk in Print*, p. 13.

23 Philip Connell and Nigel Leask, 'What is the People?', in Philip Connell and Nigel Leask (eds), *Romanticism and Popular Culture in Britain and Ireland* (Cambridge, 2009), p. 26.

24 See G. Ross Roy, 'Some Notes on Scottish Chapbooks', *Scottish Literary Journal*, 1, 1 (1974), p. 51.

25 DI, MC, Sec XIII, 27, Scrapbook, 1873–93, James Gibson to James M'Kie, 13 January 1877.

26 John Carswell (ed.), *The Autobiography of a Working Man, by Alexander Somerville* (London, 1951 edn), p. 43.

27 David Vincent (ed.), *Bread, Knowledge and Freedom: A Study of Nineteenth-Century Working Class Autobiography* (London, 1981), pp. 55, 186–7.

28 Harris and McKean, *Scottish Town*, p. 366; William Donaldson, *The Jacobite Song* (Aberdeen, 1988), pp. 72–89.

29 Matthew Gelbart, *The Invention of 'Folk Music' and 'Art Music': Emerging Categories from Ossian to Wagner* (Cambridge, 2007), pp. 80–98.

30 Erskine, 'Scotia's jewel', pp. 33–4.

31 William Thom, *Rhymes and Recollections of A Hand-Loom Weaver* (London, 1845), pp. 14–15.

32 Thomas Crawford, *Boswell, Burns and the French Revolution* (Edinburgh, 1990), pp. 61–3.

33 Robert Brown, *The History of Paisley* (Paisley, 1886, 2 vols), Vol. II, pp. 170, 181.

34 Robert Crawford, *Bannockburns: Scottish Independence and Literary Imagination, 1314–2014* (Edinburgh, 2014), pp. 57–96.

35 Patrick Joyce, *Visions of the People: Industrial England and the Question of Class, 1848–1914* (Cambridge, 1991), pp. 31–2, 37; W. Hamish Fraser, *Chartism in Scotland* (Pontypool, 2010), p. 212; Kate Bowan and Paul A. Pickering, ' "Songs for the Millions": Chartist Music and Popular Aural Tradition', *Labour History Review*, 74, 1 (April 2009), p. 55.

36 'Robert Burns and Masonry', *People's Friend*, 20 November 1872.

37 McIlvanney, *Burns the Radical*, pp. 26–7, 196–7; Bob Harris, *A Tale of Three Cities: The Life and Times of Lord Daer, 1763–1794* (Edinburgh, 2015), pp. 11–12.

38 Harris and McKean, *Scottish Town*, pp. 442–3; on freemasonry, see Margaret C. Jacob, *Living the Enlightenment: Freemasonry and Politics in Eighteenth-Century Europe* (Oxford, 1991), pp. 23–71.

39 Mark Wallace, 'Scottish Freemasons and the Struggle for Identity: Radical Scapegoats or Revolutionary Extremists?', unpublished

paper. I am grateful to Dr Wallace for letting me have a copy of this.

40 *Dumfries Courier*, 6 June 1815.

41 *Kilmarnock Standard*, 14 September 1878.

42 M. Roberts, 'Burns and the Masonic Enlightenment', in Jennifer J. Carter and Joan H. Pittock (eds), *Aberdeen and the Enlightenment* (Aberdeen, 1988), p. 333; McIntyre, *Dirt & Deity*, p. 104.

43 McGinn, 'Vehement Celebrations', p. 198.

44 McIlvanney, *Burns the Radical*, pp. 36–7.

45 John Crawford, 'Recovering the Lost Scottish Community Library: The Example of Fenwick', *Library History*, 23 (September 2007), p. 204.

46 James Mackay, *Little Boss: A Life of Andrew Carnegie* (Edinburgh and London, 1997), pp. 15–41.

47 Kay, *Mither Tongue*, pp. 108–9.

48 Roger J. Fechner, 'Burns and American Liberty', in Simpson (ed.), *Love & Liberty*, pp. 274–87.

49 Knox, *Industrial Nation*, pp. 56–7.

50 Noble and Hogg (eds), *The Canongate Burns*, pp. 825–7, 845–51; for an alternative standpoint see Gerard Carruthers and Norman R. Paton, 'Did Robert Burns Write "The Tree of Liberty"?', in Rodger and Carruthers (eds), *Fickle Man*, pp. 242–56.

51 Leith Davis, 'Burns and Transnational Culture', in Carruthers (ed.), *Edinburgh Companion*, pp. 151–3; Rhona Brown, 'Burns and Robert Fergusson', *Edinburgh Companion*, pp. 88–92.

52 Ferguson, *Letters of Robert Burns*, I, p. 107; Crawford, *Boswell, Burns and the French Revolution*, pp. 28–9.

53 Murray Pittock, *Scottish and Irish Romanticism* (Oxford, 2008), p. 153.

54 Peter Aitchison and Andrew Cassell, *The Lowland Clearances: Scotland's Silent Revolution 1760–1830* (East Linton, 2003), pp. 90–107.

55 Patrick Joyce, *Democratic Subjects: The Self and the Social in Nineteenth-Century England* (Cambridge, 1994), pp. 59–60, 173.

56 Carruthers, 'Burns and Publishing', pp. 9–11.

57 Hogg, 'First Publication', p. 5.

58 McIlvanney, *Burns the Radical*, pp. 123–35, 143–4.

59 Robert Williams Buchanan, *The Coming Terror, and Other Essays* (London, 1891), pp. 313–19.

60 Boos, *Working-Class Women*, pp. 18–19.

61 See, for example, Rev. George Gilfillan (ed.), *The National Burns* (London, Glasgow and Edinburgh, 1879–80, 2 vols), Vol. I, p. xxx.

62 DI, MC, IX, 128, *Leaves From a Peasant's Cottage Door Being Poems By Robert Davidson, Day Labourer, Morebattle, Roxburghshire* (Edinburgh, 1848), pp. 7–12.

63 Thomas M. Devine, 'Urbanisation', in Devine and Mitchison (eds), *People and Society*, p. 31.

64 Christopher A. Whatley, 'Introduction', in Christopher A. Whatley (ed.), *The Diary of John Sturrock, Millwright, Dundee, 1864–5* (East Linton, 1996), p. 8.

65 Cowan and Paterson, *Folk in Print*, pp. 36–8.

66 Thomas M. Devine, 'Introduction: Scottish Farm Service in the Agricultural Revolution', in Thomas M. Devine (ed.), *Farm Servants and Labour in Lowland Scotland, 1770–1914* (Edinburgh, 1984), p. 4.

67 Charles W. Munn, *Airdrie Savings Bank: A History* (Airdrie, 2010), p. 5.

68 John Barrel, 'Rus in urbe', in Connell and Leask (eds), *Romanticism*, pp. 113–14.

69 Quoted in Bold, *James Hogg*, p. 219.

70 Brown, *Paisley Burns Clubs*, pp. 37–53, 96–7, 122–3.

71 Alexander Stewart, *Reminiscences of Dunfermline and Neighbourhood, Illustrative of Dunfermline Life, Sixty Years Ago* (Dunfermline, 1886), p. 266; Whatley, ' "It is Said That Burns was a Radical" ', p. 661.

72 McGuirk, 'Writing Scotland', p. 176.

73 Henry Skrine, *Three Successive Tours in the North of England And a Great Part of Scotland* (London, 1795), pp. 162–3.

74 Keith M. Brown, *Noble Power in Scotland From the Reformation to the Revolution* (Edinburgh, 2013 edn), p. 244.

75 Whatley, *Scottish Society*, pp. 142–83.

76 Thomas M. Devine, 'Unrest and Stability in Rural Ireland and Scotland, 1760–1840', in Rosalind Mitchison and Peter Roebuck (eds), *Economy and Society in Scotland and Ireland, 1500–1939* (Edinburgh, 1988), pp.128–31.

77 Callum G. Brown, 'Protest in the Pews. Interpreting Presbyterianism and Society in Fracture During the Scottish

Economic Revolution', in Thomas M. Devine (ed.), *Conflict and Stability in Scottish Society, 1700–1850* (Edinburgh, 1990), pp. 91–2.

78 Quoted in Brown, *Religion*, p. 79.

79 Brown, *Religion*, pp. 67–76.

80 Devine, 'Unrest and Stability', p. 133.

81 Devine, 'Introduction', in Devine (ed.), *Farm Servants*, p. 6.

82 James H. Treble, 'The Standard of Living of the Working Class', in Devine and Mitchison (eds), *People and Society*, pp. 203–6.

83 Murray, *Scottish Handloom Weavers*, pp. 114–16, 172–8.

84 Leonard, *Radical Renfrew*, p. xix.

85 Harris, *Scottish People*, p. 86.

86 Brown, 'Protest', p. 87.

87 Ballantine, *Chronicle*, pp. 115–16.

88 Boos, *Working-Class Women*, pp. 157–9.

89 William Finlay, 'Reclaiming Local Literature: William Thom and Janet Hamilton', in Gifford (ed.), *History of Scottish Literature*, p. 361.

90 Carswell (ed.), *Autobiograhy*, p. 43.

91 David Buchan, 'The Expressive Culture of Nineteenth-Century Scottish Farm Servants', in Devine (ed.), *Farm Servants*, p. 238.

92 Martha Vicinus, *The Industrial Muse: A Study of Nineteenth Century Working Class Literature* (London, 1974), pp. 141–2.

93 Campbell, *Lanarkshire Miners*, pp. 160–1.

94 Bold, *James Hogg*, p. 283.

95 Kirstie Blair, ' "A Very Poetical Town": Newspaper Poetry and the Working-Class Poet in Dundee', *Victorian Poetry*, 52, 1 (Spring 2014), p. 89.

96 Thom, *Rhymes*, p. 40.

97 Lawrance J. Saunders, *Scottish Democracy, 1815–40* (Edinburgh, 1950), p. 260.

98 Aileen Black, *Gilfillan of Dundee, 1813–78: Interpreting Religion and Culture in Mid-Victorian Scotland* (Dundee, 2006), p. 170.

99 Boos, *Working-Class Women*, p. 156.

100 Rose, *Intellectual Life*, p. 60.

101 William Howitt, *Homes and Haunts of the British Poets* (1847), quoted in Brian Maidment (ed.), *The Poorhouse Fugitives: Self-Taught Poets and Poetry in Victorian Britain* (Manchester, 1987), p. 304.

102 Joyce, *Visions*, p. 37; Blair, ' "Poetical Town" ', pp. 94, 99.

103 Harriett Jay, *Robert Buchanan. Some Account of his Life, his Life's Work and his Literary Friendships* (London, 1903), pp. 17–30.

104 Blair, ' "Poetical Town" ', p. 91.

105 Henry Shanks, *The Peasant Poets of Scotland* (Bathgate, 1881), pp. 162–6.

106 Michael Robson, 'The Border Farm Worker', in Devine (ed.), *Farm Servants*, p. 90.

107 See, for example, Andrew Mackillop, 'Dundee, London and the Empire in Asia', in Charles McKean, Bob Harris and Christopher A. Whatley (eds), *Dundee: Renaissance to Enlightenment* (Dundee, 2009), pp. 160–85.

108 Brown, *Religion*, pp. 80–3.

109 Maidment, *Poorhouse Fugitives*, pp. 27–30.

110 *Poems and Lyrics By Robert Nicoll, with a Memoir of the Author* (Paisley, 1877 edn), pp. xxi–lxix; Peter R. Drummond, *The Life of Robert Nicoll, Poet* (Paisley and London, 1884), pp. 189–215.

111 *Northern Star*, 18 June 1842.

112 Saunders, *Scottish Democracy*, pp. 73–5; Eugenio F. Biagini, *Liberty, Retrenchment and Reform: Popular Liberalism in the Age of Gladstone, 1860–1880* (Cambridge, 1992), pp. 89–90.

113 Malcolm Chase, *Chartism: A New History* (Manchester, 2007), p. 143.

114 Vicinus, *Industrial Muse*, pp. 107–8.

115 Patrick Joyce, *Visions of the People: Industrial England and the Question of Class, 1848–1914* (Cambridge, 1991), p. 77; Biagini, pp. 87–8.

116 Chase, *Chartism*, p. 56.

117 *Northern Star*, 24 August 1844.

118 *Northern Star*, 25 August 1843.

119 *Punch*, Vol. 7, 1844, p. 129.

120 *Glasgow Herald*, 28 June 1844.

121 *Northern Star*, 24 August 1844.

122 Charles Kingsley, 'Art. V-1. Elliot's Poems, London . . . The Book of Scottish Song. By Alexander Whitelaw. Edinburgh. 1848', *The North British Review*, 16 (1851–2), pp. 149–83 (*Literature Online*, http://lion.chadwyck.co.uk).

123 Hugh Miller, *Trinity College Church versus The Burns Monument* (Edinburgh, 1856), p. 13.

124 Ian G. C. Hutchison, *A Political History of Scotland 1832–1924: Parties, Elections and Issues* (Edinburgh, 1986), p. 92.

Chapter 3

1 Fraser, *Chartism*, p. 201.
2 W. Hamish Fraser, *A History of British Trade Unionism, 1700– 1998* (Houndmills and New York, 1999), p. 25.
3 Fraser, *Chartism*, p. 142.
4 Alex Tyrrell and Mike T. Davis, 'Bearding the Tories: The Commemoration of the Scottish political Martyrs of 1793–94', in Paul Pickering and Alex Tyrrell (eds), *Contested Sites: Commemoration, Memorial and Popular Politics in Nineteenth-Century Britain* (Aldershot, 2004), pp. 29–32.
5 Johnny Rodger, 'The Burnsian Constructs', in *Fickle Man*, pp. 63–4; Tyrrell and Davis, 'Bearding the Tories', pp. 41–2.
6 Goodwillie, *World's Memorials*, p. 36; Rodger, 'Burnsian Constructs', pp. 64–5.
7 Joep Leerssen, 'Viral Nationalism: Romantic Intellectuals on the Move in Nineteenth-Century Europe', *Nations and Nationalism*, 17, 2 (2011), pp. 1–15.
8 Rigney, 'Embodied Communities', p. 87.
9 Francis Adams, *The Writings of Burns: Being a Discourse Delivered at Banchory, On the Burns Centenary* (Aberdeen, 1859), p. 5.
10 *The Celebration of the Burns Centenary at Kirkcudbright, 25th January 1859* (Liverpool, 1859).
11 Ballantine, *Chronicle*, p. 225.
12 Pittock, ' "A Long Farewell" ', p. 32.
13 Ballantine, *Chronicle*, pp. 162–6.
14 Davis, 'Robert Burns 1859 Centenary', pp. 195–6.
15 Ballantine, *Chronicle*, p. 328.
16 Gould, *Letters, Poems and Speeches*, Vol. II, p. 154.
17 Ballantine, *Chronicle*, pp. 300–6.
18 Ballantine, *Chronicle*, p. 388.
19 ML, Burns Collection, MS 55/4, 'Resumé of an address delivered to members of the London Burns Club on 25th January 1882'.
20 Rigney, 'Embodied Communities', p. 75.
21 ML, Burns Collection, MS 55/7, Circular, 1858.
22 Gould, *Poems, Letters and Speeches*, Vol. I, p. 122.

23 Ballantine, *Chronicle*, p. 23.

24 Gould, *Letters, Poems and Speeches*, Vol. I, pp. 98–9.

25 Rigney, 'Embodied Communities', p. 83.

26 Ballantine, *Chronicle*, pp. 27, 31–4.

27 Gould, *Letters, Poems and Speeches*, Vol. I, p. 64.

28 Gould, *Letters, Poems and Speeches*, Vol. III, pp. 1, 7.

29 Ballantine, *Chronicle*, p. 137.

30 Ballantine, *Chronicle*, p. 127.

31 *Illustrated London News*, 29 January 1959.

32 *Scotsman*, 27 January 1859.

33 Michie, *Enlightenment Tory*, p. 195; 'The Late Mr Colin Rae Brown', *BC* (January 1898), p. 106.

34 *Scotsman*, 27 January 1859.

35 *Lloyd's Weekly Newspaper*, 30 January 1859.

36 Whatley, ' "It is Said That Burns Was a Radical" ', p. 645.

37 Ballantine, *Chronicle*, p. 158; Callum G. Brown, 'Religion', in Abrams et al. (eds), *Gender*, p. 103.

38 Ballantine, *Chronicle*, pp. 148, 214.

39 Ballantine, *Chronicle*, p. 111.

40 Ballantine, *Chronicle*, pp. 147, 374.

41 Coleman, *Remembering the Past*, pp. 44, 54–5, 94.

42 Marsden, *Cosmo Innes*, pp. 297–320.

43 Ballantine, *Chronicle*, pp. 328–9.

44 Ballantine, *Chronicle*, p. 300.

45 Gould, *Poems, Letters and Speeches*, II, p. 5.

46 *Burns' Centenary: Are Such Honours due to the Ayrshire Bard?* (Glasgow, 1859).

47 Ballantine, *Chronicle*, p. 323.

48 Gould, *Poems, Letters and Speeches*, Vol. I, p. 89.

49 Gould, *Poems, Letters and Speeches*, Vol. I, pp. 87–8.

50 Robert Blackley Drummond, *The Religion of Robert Burns* (Edinburgh and London, 1859), p. 7.

51 Gould, *Poems, Letters and Speeches*, Vol. I, p. 84.

52 Gould, *Poems, Letters and Speeches*, Vol. I, handwritten introduction (not paginated), and pp. 124–5.

53 Steve Bruce, *Scottish Gods: Religion in Modern Scotland, 1900–2012* (Edinburgh, 2014), p. 11.

54 Peter Hately Waddell, *Life and Works of Robert Burns* (Glasgow, 1867), p. xix.

55 *Dundee Advertiser*, 16 April 1878.

56 Ballantine, *Chronicle*, p. 374.

57 Callum G. Brown, *Up-helly-aa: Custom, Culture and Community in Shetland* (Manchester, 1998), pp. 107–10.

58 Ballantine, *Chronicle*, p. 327.

59 Gould, *Poems, Letters and Speeches*, Vol. I, p. 84.

60 Reverend Fergus Ferguson, *Should Christians Commemorate the Birthday of Robert Burns?* (Edinburgh, 1869).

61 DI, MC, Section XII, 13, *Speech Delivered at the Edinburgh Burns Club, By the Rev. Dr Wallace in Proposing the 'Memory of Burns', on the 25th January 1872* (Edinburgh, 1872), p. 7.

62 Alexander Webster, *Burns and the Kirk: A Review of What the Poet Did for the Religious and Social Regeneration of the Scottish People* (Aberdeen, Glasgow and Edinburgh, 1888), p. 16.

Chapter 4

1 *Burns Day, or a History of the Movement for a Burns Statue in Detroit* (Detroit, MI, 1921), pp. 91–3.

2 John McVie, *The Burns Federation: A Bicentenary Review* (Kilmarnock, 1959), pp. 66–9.

3 *Kilmarnock Standard*, 5 September 1877.

4 McKenzie, *Public Sculpture*, pp. 114–19.

5 DI, MC, *Burns Poems: The People's Statue Edition* (Kilmarnock, 1877), p. x.

6 *Glasgow Weekly Citizen*, 3 May 1873.

7 *Kilmarnock Standard*, 20 January 1877; Ewart Library, Dumfries [ELD], Archives, WB2/10, Dumfries Town Council Minutes, 1865–78, 2 February 1877; Dundee Central Library, Lamb Collection, 228 (33), 'Inauguration of the Burns Statue' (1880).

8 *People's Journal*, 23 October 1880.

9 *Dumfries and Galloway Standard*, 8 April 1882.

10 Quoted in *Kilmarnock Standard*, 13 September 1879.

11 *Dumfries and Galloway Standard*, 15, 19 April 1882.

12 *Paisley and Renfrewshire Gazette*, 28 September, 3 October 1896.

13 Goodwillie, *World's Memorials*, p. 105.

14 David Barrie, *Police in the Age of Improvement: Police Development and the Civic Tradition in Scotland, 1775–1865* (Cullompton, 2008), p. 212.

15 *Dumfries and Galloway Herald*, 8 April 1882.

16 *Paisley and Renfrewshire Gazette*, 26 September 1896.

17 Penman, 'Bruce's Bones', 43.

18 *Times*, 30 June 1856.

19 Murphy, *Nineteenth-Century Irish Sculpture*, pp. 205–24.

20 *Kilmarnock Standard*, 9 June 1877.

21 *Art Journal* (1881), pp. 71–2.

22 Shannon H. Hurtado, *Genteel Matriarchs: Professional Women Sculptors in Victorian Britain* (Bern, 2012), p. 192.

23 National Library of Scotland [NLS], Deposit 349/76, J. Pittendrigh MacGillivray, Notes on Burns; 349/130, Burns speeches etc.

24 Peter J. M. McEwan, *The Dictionary of Scottish Art and Architecture* (Ballater, 1988), p. 534.

25 *Kilmarnock Standard*, 21 April 1877.

26 *Dumfries and Galloway Standard*, 8 January 1882; Philip Sulley, *Robert Burns and Dumfries* (Dumfries, 1896), p. 62.

27 Quoted in Robert J. Ackroyd, 'Lord Rosebery and Scottish Nationalism, 1868–1896', unpublished PhD thesis (University of Edinburgh, 1996), p. 34.

28 Nicholas Morgan and Richard Trainor, 'The Dominant Classes', in W. Hamish Fraser and Robert J. Morris (eds), *People and Society in Scotland, Volume II, 1830–1914* (Edinburgh, 1990), p. 106.

29 *James Burn: the 'Beggar Boy', An Autobiography* (London, 1882), pp. 241–2.

30 Morgan and Trainor, 'Dominant Classes', pp. 111–17.

31 See, for example, Irene Mavor, 'Glasgow's Civic Government', in W. Hamish Fraser and Irene Mavor (eds), *Glasgow, Volume II: 1830 to 1912* (Manchester, 1996), p. 449.

32 DI, MC, XIII, 24, Newspaper Cuttings, 1868–87, p. 55.

33 Brown, *Religion*, pp. 101–6.

34 Michael Lynch, 'Introduction: Scotland 1850–1979', in Michael Lynch (ed.), *Scotland, 1850–1979: Society, Politics and the Union* (London, 1993), pp. 5–9.

35 Murray G. H. Pittock, *The Invention of Scotland: The Stuart Myth and the Scottish Identity, 1638 to the Present* (London, 1991), pp. 120–33.

36 For biographies of both men, see Ayrshire Archives, Kilmarnock, AA/DC/89, Kilmarnock Burns Club Minute Book, 1855–71.

37 ML, 391557, Waverley Burns Club Minutes, 4 vols, Vol. 4, 1875–82.

38 *The Baillie*, 10 February 1875.

39 *Stirling Observer*, 5 January 1918.
40 Eugenio F. Biagini and Alastair J. Reid, 'Currents of radicalism, 1850–1914', in Eugenio F. Biagini and Alastair J. Reid (eds), *Currents of Radicalism: Popular Radicalism, Organised Labour and Party Politics in Britain, 1850–1914* (Cambridge, 1991), pp. 1–19; Smout, *Century*, pp. 246–7.
41 John Belchem, *Popular Radicalism in Nineteenth-Century Britain* (Basingstoke, 1996), pp. 102–27.
42 Ballantine, *Chronicle*, pp. 39–40.
43 ML, 22325, Printed Papers of the Waverley (Western) Burns Club, *Glasgow Waverley Burns Club* (Glasgow, n.d.), newspaper extract, 29 June 1878.
44 Ballantine, *Chronicle*, pp. 69–76.
45 Ballantine, *Chronicle*, p. 57.
46 Christopher Harvie and Peter Jones, *The Road to Home Rule: Images of Scotland's Cause* (Edinburgh, 2000), p. 17.
47 Goodwillie, *World's Memorials*, p. 86.
48 Irene Mavor, *Glasgow* (Edinburgh, 2000), p. 81.
49 *Scotsman*, 11 August 1879.
50 Goodwillie, *World's Memorials*, p. 80.
51 Dundee Central Library, Lamb Collection, 80 (15), Poems, William Harvey, 1916–25.
52 ML, No. 52910, Centenary of the Birth of Burns, 1859: Memorials Presented by C. Rae Brown, 1884, MS 55/20, Earl of Eglinton to C. Rae Brown, 28 August 1858.
53 Douglas S. Mack, *Scottish Fiction and the British Empire* (Edinburgh, 2006), p. 147.
54 Colin Kidd and James Coleman, 'Mythical Scotland', in Thomas M. Devine and Jenny Wormald (eds), *The Oxford Handbook of Modern Scottish History* (Oxford, 2012), pp. 74–5.
55 *Greenock Telegraph*, 2 April 1938.
56 DI, MC, Section XIII, 27, Scrapbook, 1873–93, cutting, *Lennox Herald*, 13 January 1877.
57 *The Baillie*, 10 February 1875.
58 *Kilmarnock Standard*, 7 September 1877; *Kilmarnock Standard Supplement*, 26 January 1877.
59 DI, MC, Section XIII, 12, Scrapbook, 1875–6, Colin Rae Brown to James M'Kie, 3 June 1875.
60 Anthony Faulkes, *The Life and Works of James Easson, The Dundee People's Poet* (Dundee, 2016), p. 72.

61 Black, *Gilfillan*, p. 192.

62 Christopher A. Whatley, 'Contesting Memory and Public Places: Albert Square and Dundee's Pantheon of Heroes', in Christopher A. Whatley, Bob Harris and Louise Miskell (eds), *Victorian Dundee: Image and Realities* (Dundee, 2011 edn), p. 191.

63 Angus Archives [AA], Burns Statue Montrose Papers, 628/4, Unveiling ceremony papers, 1912.

64 *Paisley and Renfrewshire Gazette*, 26 September 1896.

65 *The Scotsman*, 26 January 1877.

66 McVie, *Burns Federation*, pp. 79–82.

67 Kilmarnock Monument Centre, Kilmarnock Burns Club Minute Books, AA/DC/89/1/4; Robert Anderson, 'University History Teaching, National Identity and Unionism in Scotland, 1862–1914', *Scottish Historical Review*, 91, 1 (April 2012), 17–22.

68 Clarke and Dickson, 'Class', in Dickson (ed.), *Capital*, pp. 29–33.

69 www.dalryburnsclub.org.uk.

70 Hill, *Life and Works of Robert Burns*, p. 82.

71 See Clark McGinn, ' "Every Honour Except Canonisation": The Global Development of the Burns Supper', PhD thesis (University of Glasgow, 2013); *Kilmarnock Standard*, 7 September 1877.

72 See, for example, the list in *BC* (1926), pp. 190–200.

73 Brown, *Paisley Burns Clubs*, p. 284.

74 Stana Nenadic, 'The Victorian Middle Classes', in Fraser and Mavor (eds), *Glasgow*, pp. 267–71.

75 'The Aberdeen Burns Club', in John D. Ross (ed.), *Burnsiana: A Collection of Literary Odds and Ends Relating to Robert Burns* (Paisley, 1892–7, 6 vols), Vol. III, pp. 109–10.

76 Whatley, 'Contesting Memory', p. 190.

77 ML, Waverley Burns Club Minutes, Vol. I, 1860–5, 27 June 1865.

78 ML, Printed Papers, Waverley Burns Club, (17), Itinerary, 25 June 1878.

79 *The Baillie*, 13 August 1879.

80 Rose, *Intellectual Life*, p. 58.

81 Rose, *Intellectual Life*, p. 68.

82 *Dundee Advertiser*, 15 January 1900.

83 Dundee Burns Club, Minutes, 1860–4, 1873–81.

84 See Martin Hewitt, *The Dawn of the Cheap Press in Victorian Britain: the End of the 'Taxes on Knowledge', 1849–1869* (London, 2013).

85 William Donaldson, *Popular Literature in Victorian Scotland: Language, fiction and the press* (Aberdeen, 1986), pp. 1–34.

86 ML, Waverley Burns Club Minutes, Vol. I, 25 April 1865.

87 'The Late Mr Colin Rae Brown', *BC* (January 1898), pp. 104–6.

88 *Arbroath Herald*, 23 January 1959.

89 *Glasgow Herald*, 8 July 1892.

90 *Irvine Herald*, 28 June 1889.

91 Dundee Burns Club, Minutes, 1873–81, 14 August 1880.

92 Brown, *Paisley Burns Clubs*, p. 284.

93 Nancy Crathorne, *Tennant's Stalk: The Story of Tennant's of the Glen* (London, 1973), pp. 117–63.

94 Goodwillie, *World's Memorials*, p. 104.

95 *Dumfries and Galloway Standard*, 8 December 1877, 8 January 1882.

96 *Kilmarnock Standard*, 3 December 1892.

97 *Glasgow Herald*, 22 April 1896.

98 *Dumfries and Galloway Standard*, 8 January 1882.

99 Philip Sulley, *Robert Burns and Dumfries* (Dumfries, 1896), p. 34.

100 Brown, *Religion*, p. 115.

101 Sam McKinstry, 'Thomson's Architectural Theory', in Gavin Stamp and Sam McKinstry (eds), *'Greek' Thomson* (Edinburgh, 1994), p. 64.

102 Simon Gunn, *The Public Culture of the Victorian Middle Class* (Manchester, 2000), p. 53.

103 Murphy, *Nineteenth-Century Irish Sculpture*, p. vii.

104 James Schmiechen, 'Glasgow of the Imagination: Architecture, Townscape and Society', in Fraser and Mavor (eds), *Glasgow*, p. 490; Mavor, *Glasgow*, p. 174; Dianne S. Macleod, *Art and the Victorian Middle Class: Money and the Making of Cultural Identity* (Cambridge, 1996), p. 88.

105 'Unveiling of the Burns Statue at Leith', *BC* (January 1899), p. 129.

106 *The Baillie*, 18 March 1874; Mavor, *Glasgow*, p. 173.

107 *The Baillie*, 10 February 1875.

108 Whatley, 'Contesting Memory', p. 177.

109 *Piper o' Dundee*, 7 August 1889.

110 Strawhorn, *History*, p. 170.

111 *Stirling Observer*, 5 January 1918.

112 McKenzie, *Public Sculpture*, p. 141.

113 'The Flaxman Statue of Burns', *BC* (1924), p. 104.

114 *Northern Whig*, 20 September 1893.

115 *Stirling Observer*, 21 January 1913.

116 *Dumfries and Galloway Standard*, 4 April 1877.

117 William R. Turnbull, *The Heritage of Burns* (Haddington, 1896), p. 410.

118 'Prof Masson on Burns and Burns Clubs', in Ross (ed.), *Burnsiana*, I, pp. 45–7.

119 DI, MC, Sec IX, 252, pp. 158–63, Essay, 'A Plea for Scottish Literature at the Universities'.

120 Ackroyd, 'Lord Rosebery', p. 213.

121 *Scotsman*, 25 January 1892.

122 *Aberdeen Weekly Journal*, 25 January 1883.

123 See Carol McGuirk, 'The "Rhyming Trade"', in Crawford (ed.), *Heaven-Taught Fergusson*, pp. 135–59; Jenni Calder, *Scots in the USA* (Edinburgh, 2005), p. 193.

124 'Unveiling of the Burns Statue at Leith', *BC* (January 1899), p. 131.

125 *Glasgow Herald*, 16 September 1892.

126 ML, Minutes, Waverley Burns Club, Vol. I, 31 October 1865.

127 Alastair J. Durie, *Scotland For the Holidays: Tourism in Scotland c.1780–1939* (East Linton, 2003), p. 45; DI, MC, Burns Monument Visitors Book, 1879–81.

128 *Kilmarnock Standard*, 27 January 1877.

129 Strawhorn, *History*, pp. 206–7.

130 *Dumfries and Galloway Standard*, 12 April 1882.

131 'Unveiling of the Burns Statue at Leith', pp. 129–30.

132 *The Kilmarnock Burns Monument and Statue* (1882), pp. 3–4.

133 *Burns Day in Detroit*, pp. 11, 91–3.

134 *Kilmarnock Standard*, 9 June 1877.

135 Whatley, 'Contesting Memory', pp. 188–90.

136 DI, MC, XIII, 24, Newspaper Cuttings, 1868–87, 'Burns Monument for Dumfries', 25 January 1878.

137 *Dumfriesshire and Galloway Herald*, 25 April 1882.

138 *Stirling Observer*, 27 January 1914.

139 Stirling Council Archives, Stirling Burgh Records [SRB}, SB1/15/6, J. Winter Buchan to David Morris, 24 September 1912.

Chapter 5

1 *Glasgow Herald*, 11 April 1874.
2 *Glasgow Herald*, 25 January 1877.
3 *Liverpool Mercury*, 28 October 1814.
4 *Aberdeen Weekly Journal*, 31 January 1877.
5 *Aberdeen Weekly Journal*, 11 August 1879.
6 Quoted in *Glasgow Herald*, 27 January 1877.
7 *Kilmarnock Standard*, 9 June 1877.
8 Digital.nls.uk/broadsides/broadside.cfm/id/15845.
9 Whatley, 'Contesting Memory', p. 192.
10 DI, MC, Section XII, 13 (Kilmarnock, 1878).
11 *Dumfries and Galloway Standard*, 8 January 1882.
12 *People's Journal*, 23 October 1880.
13 William M. Walker, *Juteopolis: Dundee and its Textile Workers, 1885–1923* (Edinburgh, 1979), pp. 22–3, 338–43.
14 Eleanor Gordon, *Women and the Labour Movement in Scotland, 1850–1914* (Oxford, 1991), pp. 66–7.
15 Brown, 'Religion', p. 102.
16 Boos, *Working-Class Women*, p. 27.
17 Walker, *Juteopolis*, pp. 87–94.
18 *Paisley Daily Express*, 28 September 1896.
19 *Paisley Daily Express*, 5 May 1896.
20 *Dumfries and Galloway Standard*, 8 January 1882; Sulley, *Robert Burns*, p. 62.
21 Bruce Lenman, Charlotte Lythe and Enid Gauldie, *Dundee and its Textile Industry 1850–1914* (Dundee, 1969), pp. 31–2; *Dumfries and Galloway Standard*, 8 January 1882.
22 David G. Adams, 'Harbour Related Industries c.1837–1914', in Gordon Jackson and S. G. E. Lythe (eds), *The Port of Montrose* (New York and Tayport, 1993), pp. 282–4.
23 *Kilmarnock Standard*, 4 October 1879; *Dundee Advertiser*, 18 October 1880; *Dumfries and Galloway Standard*, 8 April 1882.
24 Walker, *Juteopolis*, p. 52.
25 *Glasgow Herald*, 6 November 1876.
26 *Scotsman*, 11 August 1879.
27 Smout, *Century*, pp. 246–6.
28 See Mark Nixon, Gordon Pentland and Matthew Roberts, 'The Material Culture of Scottish Reform Politics, c.1820–c.1884',

Journal of Scottish Historical Studies, 32, 1 (2012), p. 48; *Dumfries and Galloway Standard*, 8 January 1882.

29 *Glasgow Herald*, 9 August 1886.

30 Whatley, 'Contesting Memory', p. 196.

31 See, for example, *Scotsman*, 26 January 1877; 'Inauguration of the Burns Statue'; *Burns Centenary, 21st July 1896* (Dumfries, 1896), pp. 46–7.

32 *Glasgow Herald*, 9 August 1886.

33 *Burns Centenary 21st July 1896, Great Demonstration at Dumfries* (Dumfries, 1896), pp. 23–51.

34 See Vance, 'Burns in the Park', pp. 210–17.

35 See Whatley, 'Contesting Memory', pp. 190–5.

36 Ackroyd, 'Lord Rosebery', pp. 105–6, 111–12.

37 *Kilmarnock Standard*, 14 September 1878.

38 David Goldie, 'Robert Burns and the First World War', *International Journal of Scottish Literature*, 6 (Spring/Summer 2010), p. 5.

39 *Dumfries and Galloway Standard*, 8 January 1882.

40 Harvie, *Floating Commonwealth*, p. 40; 'The Burns Statue in Aberdeen', in Ross (ed.), *Burnsiana*, Vol. III, pp. 31–2.

41 Edward M. Spiers, 'Scots and the Wars of Empire, 1815–1914', in Spiers, Crang and Strickland (eds), *Military History*, p. 458.

42 *Burns Centenary*, pp. 68–9.

43 See John M. Roberts, 'Spacial Governance and Working Class Public Spheres: the Case of a Chartist Demonstration at Hyde Park', *Journal of Historical Sociology*, 14, 3 (2001), p. 309.

44 Elspeth King, *The People's Palace and Glasgow Green* (Edinburgh, 1985), pp. 19–41.

45 *People's Journal*, 27 January 1877.

46 See Corey E. Andrews, 'Radical Attribution: Robert Burns and "The Liberty Tree"', *Studies in Scottish Literature*, 41, 1 (2015), pp. 174–90.

47 Dundee Central Library, Lamb Collection, 227 (32), *Proceedings at the Unveiling of the Burns Statue in Dundee* (Dundee, 1880), p. 9.

48 Faulkes, *Life and Works of James Easson*, p. 122.

49 *Dundee Advertiser*, 23 October 1880.

50 Alex M'Donald, *Historical Sketch of the Dundee Burns Club* (Dundee, 1889), pp. 9–10.

51 James Young Geddes, *The Spectre Clock of Alyth And Other Selections* (Alyth, 1886), pp. 87–92; Bold, 'James Young Geddes', p. 22–3.

52 Boos, *Working-Class Women*, pp. 327–9.

53 *Burns Centenary*, p. 40.

54 *Dumfries and Galloway Courier*, 4 April 1882.

55 DI, MC, Section XIII, 24 and 26, pp. 81–2.

56 Ewen A. Cameron, *Impaled Upon a Thistle: Scotland Since 1880* (Edinburgh, 2010), p. 68; Smout, *Century*, p. 258.

57 William Elder, *Robert Burns as Freethinker, Poet, and Democrat* (Paisley, 1881), pp. 11, 19.

58 Boos, *Working-Class Women*, pp. 54, 60–3.

59 See Hugh MacDiarmid, 'Robert Burns: His Influence' (1959), in Duncan Glen (ed.), *Selected Essays of Hugh MacDiarmid* (London, 1969), pp. 179–80.

60 Bold, *James Hogg*, pp. 272–3.

61 Alan Reid, *The Bards of Angus and The Mearns* (Paisley, 1897), pp. 502–3.

62 *Dumbarton Herald*, 1 February 1877.

63 *Burns Centenary 21st July 1896* (Dumfries, 1896), p. 27.

64 David Swinfen, *Moncrieff: The Life and Career of James Wellwood Moncreiff, 1811–1895* (Dundee, 2015), p. 96.

65 Black, *Gilfillan*, pp. 191–9.

66 Walker, *Juteopolis*, pp. 12–20.

67 'Inauguration', n.p.

68 *Proceedings at the Unveiling of the Burns Statue in Dundee*, p. 26.

69 *The British Architect and Northern Engineer*, 2 February 1877, pp. 75–7.

70 *Aberdeen Weekly Journal*, 31 January 1877.

71 *Aberdeen Weekly Journal*, 11 August 1879.

72 'Mr Andrew Carnegie on Burns', *BC* (January 1913), pp. 69–82.

73 www.oxforddnb.com/view/article/17555, accessed 27 Nov. 2015.

74 *Glasgow Herald*, 16 September 1892.

Chapter 6

1 *Glasgow Herald*, 10 September 1875.

2 Quoted in McKenzie, *Public Sculpture*, p. 142.

3 *Aberdeen Weekly Journal*, 11 August 1879.

4 See David Hopes, 'Recollecting a Museum: A Semiotic Analysis of Burns Monument Museum, Kilmarnock', unpublished MA thesis (University of Leicester, 2002).

5 *BC* (1910); *Kilmarnock Standard*, 16 August 1879.

6 *Dumfries and Galloway Standard*, 8 April 1882.

7 Gould, *Poems, Letters and Speeches*, Vol. I, p. 181.

8 *Dumfries and Galloway Standard*, 8 January 1882.

9 *Courier & Argus*, 18 October 1880.

10 'The New York and Dundee Statue of Burns', *Art Journal* (March 1881), p. 72.

11 Ross, *Burnsiana*, Vol. III, p. 27.

12 *Paisley Daily Express*, 28 September 1896.

13 Murphy, *Irish Sculpture*, p. 5.

14 *Dumbarton Herald*, 1 February 1877; McKenzie, *Public Sculpture*, p. 131.

15 McKenzie, *Public Sculpture*, p. 482.

16 ML, 391559, Waverley Burns Club Minutes, 3, 1871–5, 27 August 1872.

17 *The Baillie*, 10 February 1875.

18 Peter J. M. McEwan, *The Dictionary of Scottish Art and Architecture* (Ballater, 1988), p. 168.

19 *Glasgow Herald*, 11 April 1874.

20 McKenzie, *Public Sculpture*, p. 142.

21 DI, MC, Section XIII, 27, Scrapbook, 1873–93, James Gibson to James M'Kie, 22 January 1877.

22 *People's Journal*, 30 October 1880.

23 AA, Burns Statue, MS 628/1/2, Andrew Carnegie to Alex Marr, 17 March 1885.

24 *Dumfries and Galloway Standard*, 2 March 1887; *Dumfries and Galloway Herald*, 8 April 1882.

25 *Dumfries and Galloway Standard*, 9 July 1887, 15 September 1894.

26 *Glasgow Herald*, 28 September 1893.

27 *Kilmarnock Standard*, 30 June 1877; Hopes, 'Recollecting a Museum', pp. 8–13.

28 Pinnington, 'Statues', p. 241.

29 John C. Hill, *The Life and Works of Robert Burns in Irvine* (London, 1933), p. 70.

30 *Paisley Daily Express*, 9 June 1896.

31 *Glasgow Herald*, 14 September 1889.

32 Ross, *Burnsiana*, Vol. I, pp. 101–4.

33 *Glasgow Herald*, 28 October 1889, 8 July 1891.

34 *Glasgow Herald*, 2 July 1894.

35 'An Art Student', 'Statues of Burns', *BC* (1895), p. 121.

36 *Paisley and Renfrewshire Gazette*, 11, 25 July 1896.

37 On portraits of Burns, see Sheila Szatkowski, 'The Paparazzo, the Publisher and the Poet', in Rodger and Carruthers (eds), *Fickle Man*, 38–49; see, too, Basil C. Skinner, *Burns: Authentic Likenesses* (Edinburgh, 1963).

38 *Glasgow Herald*, 14 September 1889.

39 'Art Student', 'Statues', pp. 122–3.

40 For a modern assessment of the 'Highland Lassie' issue, see Gerard Carruthers et al., 'Some recent discoveries in Robert Burns Studies', *Scottish Literary Review*, 2, 1 (Spring/Summer 2010), pp. 143–58.

41 Whatley, 'Contesting Memory', pp. 188–9, 195.

42 Pinnington, 'Statues', p. 242.

43 Goodwillie, *World's Memorials*, p. 79.

44 SCA, SBR, SB1/15/6, J. Winter Buchan to Andrew Morris, 24 September 1912.

45 www.oxforddnb.com/view/article/49240, accessed 27 April 2012.

46 *Glasgow Herald*, 2 July 1894.

47 Pinnington, 'Statues', p. 242.

48 NLS, Dep. 349/76, J. Pittendrigh MacGillivray, Additional note referring to the statue in Irvine; 349/124, Lecture, Sculpture in Scotland, 22 November 1917.

49 *Scotsman*, 20 August 1831.

50 McKenzie, *Public Sculpture*, p. 125.

51 *Scotsman*, 30 August 1828.

52 Vance, 'Burns in the Park', p. 219.

53 Information on Anderson provided by Sue Payne, Perth Museum; *Chambers Edinburgh Journal*, 166, 4 April 1835.

54 Murray Pittock and Isla Jack, 'Patrick Geddes and the Celtic Revival', in Manning et al. (eds), *Edinburgh History*, pp. 338–42; NLS, Dep. 349/124, J. Pittendrigh MacGillivray Lecture, 'Sculpture, Nationality and War Memorials', 22 November 1917.

55 *Scotsman*, 24 January 1925.

56 NLS, Accession 3501/28, Scrapbook, J. Pittendrigh MacGillivray, p. 220; Accession 3501/30, Record of work, J. Pittendrigh MacGillivray, pp. 8–9.

57 Murray Pittock, *Scottish Nationality* (Houndmills, 2001), pp. 97–102.

58 Calculated from 'List of Burns Clubs and Societies', *BC* (1926), pp. 190–220.

59 McVie, *Burns Federation*, pp. 83–7.

60 See 'Obituary' (of Rosebery), *BC* (1930), pp. 123–7.

61 'The Auld Brig o' Ayr', *BC* (January 1911), p. 35.

62 McVie, *Burns Federation*, pp. 119–23; 'Memorials of Robert Burns', *BC* (1928), pp. 35–40.

63 George H. Kinnear, 'Glenbervie: The Fatherland of Burns', *BC* (1898), pp. 75–84.

64 M'Donald, *Historical Sketch*, pp. 14–15.

65 *Burns Centenary*, p. 31.

66 McVie, *Burns Federation*, p. 76.

67 *Perthshire Constitutional and Journal*, 27 July 1896.

68 McVie, *Burns Federation*, p. 74.

69 For fuller information see *BC* (January 1897).

70 *Kilmarnock Standard Supplement*, 26 January 1877.

71 AA, Montrose Newspaper Cuttings, 1896–1917, Vol. 6, 7 June 1912, 'Unveiling of Montrose Burns Statue'.

72 'Proposed Burns Memorial at Mauchline', *BC* (1896), p. 48.

73 McVie, *Burns Federation*, pp. 124–6.

74 'Burns Memorial at Mauchline: "Auld Nanse Tinnock's"', *BC* (1926), pp. 85–91.

75 'National Burns Memorial at Mauchline', *BC* (January 1899), pp. 91–113.

76 AA, MS 628/1/1, James Burness to J. Birnie Rhind, 8 December 1898.

77 AA, MS 628/1/1, W. Birnie Rhind to Alex Marr, 9 October 1911.

78 Rosebery did eventually subscribe five pounds.

79 William E. Henley, *Burns: Life, Genius, Achievement* (Edinburgh and London, 1898), pp. 233–341.

80 See, for example, *Perthshire Advertiser*, 3 April 1901; NLS, Dep. 349/145, Immortal Memory, J. Pittendrigh MacGillivray, 25 January 1925.

81 *Paisley and Renfrewshire Gazette*, 3 October 1896.

82 Knox, *Industrial Nation*, p. 181.

83 Donaldson, *Popular Literature*, p. 26.

84 Goldie, 'Robert Burns', p. 3.

85 Coleman, *Remembering the Past*, p. 16.

86 *The Herald*, 17 January 2013.

87 *Arbroath Herald*, 23 January 1959.

88 Jan Merchant, ' "An Insurrection of Maids": Domestic Servants and the Agitation of 1872', in Whatley et al. (eds), *Victorian Dundee*, pp. 112–33.

89 Knox, *Industrial Nation*, pp. 134–5.

90 Callum Brown, 'Spectacle, Restraint and the Sabbath Wars: The "Everyday" Scottish Sunday', in Lynn Abrams and Callum Brown (eds), *A History of Everyday Life in Twentieth-Century Scotland* (Edinburgh, 2010), pp. 163–9.

91 Sue Innes and Jane Rendall, 'Women, Gender and Politics', in Abrams et al. (eds), *Gender in Scottish History*, pp. 60–7.

92 See Szasz, *Abraham Lincoln and Robert Burns*, p. 156.

93 Selina Todd, *The People: The Rise and Fall of the Working Class* (London, 2014), pp. 7–8.

94 *Scotsman*, 25 January 1909.

95 Knox, *Industrial Nation*, pp. 171–6.

96 Fry, *Patronage*, pp. 125–6.

97 Webster, *Burns and the Kirk*, pp. 6, 120.

98 *Forfar Review*, 30 January 1891.

99 *Reformed Presbyterian Magazine*, January 1859, pp. 12–13.

100 NLS, Dep. 349/51, James A. Morris to J. Pittendrigh MacGillivray, 2 February 1925.

101 Buchanan, *Coming Terror*, pp. 313–19.

102 DI, MC, Section XIII, 26, Letter, by J. L. to the *Weekly Chronicle*, 31 January 1891.

103 *Glasgow Herald*, 22 March 1892.

104 Dundee Burns Club, Committee Minute Book, 1881–1904.

105 Perth Museum, Minutes, Perth Burns Club, 1878–97.

106 *Glasgow Herald*, 24 March 1892.

107 Dundee Central Library, Local Studies, D5865, Dundee Burns Society Minutes, 1896–1903.

108 Gillian Shepherd, 'The Kailyard', in Gifford (ed.), *History of Scottish Literature*, p. 309; Andrew Nash, 'The Kailyard: Problem or Illusion?', in Manning et al. (eds), *Edinburgh History*, pp. 317–23.

109 *Piper o' Dundee*, 2 January 1889.

110 Valentina Bold, 'James Young Geddes (1850–1913): A Re-evaluation', *Scottish Literary Journal*, 19, 1 (1992), p. 19.

111 James Young Geddes, *In the Valhalla, and Other Poems* (Dundee, 1891), pp. 45–8.
112 Young, *In the Valhalla*, p. 51.

Chapter 7

1 'Mr Andrew Carnegie on Burns', *BC* (1913), p. 79.
2 SCA, SB1/15/6, Andrew Carnegie to David Morris, 21 August 1914.
3 *Stirling Observer*, 29 September 1914.
4 David Goldie, 'Robert Burns and the First World War', *International Journal of Scottish Literature*, 6 (Spring/Summer 2010), pp. 4–9.
5 *People's Journal*, 9, 23 January 1915.
6 Richard Price, 'Robert Burns and the Scottish Renaissance', in Simpson (ed.), *Love & Liberty*, p. 139.
7 John S. Clarke, *Robert Burns and His Politics: A Study in History and Human Nature* (Glasgow, 1925), p. 27.
8 Sir James Crichton-Browne, *Burns from a New Point of View* (London, Glasgow and Edinburgh, 1926, 1937 edn), pp. 59–67.
9 *BC* (1926), pp. 207–11.
10 On West Fife political culture see Peter Geoghegan, *The People's Referendum: Why Scotland Will Never be the Same Again* (Edinburgh, 2015), pp. 37–56.
11 Finlay, 'Burns Cult', p. 74.
12 John R. Campbell, *Burns the Democrat* (Glasgow, 1945), p. 40.
13 'The Politics of Burns', *BC* (1925), pp. 61–5.
14 Cameron, 'Politics of the Union', pp. 124–8.
15 'The Burns Federation at Greenock', *BC* (1931), p. 19.
16 *Arbroath Herald*, 30 January 1959.
17 *BC* (1930), p. 177.
18 James A. Morris, *Alloway: The Protection and Preservation of its Memorials of Robert Burns* (Ayrshire, 1930).
19 *BC* (1931), p. 27; Dumfries Museum, DUMNFM: 0198.423, Dumfries Burns Club 1938: Second Appeal.
20 McVie, *Burns Federation*, pp. 136–45.
21 George Blake, *The Heart of Scotland* (London, 1934), p. 65.
22 Tom Nairn, *The Break-Up of Britain* (London, 1977), p. 158; for further discussion and an assessment see David McCrone,

Understanding Scotland: The Sociology of a Stateless Nation (London, 1992), pp. 174–96.

23 Craig, 'National Literature', p. 59.

24 Catriona Macdonald, *Whaur Extremes Meet: Scotland's Twentieth Century* (Edinburgh, 2009), pp. 288–30.

25 Alan Riach, 'MacDiarmid's Burns', in Crawford (ed.), *Robert Burns and Cultural Authority*, pp. 199–200.

26 Alan Riach (ed.), *Hugh MacDiarmid: Contemporary Scottish Studies* (Manchester, 1995), pp. vii–xxxi.

27 Riach, 'MacDiarmid's Burns', p. 201.

28 Thomas M. Devine, *The Scottish Nation* (London, 1999), p. 320.

29 'The Burns Cult (2)', in Riach (ed.), *Hugh MacDiarmid*, pp. 360–1.

30 'The Burns Cult (1)', in Riach (ed.), *Hugh MacDiarmid*, p. 356.

31 ' "Swatches o' Hamespun" ', in Riach (ed.), *Hugh MacDiarmid*, p. 264.

32 'The Burns Cult (1)', p. 354.

33 Dundee Burns Club, Minute Book No. 8, 1934–56.

34 'The Burns Cult (1)', p. 359; 'Robert Burns: His Influence', in Glen, *Selected Essays*, p. 177.

35 Morton, *In Search of Scotland*, pp. 267–8.

36 Ewen A. Cameron, 'The Politics of the Union in an Age of Unionism', in Thomas M. Devine (ed.), *Scotland and the Union, 1707–2007* (Edinburgh, 2008), p. 127.

37 Riach, 'MacDiarmid's Burns', p. 212.

38 'Burns and Scottish Nationalism', *BC* (1936), p. 51.

39 'Burns and Scottish Nationalism', *BC* (1930), p. 57.

40 Jan Pilditch, *Catherine Carswell: A Biography* (Edinburgh, 2007), pp. 122–37.

41 Pilditch, *Catherine Carswell*, p. 132.

42 *Glasgow Herald*, 23 February 1946; Pilditch, *Catherine Carswell*, p. 173.

43 Gerard Carruthers, 'The Word on Burns', in Rodger and Carruthers (eds), *Fickle Man*, p. 33.

44 *Scotsman*, 10 January 1959.

45 Bruce, *Scottish Gods*, pp. 107–10, 131–3.

46 *Scotsman*, 7 May 1985.

47 Allan Brown and Julia Belgutay, 'Bard? He was Awful', *Sunday Times*, 17 August 2008.

48 For a long view of this topic see Sarah Dunnigan, 'Burns and Women', in Carruthers (ed.), *Edinburgh Companion*, pp. 20–33.

49 Pittock, *Road to Independence*, pp. 227–8.

50 *Courier & Advertiser*, 3 May 2016.

51 Pittock, ' "A Long Farewell" ', pp. 35–43.

52 Gerard Carruthers, 'Introduction', in Carruthers (ed.), *Edinburgh Companion*, p. 1.

53 David McCrone, Angela Morris and Richard Kiely, *Scotland – the Brand: The Making of Scottish Heritage* (Edinburgh, 1995), pp. 17–21.

54 Murray Pittock, 'Introduction: Global Burns', in Pittock (ed.), *Robert Burns*, p. 13.

55 *Daily Telegraph*, 6 June 2009.

56 David Hopes, 'Building on the Bard', *Scotland in Trust* (Autumn/ Winter 2008), pp. 20–7.

57 Information kindly supplied by David Hopes, of the NTS Robert Burns Birthplace Museum.

58 'Sunday 25th January 1959 The 200th Anniversary of the Birth of Robert Burns', *BC* (1960), pp. 53–66.

59 See Finlay, 'The Burns Cult', pp. 75–6.

60 'Statue to Burns Unveiled at Arbroath', *BC* (1960), pp. 49–52.

61 Hutchison, 'Burns, The Elastic Symbol', pp. 79–86.

62 *Dundee Courier*, 22 January 1960.

63 See, for example, Paul Scott, 'Robert Burns, Patriot', in Simpson (ed.), *Love & Liberty*, pp. 266–73.

64 David Torrance, *The Battle for Britain: Scotland and the Independence Referendum* (London, 2013), p. 197.

65 *Guardian*, 24 January 2014.

66 *Daily Record*, 12 January 2014.

67 Pittock, *Road to Independence*, p. 228.

68 *Glasgow Herald*, 30 November 1995.

69 *Glasgow Herald*, 28 September 1995.

70 See Donny O' Rourke, 'Supperman: Televising Burns', in Simpson (ed.), *Burns Now*, pp. 208–17.

71 *Glasgow Herald*, 18 December 1999.

72 Pittock, ' "A Long Farewell" ', pp. 28–9.

73 *Sunday Times*, 4 January 2009.

74 *Independent*, 15 August 2008.

75 *Daily Telegraph*, 15 August 2008.

76 See Patrick Scott Hogg, *Robert Burns: The Lost Poems* (Glasgow, 1997).

77 *Glasgow Herald*, 25 January 1996, 28 August 1998; *Scotland on Sunday*, 17 June 2001.

78 Carruthers, 'Word', pp. 35–6.

79 Pittock, ' "A Long Farewell" ', pp. 25–6.

80 Riach, 'MacDiarmid's Burns', p. 213.

81 Nigel Leask (ed.), *Commonplace Books, Tour Journals and Miscellaneous Prose* (Oxford, 2014).

82 ML, S.R.211/391560 (4), Minutes, Waverley Burns Club, John Finlay to W. Alexander, 18 January 1875.

Select bibliography

Listed below are the most relevant books, arranged thematically. Some of the edited collections contain chapters that relate to several themes. Primary sources used, chapters in edited collections, as well as articles in the specialist journals, are to be found in the endnotes for the chapters in this book. One of the most useful sources of material on Burns is the annual *Burns Chronicle* (1892–present), the journal of the World Burns Federation. Back numbers of the *Scottish Literary Journal* and *Studies in Scottish Literature* are also worth trawling through.

General Scottish histories

Devine, T. M., *The Scottish Nation, 1700–2000* (London, 1999)

Devine, T. M. and Wormald, J. (eds), *The Oxford Handbook of Modern Scottish History* (Oxford, 2012)

Fry, M., *A New Race of Men: Scotland, 1815–1914* (Edinburgh, 2013)

Fry, M., *A Higher World: Scotland, 1707–1815* (Edinburgh, 2014)

Knox, W. W., *Industrial Nation: Work, Culture and Society in Scotland, 1800–Present* (Edinburgh, 1999)

Lynch, M., *Scotland: A New History* (London, 1991)

MacDonald, C. M. M., *Whaur Extremes Meet: Scotland's Twentieth Century* (Edinburgh, 2009)

Pittock, M., *The Road to Independence? Scotland in the Balance* (London, 2013 edn)

Smout, T. C., *A Century of the Scottish People, 1830–1950* (London, 1986)

Whatley, C. A., *Scottish Society 1707–1830: Beyond Jacobitism, Towards Industrialisation* (Manchester, 2000)

Commemoration and memory (general)

Ben-Amos, A., *Funerals, Politics and Memory in Modern France, 1789–1996* (Oxford, 2000)

Berger, S. and Niven, B. (eds), *Writing the History of Memory* (London, 2014)

Gillis, J. (ed.), *Commemorations: The Politics of National Identity* (Princeton, NJ, 1994)

MacLeod, C., *Heroes of Invention: Technology, Liberalism and British Identity 1750–1914* (Cambridge, 2007)

Watson, N., *Literary Tourism and Nineteenth-Century Culture* (Basingstoke, 2009)

Wolfe, J., *Great Deaths: Grieving, Religion and Nationhood in Victorian and Edwardian Britain* (Oxford, 2000)

Commemoration, memory and identity in Scotland

Ash, M., *The Strange Death of Scottish History* (Edinburgh, 1980)

Broun, D., Finlay, R. and Lynch, M. (eds), *Image and Identity: The Making and Re-Making of Scotland Through the Ages* (Edinburgh, 1998)

Coleman, J., *Remembering the Past in Nineteenth-Century Scotland: Commemoration, Nationality and Memory* (Edinburgh, 2014)

Cowan, E. J. (ed.), *The Wallace Book* (Edinburgh, 2007)

Crawford, R., *Bannockburns: Scottish Independence and Literary Imagination 1314–2014* (Edinburgh, 2014)

Davis, L., Duncan, I. and Sorensen, J. (eds), *Scotland and the Borders of Romanticism* (Cambridge, 2004)

Donnachie, I. and Whatley, C. A. (eds), *The Manufacture of Scottish History* (Edinburgh, 1992)

Harvie, C., *A Floating Commonwealth: Politics, Culture and Technology on Britain's Atlantic Coast 1860–1930* (Oxford, 2008)

Kelly, S., *Scott-Land: The Man Who Invented A Nation* (Edinburgh, 2010)

Kidd, C., *Union and Unionisms: Political Thought in Scotland, 1500–1800* (Cambridge, 2008)

McCrone, D., *Understanding Scotland: The Sociology of a Stateless Nation* (London, 1992)

Macmillan, D., *Scottish Art 1460–1990* (Edinburgh, 1990)

Morrison, J., *Painting the Nation: Identity and Nationalism in Scottish Painting, 1800–1920* (Edinburgh, 2003)

Morton, G., *Unionist Nationalism: Governing Urban Scotland, 1830–1860* (Edinburgh, 1999)

Morton, G., *William Wallace: A National Tale* (Edinburgh, 2014)

Pittock, M. G. H., *The Invention of Scotland: The Stuart Myth and Scottish Identity, 1638 to the Present* (London, 1991)

Rigney, A., *The Afterlives of Walter Scott: Memory on the Move* (Oxford, 2012)

Clubs and associational activity

Bueltmann, T., *Clubbing Together: Ethnicity, Civility and Formal Sociability in the Scottish Diaspora to 1930* (Liverpool, 2014)

Bueltmann, T., Hinson, A. and Morton, G., *The Scottish Diaspora* (Edinburgh, 2013)

Harris, B. and McKean, C., *The Scottish Town in the Age of the Enlightenment, 1740–1820* (Edinburgh, 2014)

McGinn, C., '"Every Honour Except Canonisation": The Global Development of the Burns Supper, 1801 to 2009', unpublished PhD thesis (University of Glasgow, 2013)

McVie, J., *The Burns Federation: A Bicentenary Review* (Kilmarnock, 1959)

Burns, works, background, biography and assessments

Carruthers, G. (ed.), *The Edinburgh Companion to Robert Burns* (Edinburgh, 2009)

Crawford, R. (ed.), *Robert Burns and Cultural Authority* (Edinburgh, 1997)

Crawford, R., *Scotland's Books: The Penguin History of Scottish Literature* (London, 2007)

Crawford, R., *The Bard: Robert Burns, A Biography* (Princeton, NJ, 2009)

Low, D. (ed.), *The Songs of Robert Burns* (Aldershot, 1993)

McGuirk, C. (ed.), *Robert Burns: Selected Poems* (London, 1993)

McIntyre, I., *Dirt & Deity: A Life of Robert Burns* (London, 1995)

Noble, A, and Hogg, P. (eds), *The Canongate Burns* (Edinburgh, 2001)

Simpson, K. G. (ed.), *Burns Now* (Edinburgh, 1994)

Simpson, K. G. (ed.), *Love & Liberty: Robert Burns, A Bicentenary Celebration* (East Linton, 1997)

Burns' reputation, memorialisation and commemoration

Alker, S., Davis, L. and Nelson, H. F. (eds), *Robert Burns and Transatlantic Culture* (Farnham, 2012)

Ballantine, J., *Chronicle of the Hundredth Birthday of Robert Burns* (Edinburgh and London, 1859)

Ferguson, F. and Holmes, A. R. (eds), *Revising Robert Burns and Ulster: Literature, Religion and Politics, c.1770–1920* (Dublin, 2009)

MacKay, J. A., *Burnsiana* (Alloway, 1988)

Pittock, M. (ed.), *Robert Burns in Global Culture* (Lewisburg, PA, 2011)

Rodgers, J. and Carruthers, G. (eds), *Fickle Man: Robert Burns in the 21st Century* (Dingwall, 2009)

Szasz, F., *Abraham Lincoln and Robert Burns: Connected Lives and Legends* (Carbondale, IL, 2008)

Burns and Radicalism

Crawford, T., *Boswell, Burns and the French Revolution* (Edinburgh, 1990)

Kirk, J., Brown, M. and Noble, A. (eds), *Cultures of Radicalism in Britain and Ireland* (London, 2013)

McIlvanney, L., *Burns the Radical: Poetry and Politics in Late Eighteenth-Century Scotland* (East Linton, 2002)

Memorials, statues and sculptors

Goodwillie, E., *The World's Memorials of Robert Burns* (Detroit, MI, 1911)

Lieuallen, R., 'A Sculptor for Scotland: The Life and Work of Sir John Steell, RSA (1804–1891)', unpublished PhD, University of Edinburgh (2002)

Macdonald, M., *Scottish Art* (London, 2000)

McEwan, P. J. M., *The Dictionary of Scottish Art and Architecture* (Ballater, 2004)

McKenzie, R., *Public Sculpture of Glasgow* (Liverpool, 2002)

Murphy, P., *Nineteenth-Century Irish Sculpture: Native Genius Reaffirmed* (New Haven, CT and London, 2010)

Rodger, J., *The Hero Building: An Architecture of Scottish National Identity* (Farnham, 2015)

Ross Roy, G. (ed.), *Robert Burns & America* (Columbia, SC, 2001)

Working-class readers, poets and the autodidacts

Black, A., *Gilfillan of Dundee, 1813–1878: Interpreting Religion and Culture in Mid-Victorian Scotland* (Dundee, 2006)

Bold, V., *James Hogg: A Bard of Nature's Making* (Oxford, 2007)

Boos, F. S., *Working-Class Women Poets in Victorian Britain* (Peterborough, Canada, 2008)

Cowan, E. J. and Paterson, M., *Folk in Print: Scotland's Chapbook Heritage, 1750–1850* (Edinburgh, 2007)

Leonard, T. (ed.), *Radical Renfrew: Poetry from the French Revolution to the First World War* (Edinburgh, 1990)

Maidment, B. (ed.), *The Poorhouse Fugitives: Self-taught Poets and Poetry in Victorian Britain* (Manchester, 1987)

Rose, J., *The Intellectual Life of the British Working Classes* (New Haven, CT and London, 2010 edn)

Vicinus, M., *The Industrial Muse: A Study of Nineteenth Century Working Class Literature* (London, 1974)

Index